ÉDITION FRANÇAISE
ENGLISH
FOR EVERYONE

EXERCICES
NIVEAU **4** AVANCÉ

AUDIO OFFERT
Site Internet et appli
www.dkefe.com

L'auteur

Claire Hart est auteur indépendant de documents en langue anglaise. Elle a publié une gamme de documents imprimés et créé plusieurs cours en ligne. Elle enseigne également l'anglais à l'université de sciences appliquées d'Ulm en Allemagne.

Les consultants pédagogiques

Tim Bowen a enseigné l'anglais et formé des enseignants dans plus de trente pays. Il est le coauteur d'ouvrages sur l'enseignement de la prononciation et sur la méthodologie de l'enseignement des langues, et est l'auteur de nombreux ouvrages pour les enseignants d'anglais. Il travaille actuellement comme auteur indépendant de matériels pédagogique, éditeur et traducteur. Il est membre du Chartered Institute of Linguists.

Kate O'Donovan, irlandaise, est titulaire d'un PDGE, et d'une licence d'histoire et d'anglais. Elle a travaillé en Suisse, à Oman et au Bahreïn. Depuis 2014 à Paris, elle enseigne l'anglais au British Council où elle est aussi coordinatrice.

La consultante linguistique

Susan Barduhn est professeur d'anglais et formatrice expérimentée d'enseignants. Elle a, en tant qu'auteur, contribué à de nombreuses publications. Elle donne non seulement des cours d'anglais dans le monde entier, mais est également présidente de l'Association internationale des professeurs d'anglais langue étrangère et conseillère auprès du Conseil britannique et du département d'État américain. Elle est actuellement professeur à la School for International Training dans le Vermont, aux États-Unis.

ÉDITION FRANÇAISE
ENGLISH
FOR EVERYONE

EXERCICES
NIVEAU 4 AVANCÉ

DK Inde
Rédacteurs en chef Vineetha Mokkil, Anita Kakar
Éditeur artistique senior Chhaya Sajwan
Éditeur de projet Antara Moitra
Editeurs Agnibesh Das, Nisha Shaw, Seetha Natesh
Éditeurs artistiques Namita, Heena Sharma, Sukriti Sobti,
Shipra Jain, Aanchal Singhal
Rédacteurs en chef adjoints Ira Pundeer, Ateendriya Gupta,
Sneha Sunder Benjamin, Ankita Yadav
Assistant éditeur artistique Roshni Kapur,
Meenal Goel, Priyansha Tuli
Illustrateurs Ivy Roy, Arun Pottirayil, Bharti Karakoti, Rahul Kumar
Iconographie Deepak Negi
Rédacteur en chef Pakshalika Jayaprakash
Éditeur artistique en chef Arunesh Talapatra
Directeur de la production Pankaj Sharma
Directeur de la préproduction Balwant Singh
Concepteur PAO en chef Vishal Bhatia, Neeraj Bhatia
Concepteur PAO Sachin Gupta
Concepteur couverture Surabhi Wadhwa
Rédacteur en chef couvertures Saloni Singh
Concepteur PAO en chef (couvertures) Harish Aggarwal

DK Royaume-Uni
Assistants d'édition Jessica Cawthra, Sarah Edwards
Illustrateurs Edwood Burn, Denise Joos, Michael Parkin,
Jemma Westing
Producteur audio Liz Hammond
Rédacteur en chef Daniel Mills
Éditeur artistique en chef Anna Hall
Gestionnaire de projet Christine Stroyan
Concepteur couverture Natalie Godwin
Éditeur couverture Claire Gell
Responsable conception couverture Sophia MTT
Production, préproduction Luca Frassinetti
Production Mary Slater
Éditeur Andrew Macintyre
Directeur artistique Karen Self
Directeur de publication Jonathan Metcalf

Publié en Grande-Bretagne en 2016
par Dorling Kindersley Limited
80 Strand, London, WC2R 0RL

Titre original : *English for Everyone. Practice Book.
Level 4. Advanced.*

Copyright © 2016 Dorling Kindersley Limited
Une société faisant partie du groupe Penguin Random House

Pour la version française
© 2017 Dorling Kindersley Limited

Adaptation et réalisation : Édiclic
Révision pédagogique : Kate O'Donovan
Traduction : Estelle Demontrond-Box pour Édiclic
Lecture-correction : Paul Cléonie

ISBN : 978-0-2413-0364-1
Imprimé et relié en Chine

A WORLD OF IDEAS:
SEE ALL THERE IS TO KNOW

www.dk.com

Sommaire

Fonctionnement du cours

English for everyone est un ouvrage conçu pour toutes les personnes désireuses d'apprendre l'anglais par elles-mêmes. Comme tout cours de langue, il porte sur les compétences de base : grammaire, vocabulaire, prononciation, compréhension orale, expression orale, compréhension écrite et expression écrite. Ici, les compétences sont enseignées de façon visuelle, à l'aide d'images et de schémas pour vous aider à comprendre et à bien mémoriser. Pour être plus efficace, suivez la progression du livre en veillant à utiliser les enregistrements à votre disposition sur le site Internet et sur l'application. À la fin de chaque unité, vous pouvez effectuer les exercices supplémentaires dans le cahier d'exercices afin de renforcer votre apprentissage.

MANUEL D'APPRENTISSAGE

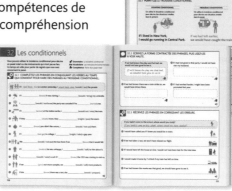

LIVRE D'EXERCICES

Numéro de chapitre Le livre est réparti en chapitres. Chaque chapitre du livre d'exercices teste les points linguistiques enseignés dans le chapitre du manuel d'apprentissage correspondant.

Les points de pratique Chaque chapitre débute par un résumé des points de pratique clés.

59 Le futur perfect

Vous pouvez utiliser le « futur perfect » pour parler d'événements qui vont chevaucher, ou finir avant, un autre événement du futur.

Grammaire Le futur perfect
Aa Vocabulaire Les projets de vie
Compétence Faire des projets et des prédictions

59.1 COMPLÉTEZ LES PHRASES EN CONJUGUANT LES VERBES AU FUTUR PERFECT.

By next March, I _____will have bought_____ (buy) my own house.

1. I _____ (finish) my degree by the time I am 22.

2. You _____ (be) married for one year in a week's time.

3. We _____ (complete) all our essays by the end of June.

4. By the time I am 24, I _____ (find) a good job.

5. I think my son _____ (propose) to his girlfriend by the end of the year.

6. By the time we are 30, we _____ (have) our first child.

7. Liza _____ (move) to London by the end of the month.

8. I _____ (graduate) from college by this time next year.

9. By the time I am 25, I _____ (leave) my parents' house.

10. I _____ (make) one million dollars by the time I'm 40.

11. They _____ (start) their new business by the end of the month.

196

Modules Chaque chapitre est divisé en modules, qui doivent être réalisés dans l'ordre. Vous pouvez faire une pause à la fin de chaque module.

59.2 RÉCRIVEZ LES PASSAGES SURLIGNÉS EN CORRIGEANT LES ERREURS.

will have taken

1.
2.
3.
4.
5.
6.
7.
8.
9.

59.3 COMPLÉTEZ LES PHRASES, PUIS LIS

Ken _____will have read_____ (read) all his text

1. They _____ (choose) the

2. Jenny _____ (buy) a new

3. By the end of the year, I _____

4. I _____ (open) all my pres

5. By the time he starts his new job, Hans _____

6. We _____ (visit) 15 counte

Vocabulaire Tout au long du livre, des pages de vocabulaire évaluent vos connaissances des expressions et mots anglais clés enseignés dans le manuel d'apprentissage.

Pratique visuelle Des images et graphiques vous donnent des indices visuels pour vous aider à mémoriser les mots anglais les plus utiles et les plus importants.

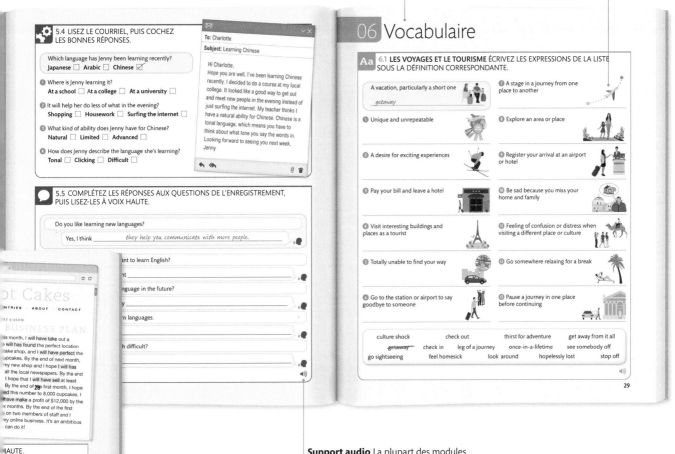

5.4 LISEZ LE COURRIEL, PUIS COCHEZ LES BONNES RÉPONSES.

Which language has Jenny been learning recently?
Japanese ☐   Arabic ☐   Chinese ☑

1 Where is Jenny learning it?
At a school ☐   At a college ☐   At a university ☐

2 It will help her do less of what in the evening?
Shopping ☐   Housework ☐   Surfing the internet ☐

3 What kind of ability does Jenny have for Chinese?
Natural ☐   Limited ☐   Advanced ☐

4 How does Jenny describe the language she's learning?
Tonal ☐   Clicking ☐   Difficult ☐

To: Charlotte
Subject: Learning Chinese

Hi Charlotte,
Hope you are well. I've been learning Chinese recently. I decided to do a course at my local college. It looked like a good way to get out and meet new people in the evening instead of just surfing the internet. My teacher thinks I have a natural ability for Chinese. Chinese is a tonal language, which means you have to think about what tone you say the words in.
Looking forward to seeing you next week.
Jenny

5.5 COMPLÉTEZ LES RÉPONSES AUX QUESTIONS DE L'ENREGISTREMENT, PUIS LISEZ-LES À VOIX HAUTE.

Do you like learning new languages?
Yes, I think _____ they help you communicate with more people.

...ant to learn English?
...nt

...language in the future?
...y

...rn languages.

...h difficult?

197

06 Vocabulaire

Aa 6.1 **LES VOYAGES ET LE TOURISME** ÉCRIVEZ LES EXPRESSIONS DE LA LISTE SOUS LA DÉFINITION CORRESPONDANTE.

A vacation, particularly a short one
getaway

1 Unique and unrepeatable

2 A desire for exciting experiences

3 Pay your bill and leave a hotel

4 Visit interesting buildings and places as a tourist

5 Totally unable to find your way

6 Go to the station or airport to say goodbye to someone

7 A stage in a journey from one place to another

8 Explore an area or place

9 Register your arrival at an airport or hotel

10 Be sad because you miss your home and family

11 Feeling of confusion or distress when visiting a different place or culture

12 Go somewhere relaxing for a break

13 Pause a journey in one place before continuing

culture shock   check out   thirst for adventure   get away from it all
~~getaway~~   check in   leg of a journey   once-in-a-lifetime   see somebody off
go sightseeing   feel homesick   look around   hopelessly lost   stop off

29

Support audio La plupart des modules sont accompagnés d'enregistrements sonores de locuteurs anglophones pour vous aider à améliorer vos compétences en matière de compréhension et d'expression orales.

Modules d'exercices

Chaque exercice est soigneusement conçu pour pratiquer et évaluer les nouveaux points linguistiques enseignés dans les chapitres correspondants du manuel d'apprentissage. Les exercices accompagnant le manuel vous aideront à mieux mémoriser ce que vous avez appris, et donc à mieux maîtriser la langue anglaise. Chaque exercice est introduit par un symbole indiquant la compétence étudiée.

GRAMMAIRE
Appliquez les nouvelles règles grammaticales dans des contextes différents.

COMPRÉHENSION ÉCRITE
Étudiez la langue cible dans des contextes anglophones authentiques.

COMPRÉHENSION ORALE
Évaluez votre niveau de compréhension de l'anglais oral.

VOCABULAIRE
Consolidez votre compréhension du vocabulaire clé.

EXPRESSION ÉCRITE
Entraînez-vous à rédiger des textes en anglais.

EXPRESSION ORALE
Comparez votre anglais oral aux enregistrements audio types.

Numéro de module Chaque module est identifié par un numéro unique qui vous permet de trouver facilement les réponses et les enregistrements associés.

Consignes des exercices Chaque exercice est introduit par une consigne courte qui vous explique ce que vous devez faire.

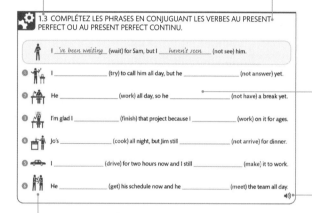

1.3 COMPLÉTEZ LES PHRASES EN CONJUGUANT LES VERBES AU PRESENT PERFECT OU AU PRESENT PERFECT CONTINU.

I _'ve been waiting_ (wait) for Sam, but I _haven't seen_ (not see) him.

1. I _____ (try) to call him all day, but he _____ (not answer) yet.

2. He _____ (work) all day, so he _____ (not have) a break yet.

3. I'm glad I _____ (finish) that project because I _____ (work) on it for ages.

4. Jo's _____ (cook) all night, but Jim still _____ (not arrive) for dinner.

5. I _____ (drive) for two hours now and I still _____ (make) it to work.

6. He _____ (get) his schedule now and he _____ (meet) the team all day.

Espace pour écrire Il est recommandé que vous écriviez vos réponses dans le livre pour garder une trace et évaluer vos résultats.

Supports audio Ce symbole indique que les réponses de l'exercice sont disponibles sous forme d'enregistrements audio. Écoutez-les une fois l'exercice terminé.

Supports graphiques
Des images ou pictos vous aideront à comprendre les exercices.

Exercice de compréhension orale
Ce symbole indique que vous devez écouter un enregistrement audio afin de répondre aux questions de l'exercice.

Exemple de réponse
La réponse de chaque première question de chaque exercice vous est donnée pour vous aider à mieux comprendre la consigne.

68.6 ÉCRIVEZ LES PHRASES EN AJOUTANT « SO » OU « SUCH » AU BON ENDROIT, PUIS LISEZ-LES À VOIX HAUTE.

The party was a success. [such]
The party was such a success.

1. These stray cats are a nuisance. [such]

2. I feel much calmer after a walk in the rain. [so]

3. You opened the door quietly last night. [so]

4. Color was amazing that I watched it again. [so]

5. There are many shirts to choose from. [so]

6. It's a lovely dress that I'm going to buy it. [such]

7. My dog is always hungry. She eats much. [so]

Exercice d'expression orale
Ce symbole indique que vous devez donner les réponses à voix haute, puis les comparer aux enregistrements fournis dans les fichiers audio.

10.2 ÉCOUTEZ L'ENREGISTREMENT, PUIS INDIQUEZ SI CHAQUE ACTIVITÉ A DES CHANCES D'AVOIR LIEU OU PAS.

Likely ✓ Unlikely ☐

1. Likely ☐ Unlikely ☐

2. Likely ☐ Unlikely ☐

3. Likely ☐ Unlikely ☐

4. Likely ☐ Unlikely ☐

42

Audio

English for everyone contient de nombreux documents audio. Il vous est recommandé de les utiliser autant que possible, afin d'améliorer votre compréhension de l'anglais parlé et d'acquérir un accent et une prononciation plus naturels. Chaque dossier peut être lu, mis en pause ou répété aussi souvent que vous le désirez jusqu'à ce que vous soyez sûr d'avoir pleinement compris ce qui a été dit.

EXERCICES DE COMPRÉHENSION ORALE

Ce symbole indique que vous devez écouter un enregistrement afin de pouvoir répondre aux questions d'un exercice.

AUDIO ASSOCIÉ

Ce symbole indique qu'un enregistrement supplémentaire est à votre disposition une fois le module terminé.

AUDIO OFFERT
Site internet et appli
www.dkefe.com

Réponses

À la fin du livre, une section répertorie toutes les réponses de chaque exercice. Référez-vous à ces pages lorsque vous avez terminé un module et comparez vos réponses avec celles du livre. Vous pourrez ainsi évaluer si vous avez bien compris chaque point d'apprentissage.

24

24.1 ◄))
1 She finally managed **to cut** down the number of hours she works from 40 to 35.
2 I think our manager should allow us **to leave** work a bit earlier on Friday afternoon.
3 This new piece of software enables me **to make** updates very quickly.
4 Sam threatened **to leave** if the boss doesn't find a new employee to help him.
5 I'm the person in my office who always **volunteers** to stay late.
6 This is the first time that a colleague has invited me **to have** dinner at their home.
7 The merger deal we completed last month has caused our profits **to increase**.
8 He doesn't like people **telling** him what to do while he's at work.
9 The boss has offered **to send** me on a training course to improve my computer skills.
10 He enjoys **playing** the role of the hot-shot manager when visitors come.

24.2 ◄))
1 My colleague enjoys **hearing** from satisfied customers.
2 My new smartphone **enables** me to stay connected with my office wherever I am.
3 She hates her colleagues **telling** her what she should do in her department.
4 We like our customers **to give** us feedback on the services we provide them.
5 My boss **offered** to give me an office of my own next year.

24.3
1 False 2 True 3 Not given
4 True 5 False

24.4 ◄))
1 She always stops **to look** at what's on at the movie theater when we walk past it.
2 I remember **watching** that movie with Brian Owen, but it was a very long time ago.
3 She reminded him **to go** to the supermarket after work, but he still forgot!
4 I wish they would stop **looking** at us like that. They're making me nervous.
5 He finally remembered **to buy** me some flowers for my birthday. He usually forgets.
6 When I was a child, my mother always encouraged me **to eat** fruit and vegetables.
7 The turbulence caused the airplane **to move** from side to side for about 10 minutes.
8 He knew that we weren't interested in what he had to say, but he still went on **talking**.
9 I would advise you **to take** an aspirin for your headache.

Réponses Vous trouverez les réponses de chaque exercice à la fin du livre.

Audio Ce symbole indique qu'il vous est également possible d'écouter les réponses.

Numéros des exercices Faites correspondre ces nombres avec l'identifiant unique situé au coin supérieur gauche de chaque exercice.

01 Converser

Les verbes ont plusieurs formes au présent, y compris la forme continue et la forme parfaite (perfect). Vous devez comprendre ces différences pour formuler des question tags.

⚙ **Grammaire** Les temps du présent
Aa **Vocabulaire** Faire de nouvelles rencontres
🧩 **Compétence** Utiliser les question tags

⚙ 1.1 COCHEZ LES PHRASES CORRECTES.

Today is being my first day in my new job at the bank. ☐
Today is my first day in my new job at the bank. ☑

① I'm being a sales assistant in a department store that opened recently. ☐
I'm a sales assistant in a department store that opened recently. ☐

② Hurry up! The bus is coming. If we miss it, we will be late for work. ☐
Hurry up! The bus comes. If we miss it, we will be late for work. ☐

③ I'm meeting my new team leader right now to discuss plans for next year. ☐
I meet my new team leader right now to discuss plans for next year. ☐

④ I'm getting up at 7 o'clock every day to get to the office on time. ☐
I get up at 7 o'clock every day to get to the office on time. ☐

⑤ I'm always having a coffee break at 10 o'clock so I can work faster. ☐
I always have a coffee break at 10 o'clock so I can work faster. ☐

⑥ Today I'm wearing a new white blouse I bought from the store near my office. ☐
Today I wear a new white blouse I bought from the store near my office. ☐

⑦ She's working in the New York office at the moment, but she's planning to move to California. ☐
She working in the New York office at the moment, but she's planning to move to California. ☐

⑧ I'm thinking I'm in the wrong building. Cathy lives in building number seven. ☐
I think I'm in the wrong building. Cathy lives in building number seven. ☐

⑨ I'm having lunch in 30 minutes. Would you like to join me? ☐
I have lunch in 30 minutes. Would you like to join me? ☐

⑩ I'm going home at 5 o'clock every day after I finish work. ☐
I go home at 5 o'clock every day after I finish work. ☐

🔊

1.2 RÉCRIVEZ LES PHRASES EN CORRIGEANT LES ERREURS.

> My boss is being a lot older than me.
> _My boss is a lot older than me._

① I'm being the new member of the team.

_____

② He is always sits at that desk. You'll have to move!

_____

③ The train is arriving at 7:22am every morning.

_____

④ The bus is usually being on time, but not today.

_____

⑤ I talk to my boss at the moment.

_____

⑥ I work on the new project with David today.

_____

⑦ We are being a very good team!

_____

⑧ I'm having a meeting at 9 o'clock every day.

_____

⑨ I wait for you in front of the office.

_____

🔊

1.3 COMPLÉTEZ LES PHRASES EN CONJUGUANT LES VERBES AU PRESENT PERFECT OU AU PRESENT PERFECT CONTINU.

> I _'ve been waiting_ (wait) for Sam, but I _____haven't seen_____ (not see) him.

① I _____ (try) to call him all day, but he _____ (not answer) yet.

② He _____ (work) all day, so he _____ (not have) a break yet.

③ I'm glad I _____ (finish) that project because I _____ (work) on it for ages.

④ Jo's _____ (cook) all night, but Jim still _____ (not arrive) for dinner.

⑤ I _____ (drive) for two hours now and I still _____ (make) it to work.

⑥ He _____ (get) his schedule now and he _____ (meet) the team all day.

🔊

John is our new team leader,

shouldn't he?

1 Rebecca is from Australia,

aren't you?

2 Gary doesn't live far from the office,

hasn't he?

3 They went to college in the US,

isn't he?

4 You're working in the Singapore office,

haven't you?

5 The new employees have their badges,

hasn't she?

6 She's been waiting for 20 minutes,

didn't they?

7 Angelina worked as an engineer in New York,

isn't she?

8 Mark has traveled to many countries in Europe,

does he?

9 They are planning to move out of the city,

aren't they?

10 Alan should go on the training course next week,

don't they?

11 You have been to Singapore on a business trip,

didn't she?

1.5 ÉCOUTEZ L'ENREGISTREMENT, PUIS COCHEZ LES BONNES RÉPONSES.

Heather Miller, auteur célèbre
de récits de voyage, est interviewée.

Heather Miller comes from the UK.
True ☑ False ☐

1 Heather started travel writing 12 years ago.
True ☐ False ☐

2 Heather has been to fewer than 20 countries.
True ☐ False ☐

3 Heather has been to Central America.
True ☐ False ☐

4 Heather writes recipes in a notebook.
True ☐ False ☐

5 Heather thinks scorpion soup tastes awful.
True ☐ False ☐

1.6 AJOUTEZ DES QUESTION TAGS AUX PHRASES, PUIS LISEZ-LES À VOIX HAUTE.

Robin should tell us when he's going to be out of the office, _____*shouldn't he*_____ ?

1 Maxine always takes the 7:45 train to work like Paul, _____ ?

2 Your car is parked on the road in front of the company reception, _____ ?

3 Jonathan doesn't work in the sales department anymore, _____ ?

4 She worked for one of our competitors before she started working here, _____ ?

5 Nick and Philip have visited a lot of different countries on business trips, _____ ?

6 You would like to join us for lunch in the cafeteria today, _____ ?

7 Jessica didn't go to the strategy meeting we had last Tuesday, _____ ?

8 The boss should be showing the new employees around the office, _____ ?

9 Katrina and John know each other from their days in college, _____ ?

10 He's been waiting for some time to talk to the boss about his promotion, _____ ?

11 James isn't going to be the next head of the Human Resources department, _____ ?

12 Daniel should present the results of his research to the rest of the team, _____ ?

13 You worked with Janet on the project we did in Singapore, _____ ?

14 He works from home two days a week so he can spend time with his family, _____ ?

15 Simon and Gregory are working on a prototype for the new product, _____ ?

◀))

02 Les verbes d'action et d'état

On appelle « verbes d'action » ou « verbes dynamiques », les verbes qui décrivent des actions ou des événements ; on appelle « verbes d'état » ou « verbes statifs », ceux qui décrivent des états.

⚙ **Grammaire** Les verbes d'état aux formes continues
Aa Vocabulaire Les verbes d'action et les verbes d'état
🧩 **Compétence** Décrire les états

2.1 INDIQUEZ SI LE VERBE DÉCRIT UNE ACTION OU UN ÉTAT.

I **think** we should go home now.
Action ☐ State ☑

1 The train **arrives** in 10 minutes.
Action ☐ State ☐

2 I'll **send** her an email about it.
Action ☐ State ☐

3 This tomato soup **tastes** delicious.
Action ☐ State ☐

4 I **love** hiking in the mountains.
Action ☐ State ☐

5 I **understand** exactly how you feel.
Action ☐ State ☐

6 We're **watching** a film in the living room.
Action ☐ State ☐

7 I **belong** to a sports club in my town.
Action ☐ State ☐

8 They **seem** to be very open and friendly.
Action ☐ State ☐

9 Someone's **knocking** on the door.
Action ☐ State ☐

10 I **spoke** to my parents about it yesterday.
Action ☐ State ☐

🔊

2.2 COCHEZ LES PHRASES CORRECTES.

Are you having a dictionary? ☐
Do you have a dictionary? ☑

1 She's concentrating hard at the moment. ☐
She concentrates hard at the moment. ☐

2 I'm hating video games. They're so boring. ☐
I hate video games. They're so boring. ☐

3 He's wanting to move to a bigger place. ☐
He wants to move to a bigger place. ☐

4 She is seeming to be a reliable employee. ☐
She seems to be a reliable employee. ☐

5 He's reading a science-fiction novel. ☐
He reads a science-fiction novel. ☐

6 I'm just cooking some pasta for dinner. ☐
I just cook some pasta for dinner. ☐

7 The package is weighing four pounds. ☐
The package weighs four pounds. ☐

8 I'm not hearing you at all. ☐
I can't hear you at all. ☐

9 Laura is appearing in the show this evening. ☐
Laura appearing in the show this evening. ☐

10 What are you thinking of me? ☐
What do you think of me? ☐

🔊

2.3 RÉCRIVEZ LES PHRASES EN CORRIGEANT LES ERREURS.

I was loving pop music when I was a teenager.
I loved pop music when I was a teenager.

1 The items that the bags are containing are heavy.

_____

2 I'm seeing the mountains in the distance.

_____

3 He weighs the boxes on the scales right now.

_____

4 We were spending two hours doing our work.

_____

5 I am believing everything you say.

_____

6 I'm sorry, but I'm feeling that you're wrong.

_____

7 I listened to the radio when you came in.

_____

8 This milk is smelling bad.

_____

9 Shaun is usually arriving at work at 8am.

_____

🔊

2.4 CONJUGUEZ LES VERBES AU TEMPS QUI CONVIENT, PUIS LISEZ LES PHRASES À VOIX HAUTE.

We're _____ _expecting_ _____ (expect) some guests for an early dinner this evening. 🗣

1 William _____ (want) to travel around the world when he's older. 🗣

2 I _____ (taste) the soup to see if it needs more salt or pepper. 🗣

3 I _____ (see) my dentist later this afternoon for a consultation. 🗣

4 My knees _____ (hurt) when I walk too far or sit for too long. 🗣

5 My colleagues _____ (have) lunch right now in the cafeteria. 🗣

6 Michael _____ (be) all shy and quiet now that you're here to visit. 🗣

🔊

Utiliser les collocations

Les collocations sont généralement composées de deux mots, parfois plus. Votre anglais sera plus fluide si vous les utilisez.

⚙ **Grammaire** Les collocations
Aa Vocabulaire Les opinions et les croyances
🧩 **Compétence** Parler de votre vie

⚙ **3.1 COMPLÉTEZ LES PHRASES AVEC LES COLLOCATIONS DE LA LISTE.**

All their lives Jim and Alice appeared to be _____ *happily married* _____.

1. Laura _____ straight after school, at the age of 18.

2. The difference between these two cars is _____.

3. You've studied so much for the exam. Now all that's left is to _____.

4. I _____ asking you to pack the passports. Don't tell me you forgot!

5. I think it's _____ that you'll win the lottery tonight.

6. I don't think Steffi likes me. She seems to have a _____ of me.

7. The smell of fresh bread always _____ of my grandma.

8. Bill made a big mistake at work and it has _____.

9. I'm very lucky to have a _____. We meet up every Sunday for lunch.

happily married	clearly visible	close family	distinctly remember	do your best
extremely unlikely	low opinion	ruined his career	stirs up memories	went into business

🔊

34 Global Beat

ENIGMA FOREVER

Seventy years on, the mystery of Amelia endures

Amelia Earhart, one of the first female aviators, has been missing since 1937. She was attempting a round-the-world flight when, on July 2 1937, her plane disappeared over the Pacific Ocean. Despite a huge search effort, no body or wreckage was ever found.

Opinions are divided as to what happened to Amelia. Jack Berger, an aviation expert, firmly believes that the plane ran out of fuel and crashed into the ocean, where Amelia drowned. Berger's reasonable theory is poles apart from other, more outlandish,

explanations. For example, another popular belief is that Amelia ditched her plane on purpose, and went to spy on the Japanese. Even more unlikely is that she completed the round-the-world trip, but didn't want to be in the spotlight anymore, so moved

to a small town in the US and changed her name.

It seems extremely unlikely that we will ever know for sure what happened to Amelia. What is not a matter of opinion however, is that Amelia was declared dead in 1939, despite no body ever being found.

A LOCKHEED VEGA SIMILAR TO THE ONE FLOWN BY AMELIA EARHART

Not many women had flown a plane in 1937.
True ☑ False ☐ Not given ☐

❶ Amelia's plane disappeared over water.
True ☐ False ☐ Not given ☐

❷ Amelia's plane was found.
True ☐ False ☐ Not given ☐

❸ Jack Berger has written a book about Amelia.
True ☐ False ☐ Not given ☐

❹ Berger's theory seems reasonable.
True ☐ False ☐ Not given ☐

❺ Amelia could speak fluent Japanese.
True ☐ False ☐ Not given ☐

❻ Some people believe Amelia is still alive.
True ☐ False ☐ Not given ☐

❼ A woman with Amelia's name lives in the US.
True ☐ False ☐ Not given ☐

❽ Experts are close to solving the mystery.
True ☐ False ☐ Not given ☐

❾ Officially, Amelia has been dead since 1939.
True ☐ False ☐ Not given ☐

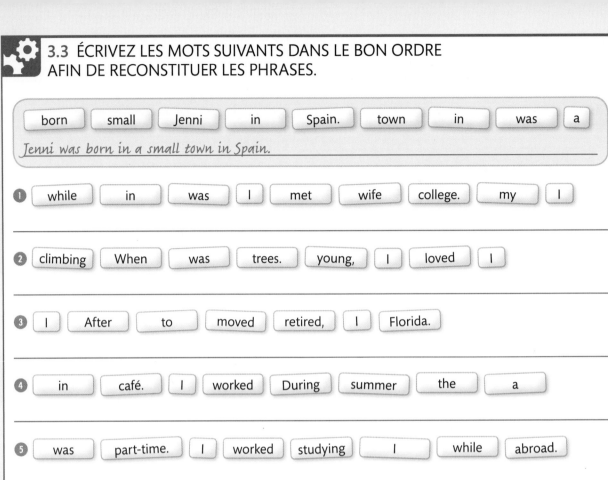

3.3 ÉCRIVEZ LES MOTS SUIVANTS DANS LE BON ORDRE AFIN DE RECONSTITUER LES PHRASES.

| born | small | Jenni | in | Spain. | town | in | was | a |

Jenni was born in a small town in Spain.

1. | while | in | was | I | met | wife | college. | my | I |

2. | climbing | When | was | trees. | young, | I | loved | I |

3. | I | After | to | moved | retired, | I | Florida. |

4. | in | café. | I | worked | During | summer | the | a |

5. | was | part-time. | I | worked | studying | I | while | abroad. |

3.4 ÉCOUTEZ L'ENREGISTREMENT, PUIS RELIEZ CHAQUE ÉVÉNEMENT AU MOMENT OÙ IL S'EST PRODUIT.

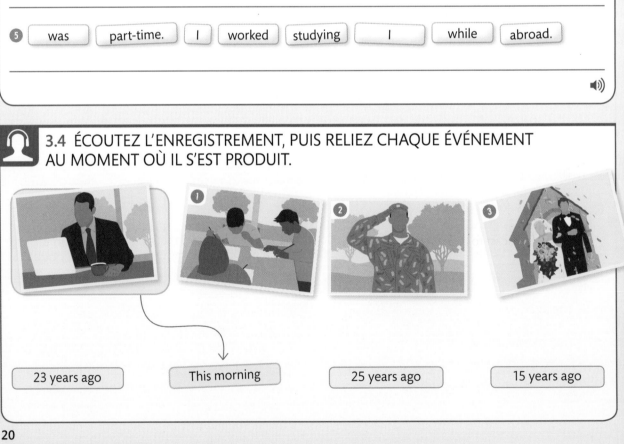

| 23 years ago | This morning | 25 years ago | 15 years ago |

3.5 BARREZ LES MOTS INCORRECTS DANS CHAQUE PHRASE.

I think Adrian ~~was having~~ / had an interview for a new job this afternoon / ~~every afternoon~~.

1. Stephanie has graduated / graduated from college with an honors degree last / before year.

2. Bill had been running / was running for many years when he decided / has decided to run a marathon.

3. Matthew was starting / started working at the company 33 years since / ago.

4. Leah was having / had a baby previous / last month. Her name's Sophie and she's beautiful.

5. Peter arrived / has arrived very early this / previous morning because he has an important meeting.

6. Jenny was working / worked in a bar in London when she has met / met Stephen.

7. Jenny and Stephen were getting married / got married this year on / in June 7.

8. Stuart had been living / has lived in the US since / for 10 years before he moved to the UK.

9. When they were / had been five years old, Anna and Jasmine were / have been best friends.

Aa 3.6 RELIEZ LE DÉBUT DE CHAQUE PHRASE À LA FIN CORRESPONDANTE.

I firmly believe → that there is someone for everyone.

1. Whether too much sleep is bad for you — so take an umbrella.

2. There is a popular belief that — her career in athletics.

3. Lionel has gone into business, — up memories of my first love.

4. There's forecast to be light rain later on, — it's extremely unlikely we'll fly today.

5. When I smelled that perfume, it stirred — such a low opinion of me.

6. The airport is still closed, so — selling clothes he has designed himself.

7. I'm not sure why Rebecca has — the number 13 is unlucky.

8. The scandal over drug-taking ruined — is a matter of opinion.

04 Les descriptions complexes

Lorsque vous décrivez quelque chose avec plusieurs adjectifs, ces derniers doivent suivre un ordre précis. Il y a plusieurs catégories d'adjectifs.

✿ **Grammaire** Les adjectifs d'ordre général et spécifique
Aa Vocabulaire Les personnalités
🧩 **Compétence** L'ordre des adjectifs

 4.1 RÉCRIVEZ LES PHRASES EN CORRIGEANT LES ERREURS.

> That looks like a new interesting movie. We should go to see it.
> _That looks like an interesting new movie. We should go to see it._

1 She's a little intelligent girl. She always does well at school.

_____

2 It's a old, horrible ugly car. I'm not going to buy it as I don't like it.

_____

3 We're going on a cheap, fantastic train trip across Europe for our vacation.

_____

4 This is such an old comfortable sweater. I love wearing it in winter.

_____

5 Gio always wears Italian stylish clothes. He is a fashion designer in London.

_____

6 Today we're going to present our new innovative tablet to you for the first time.

_____

7 Don't forget to try these spicy delicious sauces, which we've created ourselves.

_____

8 I was one of the first to ride in a high-speed unique train while I was there.

_____

9 Sometimes a low-tech reliable product is a better option than a more hi-tech one.

_____

◀))

Aa 4.2 ENTOUREZ 8 ADJECTIFS D'OPINION DANS LA GRILLE, PUIS CLASSEZ-LES.

U	R	I	T	T	N	A	T	E	E	I	L	F
F	E	U	N	A	D	W	S	V	L	A	P	K
L	S	Y	R	S	T	F	T	D	E	S	A	D
M	X	R	D	T	E	U	I	L	X	Z	N	L
N	O	A	S	Y	E	L	B	Z	C	P	G	O
E	B	S	S	E	T	U	G	L	Y	K	L	V
N	B	S	S	I	R	I	I	T	T	I	U	E
R	I	G	A	R	L	X	I	Y	I	T	G	L
R	D	C	O	N	F	K	I	N	D	W	M	Y
R	N	H	E	T	P	D	A	O	G	E	Y	R

GENERAL OPINION

nice

_____

_____

_____

SPECIFIC OPINION

kind

_____

_____

_____

4.3 COMPLÉTEZ LES PHRASES EN METTANT LES ADJECTIFS DANS LE BON ORDRE.

uncomfortable	wooden	horrible

It's a ___*horrible*___ , ___*uncomfortable*___ ___*wooden*___ chair.

old	wonderful	generous

❶ My grandma is a _____ , _____ _____ lady.

ugly	awful	expensive

❷ I bought this _____ , _____ _____ dress on the internet.

pleasant	young	friendly

❸ What a _____ , _____ _____ man Peter is!

stylish	beautiful	new

❹ Jon's got a _____ , _____ _____ car.

🔊

4.4 COMPLÉTEZ LES PHRASES AVEC LES PRÉFIXES DE LA LISTE.

> Tom was very rude and __un__ friendly toward my friends.

❶ Lana's _____ honest. She hides information and never tells the truth.

❷ You're so _____ considerate! Think about other people for a change!

❸ It was very _____ kind of you to make your sister cry. You should apologize to her.

❹ Leon always has a solution for a problem. Unfortunately, he's often _____ correct.

❺ Susanne is always being rude to her parents. She's so _____ respectful.

❻ Stop behaving like a five-year-old! You're so _____ mature!

in	dis	~~un~~	dis	in	im	un

4.5 ÉCOUTEZ L'ENREGISTREMENT, PUIS COCHEZ LES BONNES RÉPONSES.

Richard et Jenni discutent d'un poste à pourvoir dans leur société.

Jenni thinks the person they choose must be...
- blunt ☐
- fair-minded ☐
- resourceful ☑

❸ The person that Richard is considering is...
- Anna ☐
- Esther ☐
- Mary ☐

❶ The person they choose must not be...
- rude ☐
- inexperienced ☐
- mature ☐

❹ Esther has been working with the company for...
- five years ☐
- six years ☐
- seven years ☐

❷ Richard thinks Sonia is reliable, but also...
- lazy ☐
- efficient ☐
- arrogant ☐

❺ Jenni thinks Esther is...
- trustworthy ☐
- arrogant ☐
- popular ☐

4.6 LISEZ L'ÉVALUATION DES COMPÉTENCES, PUIS RÉPONDEZ AUX QUESTIONS.

Name: Jenson Lee
Position: Website administrator
Subject: Performance Review

Jenson joined the company just over a year ago. He appeared rather quiet to begin with, but has proved himself to be hardworking and proactive. For example, in June the company website crashed while May Wong, Jenson's boss, was on vacation. Jenson took charge of the situation and sought help from others on the team. He was incredibly organized, and thanks to his excellent planning, the website was back online within six hours. Jenson is also clearly ambitious, and he has expressed a desire to be promoted into management.

Because Jenson is so shy, some people think he is unfriendly and insensitive. We discussed this and he agreed he sometimes feels uncomfortable in social situations. We will look for training courses that will help him with this. Jenson needs to improve his social skills before he can be considered for promotion.

When Jenson first started working for the company, what was his personality like?

Jenson was very quiet when he first started working for the company.

1 How did Jenson solve the problem with the website?

_____

2 What are Jenson's hopes for his future career?

_____

3 Why might Jenson sometimes appear rude?

_____

4 What solution has Jenson's company come up with to help him overcome his shyness?

_____

5 How can Jenson improve his chances of getting promoted?

_____

6 Would you say the review is generally positive or negative?

_____

Faire des déclarations d'ordre général

Il est très utile de savoir comment commencer une phrase avec le mot « it » en anglais. Vous pouvez utiliser « it is » en début de phrase pour faire une déclaration d'ordre général.

⚙ **Grammaire** Le « it » introductif
Aa Vocabulaire Les talents et les aptitudes
🧩 **Compétence** Exprimer des vérités générales

5.1 COMPLÉTEZ LES PHRASES AVEC LES EXPRESSIONS DE LA LISTE.

It is ___*not important that*___ we lost the first game. You should forget about that.

1. It's _____ some people aren't interested in learning languages.

2. It's _____ you chose that book because it's the book that I chose, too.

3. It's _____ win. What you should be focused on is doing your very best.

4. It is _____ learn English vocabulary, but it's difficult to learn the grammar.

5. It's _____ our neighbors are so understanding because we make a lot of noise!

6. When it's so cold outside, it's _____ wrap yourself up as warmly as possible.

7. It's _____ everyone has enough water to drink while we're out walking in the heat.

8. It's _____ look at your phone while you're driving. You could have an accident.

9. Joshua has been doing so badly at school that he's _____ do well in his exams.

10. It is _____ understand people when they speak English very quickly.

11. Look at those black clouds over there. I think it's _____ rain sometime soon.

12. Our train is so delayed. I think it's _____ we'll get home before midnight!

13. It's really _____ some people don't care about the environment. They should!

14. It's _____ our children do their best at school and get a good education.

15. It's _____ have all of the family here together again. I've missed everyone.

---

interesting that	important to	important that	not important to	essential that
difficult to	unlikely that	unlikely to	likely to	bad that	bad to
good that	good to	easy to	~~not important that~~	a shame that

🔊

5.2 BARREZ LES MOTS INCORRECTS DANS CHAQUE PHRASE.

 To / ~~That~~ / ~~It~~ get to the school, go straight ahead and then turn left.

❶ That / To / It is unlikely that I will finish this assignment on time.

❷ It's difficult that / to / it decide what to order because it all sounds delicious.

❸ That / To / Them lose at this point would be very difficult after coming so far.

❹ It's easy that / to / they start writing an essay, but it's not always easy to finish one!

❺ It's essential that / to / they everyone follows the rules and does what they're told.

❻ That / To / They read English is easy, but to write in English is more difficult.

❼ It's important that / to / it choose an interesting topic to give a presentation about.

🔊

Aa **5.3 RELIEZ LE DÉBUT DE CHAQUE PHRASE À LA FIN CORRESPONDANTE.**

My brother surprised us with his   to plan ahead. He's always late!

❶ I have a certain aptitude for   navigating with a map, but I still get lost.

❷ My friend has a complete inability   to memorize huge passages of text.

❸ It seems like some people have a   hidden talent for baking cakes.

❹ Dr. Finn had a remarkable capacity   natural ability to run long distances.

🔊

5.4 LISEZ LE COURRIEL, PUIS COCHEZ LES BONNES RÉPONSES.

To: Charlotte
Subject: Learning Chinese

Hi Charlotte,
Hope you are well. I've been learning Chinese recently. I decided to do a course at my local college. It looked like a good way to get out and meet new people in the evening instead of just surfing the internet. My teacher thinks I have a natural ability for Chinese. Chinese is a tonal language, which means you have to think about what tone you say the words in. Looking forward to seeing you next week.
Jenny

Which language has Jenny been learning recently?
Japanese ☐ **Arabic** ☐ **Chinese** ☑

① Where is Jenny learning it?
At a school ☐ **At a college** ☐ **At a university** ☐

② It will help her do less of what in the evening?
Shopping ☐ **Housework** ☐ **Surfing the internet** ☐

③ What kind of ability does Jenny have for Chinese?
Natural ☐ **Limited** ☐ **Advanced** ☐

④ How does Jenny describe the language she's learning?
Tonal ☐ **Clicking** ☐ **Difficult** ☐

5.5 COMPLÉTEZ LES RÉPONSES AUX QUESTIONS DE L'ENREGISTREMENT, PUIS LISEZ-LES À VOIX HAUTE.

Do you like learning new languages?

Yes, I think ___*they help you communicate with more people.*___

① Why do so many people want to learn English?

Because it's important _____

② Will English be a popular language in the future?

I think English is likely _____

③ Describe your ability to learn languages.

I think I have _____

④ What makes learning English difficult?

It's difficult _____

06 Vocabulaire

Aa 6.1 **LES VOYAGES ET LE TOURISME** ÉCRIVEZ LES EXPRESSIONS DE LA LISTE SOUS LA DÉFINITION CORRESPONDANTE.

A vacation, particularly a short one

getaway

1 Unique and unrepeatable

2 A desire for exciting experiences

3 Pay your bill and leave a hotel

4 Visit interesting buildings and places as a tourist

5 Totally unable to find your way

6 Go to the station or airport to say goodbye to someone

7 A stage in a journey from one place to another

8 Explore an area or place

9 Register your arrival at an airport or hotel

10 Be sad because you miss your home and family

11 Feeling of confusion or distress when visiting a different place or culture

12 Go somewhere relaxing for a break

13 Pause a journey in one place before continuing

culture shock	check out	thirst for adventure	get away from it all
getaway	check in	leg of a journey	once-in-a-lifetime	see somebody off
go sightseeing	feel homesick	look around	hopelessly lost	stop off

07 Les verbes à particule

Les verbes à particule se présentent sous différentes formes. Ils sont composés de 2 ou 3 éléments qui sont parfois séparables. Ils sont très communs, surtout en anglais parlé.

⚙ **Grammaire** Vue d'ensemble des verbes à particule
Aa Vocabulaire Le voyage
🧩 **Compétence** Utiliser des verbes à particule complexes

⚙ 7.1 ÉCRIVEZ LES MOTS SUIVANTS DANS LE BON ORDRE AFIN DE RECONSTITUER LES PHRASES.

all | It | on | raining | kept | night.

It kept on raining all night.

① get | at | I | up | 7am. | usually

_____

② would | in | early. | like | to | check | I

_____

③ out | need | by | I | to | check | 9am.

_____

④ works | two | He | hours. | out | for

_____

⑤ Fridays. | We | go | always | out | on

_____

⑥ up | in. | Please | go | line | here | to

_____

⑦ the | Martin | showed | at | party. | up

_____

🔊

⚙ 7.2 COCHEZ LES PHRASES CORRECTES.

This is where you have to line up. ☑
This is where you have to lines up. ☐

① They want to check in at the hotel. ☐
They want to check up at the hotel. ☐

② He keeps on complaining about his job. ☐
He keeps complaining on about his job. ☐

③ She doesn't like getting up early. ☐
She doesn't like getting on early. ☐

④ She works down in the morning. ☐
She works out in the morning. ☐

⑤ We're going for Sheila's birthday out. ☐
We're going out for Sheila's birthday. ☐

⑥ He shows up late to work yesterday. ☐
He showed up late to work yesterday. ☐

⑦ Jo, please come in and join us here. ☐
Jo, please come into and join us here. ☐

⑧ Tim is coming down for my birthday. ☐
Tim is coming under for my birthday. ☐

⑨ Cooking is hard, but you should keep it at. ☐
Cooking is hard, but you should keep at it. ☐

⑩ He always checks down early. ☐
He always checks out early. ☐

🔊

7.3 RÉCRIVEZ LES PHRASES EN PLAÇANT LA PARTICULE DES VERBES AU BON ENDROIT.

> We seem to throw away too much food. We should buy less when we go to the supermarket.
> *We seem to throw too much food away. We should buy less when we go to the supermarket.*

1 She really needs to clean up her desk. It's full of papers and old coffee cups.

_____

2 The sixth grade students are putting on a show to celebrate the end of their time at this school.

_____

3 Everyone needs to hand in their forms by Friday. Otherwise you can't go on the trip.

_____

4 I need you to look up a few words in the dictionary for me. Can you do that?

_____

5 I'll check out the hotels in Monte Carlo and let you know what the prices are.

_____

7.4 RÉCRIVEZ LES PHRASES EN UTILISANT DES PRONOMS.

> We're getting a new gymnasium at school. They're putting the building up this year.
> *We're getting a new gymnasium at school. They're putting it up this year.*

1 It's not a problem. We'll come over and pick up the sofa from your place.

_____

2 He was so angry he tore up the contract and threw the pieces around the room.

_____

3 You should put on that pullover when you go outside. It's absolutely freezing.

_____

4 If you cut out that coupon, you can use it to get two for the price of one at the supermarket.

_____

7.5 COMPLÉTEZ LES PHRASES AVEC LES VERBES À PARTICULE DE LA LISTE, PUIS LISEZ-LES À VOIX HAUTE.

CONSEIL
N'oubliez pas que lorsque vous prononcez un verbe à particule de 3 mots, vous devez accentuer le deuxième.

I'm lucky that I ___*get along with*___ all of my colleagues really well.

1 He's always trying to _____ his reputation as a big spender.

2 We're _____ some really good ideas at the moment.

3 I should just _____ the things that I don't need.

4 She's so fast. I can't _____ her.

5 Melissa's great. I really _____ her.

get rid of

coming up with

live up to

keep up with

look up to

~~get along with~~

7.6 COMPLÉTEZ LES PHRASES EN CONJUGUANT LES VERBES AU TEMPS QUI CONVIENT.

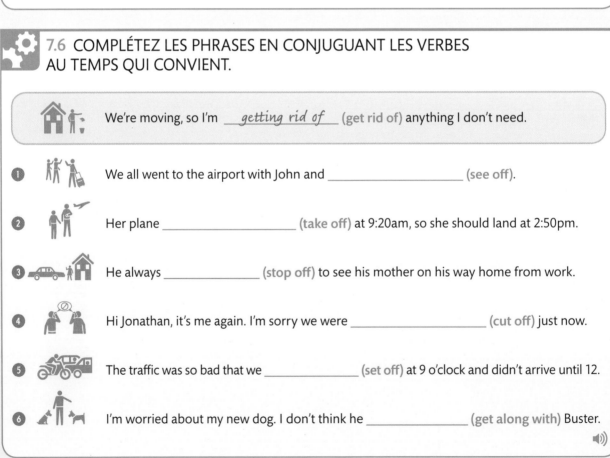

We're moving, so I'm ___*getting rid of*___ (get rid of) anything I don't need.

1 We all went to the airport with John and _____ (see off).

2 Her plane _____ (take off) at 9:20am, so she should land at 2:50pm.

3 He always _____ (stop off) to see his mother on his way home from work.

4 Hi Jonathan, it's me again. I'm sorry we were _____ (cut off) just now.

5 The traffic was so bad that we _____ (set off) at 9 o'clock and didn't arrive until 12.

6 I'm worried about my new dog. I don't think he _____ (get along with) Buster.

TEAM-BUILDING UPDATE

A trip to Salzburg

How a weekend in the mountains brought a team together

Last year our boss, Robert, suggested we go on a team-building trip to help us get along with each other better. Robert said we needed to keep up with other companies and live up to our reputation as an efficient company. We set off early one morning and our plane to Salzburg took off at 8am. When we landed, someone from our hotel came to pick us up. As soon as we arrived we had to put some extra layers on because it was freezing cold.

We went climbing in the mountains and at one point, I got cut off from the others. Luckily Sebastian, our guide, called out to me and I found the group again. Sebastian said we needed to get rid of our inhibitions and just climb. At the end of the weekend, we all agreed that the trip had been enjoyable and we even came up with some ideas for a new sales campaign!

They went on the team-building trip this year.　　　**True** ☐　**False** ☐　**Not given** ☑

① Their boss suggested the team-building trip.　　　**True** ☐　**False** ☐　**Not given** ☐

② The aim of the trip was to improve team relationships.　　　**True** ☐　**False** ☐　**Not given** ☐

③ Other people don't see the company as being efficient.　　　**True** ☐　**False** ☐　**Not given** ☐

④ The team flew from London Heathrow airport.　　　**True** ☐　**False** ☐　**Not given** ☐

⑤ Their plane arrived in Salzburg at 8am.　　　**True** ☐　**False** ☐　**Not given** ☐

⑥ The team took the bus to the hotel in Salzburg.　　　**True** ☐　**False** ☐　**Not given** ☐

⑦ The team discovered they weren't dressed warmly enough.　　　**True** ☐　**False** ☐　**Not given** ☐

⑧ The writer lost the group and couldn't find them again.　　　**True** ☐　**False** ☐　**Not given** ☐

⑨ Sebastian encouraged the group to feel inhibited.　　　**True** ☐　**False** ☐　**Not given** ☐

⑩ The team thought of some new ideas while on the trip.　　　**True** ☐　**False** ☐　**Not given** ☐

08 Les temps narratifs

Lorsque vous racontez une histoire (même s'il ne s'agit que de ce qui vous est arrivé récemment), vous devez utiliser plusieurs temps pour être bien compris.

⚙ **Grammaire** Le past perfect continu
Aa **Vocabulaire** Les adjectifs et les idiomes du voyage
🧩 **Compétence** Parler de plusieurs actions passées

 8.1 COMPLÉTEZ LES PHRASES EN CONJUGUANT LES VERBES AU PRÉTÉRIT OU AU PRÉTÉRIT CONTINU.

> We __decided__ (decide) to order a bottle of wine while we __were having__ (have) dinner.

❶ I _____ (learn) a lot of Japanese while I _____ (live) in Japan.

❷ While I _____ (wait) for the train, I _____ (meet) my favorite singer.

❸ As we _____ (walk) home last night, we _____ (see) a firework display.

❹ We _____ (stop) at the café while we _____ (visit) the castle.

❺ I _____ (get) off my bike a few times while I _____ (cycle) to work.

❻ I _____ (see) a lot of cafés when I _____ (stroll) around town.

❼ While I _____ (wander) around, I _____ (find) a good bookstore.

❽ She _____ (take) so many pictures when she _____ (travel).

❾ I _____ (have) problems with my car until he _____ (help) me.

🔊

34

8.2 COMPLÉTEZ LES PHRASES EN UTILISANT LE PAST PERFECT, PUIS LISEZ-LES À VOIX HAUTE.

They **decided** to travel around the country, so they rented a car at the airport.

They rented a car at the airport because *they had decided to travel around the country.*

❶ The hotel receptionist **recommended** a local restaurant to us, so we tried it.

We tried a local restaurant because _____

❷ I **went** in the swimming pool at the hotel and then I went in the sauna.

I went in the sauna after I _____

❸ A friend of ours **said** it was a good idea to rent a bike, so we did.

We rented a bike because _____

❹ Just after we **arrived** at the hotel, they gave us a welcome drink.

They gave us a welcome drink just after _____

❺ We **bought** advance tickets, so didn't have to wait in line to go into the museum.

We didn't have to wait in line to go in because _____

8.3 COMPLÉTEZ LES PHRASES EN CONJUGUANT LES VERBES AU PAST PERFECT CONTINU.

They ____*had been walking*____ (walk) around Rome for two hours before they found the restaurant.

❶ The Miller family _____ (go) to Croatia for years before it became popular with tourists.

❷ We needed to move around after we _____ (sit) on the plane for 14 hours.

❸ I _____ (wait) for them at the airport for half an hour before they arrived.

❹ Our team _____ (lose) in the first half of the game, but they came back in the second.

❺ She _____ (study) Spanish for six months before she went to Mexico.

❻ It _____ (rain) for five days in a row before we had some sunshine.

8.4 COMPLÉTEZ LES PHRASES EN CONJUGUANT LES VERBES DE LA LISTE AU TEMPS QUI CONVIENT.

We ___*had been waiting*___ in line for an hour before we ___*were able to*___ buy our train tickets.

❶ She _____ to cycle across China, but then she _____ an accident on her bike.

❷ When they _____ back home, they discovered that someone _____ their house.

❸ After I _____ around Asia for six months, I _____ very happy to be back home.

❹ Before I _____ to South America, I _____ tango dancing.

❺ He _____ to visit the fjords because he _____ they were beautiful.

go	want	~~be able to~~	travel	not try	get
plan	hear	feel	burgle	have	~~wait~~

🔊

8.5 RELIEZ LE DÉBUT DE CHAQUE PHRASE À LA FIN CORRESPONDANTE.

After I left home, I realized → that I had forgotten my umbrella.

I realized that someone had stolen my car.

❶ I had written some practice answers

but they decided to go to bed early.

❷ When I got back to the parking lot,

been working in the US for six months.

❸ Before I started working here, I had

that I had forgotten my umbrella.

❹ I had given the matter a lot of thought

before I decided to change jobs.

❺ They were eating at a restaurant when

I had not been sleeping very well.

❻ She wanted to go to Spain because

her parents had told her it was fantastic.

❼ They had been planning to go out,

a famous author came in.

❽ I was feeling extremely tired because

before the exam, so I was well prepared.

🔊

TRUE STORIES

An unusual friendship

Two strangers became friends without even knowing each other's names

Jason works in an office in New York. One Monday morning, he looked out of the window and saw a woman working in the building across the street. To his surprise, she smiled and waved. Jason had moved to New York a few months earlier. Before that, he had been doing an internship in London, and he was certain he and the woman in the window had never met.

A few days later, Jason saw the woman again. This time she was holding up a piece of paper with the word "hi" written on it. Jason found a piece of paper and wrote "hi" back. From that day on, they sent regular messages using pieces of paper, without ever meeting face-to-face. Finally, some weeks later, the mystery woman wrote: "Do you want to meet for coffee?" Jason wrote back: "Yes, sure."

Their unusual meeting had led to a genuine friendship, which has lasted many years.

When did Jason first see the woman in the office building across the street?

Jason first saw the woman on a Monday morning.

❶ How long had Jason been living in New York at the time?

_____

❷ What had Jason been doing before he moved to New York?

_____

❸ How long was it before Jason saw the woman a second time?

_____

❹ Who was the first person to start writing messages?

_____

Lorsque vous voulez donner un conseil ou faire une recommandation, vous pouvez utiliser plusieurs modaux. Vous pouvez moduler l'intensité de votre conseil en employant différents modaux.

⚙ **Grammaire** Les modaux pour le conseil et l'opinion
Aa Vocabulaire Les recommandations
🧩 **Compétence** Donner des conseils et votre opinion

 9.1 COCHEZ LES RECOMMANDATIONS.

It's difficult to find a hotel in the center of Paris that isn't really expensive.

You could try the Hôtel du Théâtre. It's quite cheap. ✓

③ You might want to take a boat trip around the lake while you're here.

That sounds like a good idea. We couldn't do that last time.

① When you're in Berlin, you ought to visit the television tower.

Oh yes. I heard there are some great views from the top.

④ Jonas could make a reservation. Then he'll definitely get a seat on the train.

You're right. I'll tell him to do that.

② It's so hot today, I can't believe it!

I know! You really should take the kids down to the swimming pool.

⑤ We could go to visit the Great Wall on our third day in Beijing.

Yes, it's awesome. You really must do that.

🔊

 **9.2 ÉCOUTEZ L'ENREGISTREMENT, PUIS COCHEZ LA CRITIQUE QUI CORRESPOND LE PLUS À L'OPINION DE CHARLOTTE.**

① Charlotte liked the restaurant's location by the canal and thought the food was very fresh. ☐

② Charlotte thought the restaurant was noisy and the service was bad. ☐

③ Charlotte didn't like the inside of the restaurant and thought the food wasn't very fresh. ☐

9.3 COMPLÉTEZ LES PHRASES AVEC LES RECOMMANDATIONS DE LA LISTE.

The science museum is a lot of fun for all the family!

You really should take your kids there soon.

We can't praise our tour guide enough. She gave us such a lot of interesting information.

③ _____

We had some outstanding food at Lionel's restaurant!

① _____

I had trouble sleeping because the sheets were very rough.

④ _____

The room wasn't bad, although ours was a lot smaller than some of the others.

② _____

The staff at the bar had fantastic recommendations for drinks.

⑤ _____

You might want to bring a sheet!   You could ask for a larger room if this is an issue.

You really must try the cocktails.   ~~You really should take your kids there soon~~.

You must ask for Irene if you go there.   You ought to try the pasta.

9.4 ÉCOUTEZ L'ENREGISTREMENT, PUIS COCHEZ SI VICTOR A AIMÉ OU PAS CHAQUE ACTIVITÉ.

Like ☐   Dislike ☑

① Like ☐   Dislike ☐

① Like ☐   Dislike ☐

③ Like ☐   Dislike ☐

④ Like ☐   Dislike ☐

9.5 CHOISISSEZ LA BONNE PROPOSITION, PUIS LISEZ LES PHRASES À VOIX HAUTE.

You **should** / ~~had better~~ take some photographs when you get to the top of the tower.

1 You **must** / **could** put on a lot of sun cream or you'll burn.

2 You **could** / **had better** take your walking boots if you're going to go hiking while you're there.

3 The firework display will be absolutely stunning. You **would** / **must** go and see it.

4 If I were you, I **would** / **could** take the train from Paris to London instead of flying.

5 You **would** / **should** ask if they have any vacancies at the Hotel Bennetton.

9.6 LISEZ LE COURRIEL, PUIS COCHEZ LES BONNES RÉPONSES.

Severine went on vacation to...
France ☐ **South Africa** ☑ **Belgium** ☐

1 Severine recommends traveling around by...
car ☐ **bus** ☐ **plane** ☐

2 Severine recommends taking a lot of...
cameras ☐ **photographs** ☐ **videos** ☐

3 Severine advises locking your...
car doors ☐ **trunk** ☐ **car windows** ☐

4 Severine recommends trying a South African...
safari ☐ **car** ☐ **dish** ☐

5 Severine wants to show Tim her...
photographs ☐ **camera** ☐ **South African dishes** ☐

✉

To: Tim

Subject: Our trip!

Hi Tim,
Robert and I have just come back to Belgium after our trip to South Africa! We flew from Paris to Cape Town and took a bus along the coast. If I were you, I'd rent a car when you come. You ought to take a good camera with you, so you can take lots of photos because there are animals everywhere. Some of them can be dangerous, so you'd better keep your car doors locked! The food was also great. You should try bobotie, a typical South African dish. You should come over some time so we can show you all our photos.
Best wishes,
Severine

9.7 ÉCRIVEZ UNE LETTRE DANS LAQUELLE VOUS RECOMMANDEZ UN VOYAGE EN UTILISANT LES SYNTAGMES VERBAUX DE LA LISTE.

Hi Jake!

How are you? It's been a long time since I sent you a letter, so I thought I would tell you about our family trip to Paris.

We went to	I really enjoyed the	You ought to	You'd better
If I were you, I'd	Best wishes	You must	The highlight for me was

10 Faire des prédictions

Lorsque vous parlez d'un événement futur, vous pouvez être amené à évaluer le degré de probabilité qu'il a de se produire. Il y a plusieurs méthodes pour y parvenir.

⚙️ **Grammaire** Les degrés de probabilité
Aa **Vocabulaire** Les idiomes temporels
🧩 **Compétence** Parler de possibilité

10.1 RELIEZ LE DÉBUT DE CHAQUE PHRASE À LA FIN QUI LUI CORRESPOND.

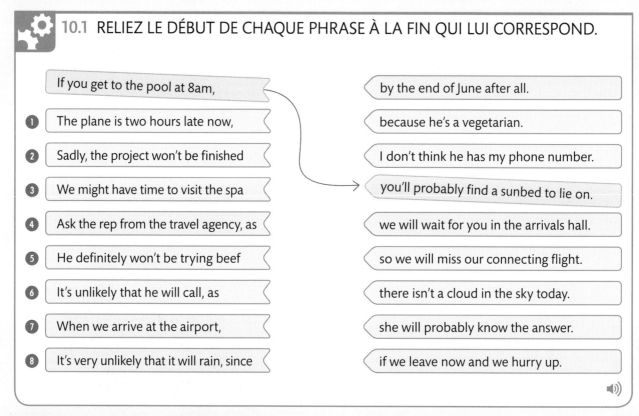

If you get to the pool at 8am,

① The plane is two hours late now,

② Sadly, the project won't be finished

③ We might have time to visit the spa

④ Ask the rep from the travel agency, as

⑤ He definitely won't be trying beef

⑥ It's unlikely that he will call, as

⑦ When we arrive at the airport,

⑧ It's very unlikely that it will rain, since

by the end of June after all.

because he's a vegetarian.

I don't think he has my phone number.

you'll probably find a sunbed to lie on.

we will wait for you in the arrivals hall.

so we will miss our connecting flight.

there isn't a cloud in the sky today.

she will probably know the answer.

if we leave now and we hurry up.

10.2 ÉCOUTEZ L'ENREGISTREMENT, PUIS INDIQUEZ SI CHAQUE ACTIVITÉ A DES CHANCES D'AVOIR LIEU OU PAS.

Likely ✓ Unlikely ☐

① Likely ☐ Unlikely ☐

② Likely ☐ Unlikely ☐

③ Likely ☐ Unlikely ☐

④ Likely ☐ Unlikely ☐

10.3 BARREZ LE MOT INCORRECT DANS CHAQUE PHRASE.

He looked surprisingly / ~~fortunately~~ good in his suit and tie at the wedding.

❶ The internet has fundamentally / essentially changed how we book our vacations.

❷ Luckily / Fundamentally, we had nice weather every day when we were on vacation.

❸ Unfortunately / Essentially, Emma was sick when we were on vacation.

❹ The trip home was surprisingly / predictably slow. There are always problems on that route.

❺ They make their pancakes in luckily / essentially the same way that we do.

❻ Interestingly / Predictably, Winston Churchill had stayed at our hotel when he was in the region.

❼ Unfortunately / Fortunately, we were fit enough to be able to hike back down the coast.

10.4 COMPLÉTEZ LES PHRASES AVEC LES MOTS DE LA LISTE, PUIS LISEZ-LES À VOIX HAUTE.

Fundamentally , this is an absolutely awful hotel and I would advise you not to stay here.

❶ _____ , we made it to the hotel before the reception closed for the night.

❷ Windsurfing is _____ sailing with a surfboard.

❸ _____ , the hotel is completely booked up.

❹ _____ , the café was also an art gallery.

❺ _____ , Richard actually went in the pool. You know how he normally hates water.

❻ _____ , Donald got sunburned again. He never puts any sun tan lotion on.

~~Fundamentally~~   essentially   Surprisingly   Predictably   Unfortunately   Luckily   Interestingly

43

36 CITY PULSE

CITY TO GET MEGA-MALL

Authorities announce plans to build new mega-mall in Graysonville

The local authorities have announced plans to build a new mega-mall in Graysonville. Spokesman William Peters said mega-malls are the shape of things to come and it was only a matter of time before Graysonville built one. Interestingly, the mayor of Graysonville rejected plans to build a mega-mall 10 years ago, but now he's saying that it's essentially a very positive step forward for the town. In the short-term, there's probably going to be construction work going on for the next two years. Luckily, the construction company can use the plans that were drawn up 10 years ago.

The mayor will probably make a statement to explain why the mall will be built, when this had seemed so unlikely. In the long-term, the new development means that Graysonville residents won't have to go out of town to shop because they'll have everything they need right here.

	True	False	Not given
A large new mall is going to be built in Graysonville.	☑	☐	☐
❶ The mall will contain over 200 shops.	☐	☐	☐
❷ The spokesman thinks malls are the future of shopping.	☐	☐	☐
❸ He also said it was inevitable one would be built in Graysonville.	☐	☐	☐
❹ The mayor agreed to plans to build a mall 10 years ago.	☐	☐	☐
❺ It's unlikely that construction work will go on for two years.	☐	☐	☐
❻ It's a good thing that the old plans can be used.	☐	☐	☐
❼ There's a good chance the mayor will make a statement.	☐	☐	☐
❽ Graysonville residents will no longer shop in Buntstown.	☐	☐	☐
❾ Residents will have all the shops they need in their city.	☐	☐	☐

11 Vocabulaire

Aa 11.1 LA FAMILLE ET LES RELATIONS ÉCRIVEZ LES EXPRESSIONS DE LA LISTE SOUS LA DÉFINITION CORRESPONDANTE.

Share an interest or opinion

have something in common

1 Develop from a child to an adult

2 Be a common feature of a family

3 Speak out in support of somebody

4 Agree with or have similar opinions to somebody

5 Become friendly with a person

6 Like somebody quickly and easily

7 Have a child

8 Slowly become less friendly or close to somebody

9 Meet someone unexpectedly

10 Be strict about something

11 Have respect and admiration for someone

12 A friend who you know very well

13 End a romantic relationship

---

put your foot down   make friends with somebody   give birth   close friend   run in the family

break up with somebody   grow up   drift apart   bump into somebody   ~~have something in common~~

look up to somebody   stick up for somebody   click with somebody   see eye to eye with somebody

12 Utiliser des marqueurs rhétoriques

Les marqueurs rhétoriques peuvent être utilisés pour indiquer une relation entre deux phrases, ou segments de phrase. Cette relation peut être une relation de cause, effet, emphase, contraste ou comparaison.

Grammaire Lier l'information
Aa Vocabulaire L'histoire familiale
Compétence Parler de relations

12.1 RELIEZ LE DÉBUT DE CHAQUE PHRASE À LA FIN QUI LUI CORRESPOND.

I call my mother when I arrive at work, ———→ so she knows I got there safely.

particularly chess.

1. I have bright blue eyes — especially my brother, who's a scientist.

2. We live in different countries, — as a result, he always gets socks!

3. My siblings are all very intelligent, — so she knows I got there safely.

4. My dad loves to play board games, — because we're all so busy now.

5. They like different TV channels — so he always makes dinner for us.

6. We can video chat with each other — like my mother.

7. She is interested in my life at college — especially when they all get together.

8. I enjoy going fishing — just as we used to do when we were kids.

9. My father is a great cook, — but we all get together at Christmas.

10. We only see each other once a month — because she wasn't able to go.

11. It's hard to buy a present for dad and, — since we all have smartphones or laptops.

12. We cook something different for her — so they watch them in different rooms.

13. My relatives all talk a lot, — though my family doesn't eat it often.

14. Ann and I still stay up late chatting — just as my father does. He's great at it.

15. I love cooking Chinese food, — as she's a vegetarian.

12.2 BARREZ LES MOTS INCORRECTS DANS CHAQUE PHRASE.

I always call my mother when I have a problem because / ~~though~~ she gives me good advice.

1 My brother loves sports, especially / but ice hockey.

2 Our family usually goes to Greece on vacation, since / though last year we went to Turkey.

3 My brother got great grades at school, so / particularly he studied at a good university.

4 My dad works in the garden every day though / as he has a lot of free time after retiring.

5 My mother loves cats just as / but my grandmother did.

6 My sister loves music, since / particularly rock and pop bands.

7 My mother's always wanted to go to Paris, like / so we organized a trip for her 50th birthday.

8 We do sometimes argue with each other, since / but we never stay angry at each other for long.

9 My two younger brothers are very close but / as they shared a room when they were growing up.

10 My family isn't very big like / since my husband's.

11 We will have a big family gathering this year as / especially all my cousins will be here.

12 Sonya is a talented painter just as / as a result her grandmother was.

13 All my relatives are good singers, though / particularly my aunt.

12.3 RELIEZ LE DÉBUT DE CHAQUE PHRASE À LA FIN QUI LUI CORRESPOND.

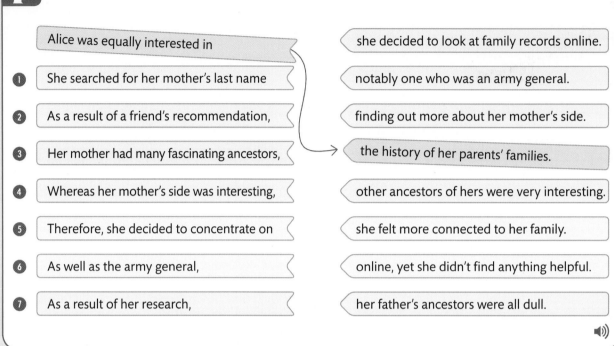

Alice was equally interested in

she decided to look at family records online.

1 She searched for her mother's last name

notably one who was an army general.

2 As a result of a friend's recommendation,

finding out more about her mother's side.

3 Her mother had many fascinating ancestors, → the history of her parents' families.

4 Whereas her mother's side was interesting,

other ancestors of hers were very interesting.

5 Therefore, she decided to concentrate on

she felt more connected to her family.

6 As well as the army general,

online, yet she didn't find anything helpful.

7 As a result of her research,

her father's ancestors were all dull.

12.4 BARREZ LE MARQUEUR RHÉTORIQUE QUI CONVIENT LE MOINS, PUIS LISEZ LES PHRASES À VOIX HAUTE.

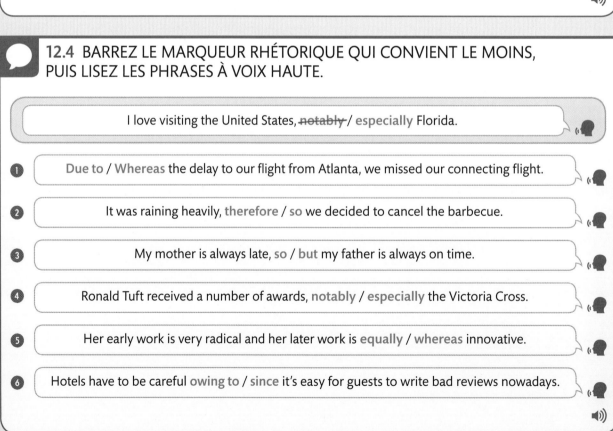

I love visiting the United States, ~~notably~~ / especially Florida.

1 Due to / Whereas the delay to our flight from Atlanta, we missed our connecting flight.

2 It was raining heavily, therefore / so we decided to cancel the barbecue.

3 My mother is always late, so / but my father is always on time.

4 Ronald Tuft received a number of awards, notably / especially the Victoria Cross.

5 Her early work is very radical and her later work is equally / whereas innovative.

6 Hotels have to be careful owing to / since it's easy for guests to write bad reviews nowadays.

12.5 LISEZ L'ARTICLE, PUIS COCHEZ LES BONNES RÉPONSES.

GENEALOGY

Top tips for researching your family

Start by talking to your family about their memories, particularly your grandparents or older family members. Remember that they won't be around forever, so it's a good idea to record anything they tell you.

Look at any documents your family has kept. These can give important information about births, marriages, and deaths.

Censuses primarily contain information about people's ages and addresses, but they can also tell you the occupations of your ancestors.

Write down any information you find out. Make copies of family documents and keep them together with this information.

You might think family history research is something you do alone, but this doesn't have to be the case. Why not join a local family history society where you can share tips with others?

The article gives advice on how to research your family history.
True ☑ **False** ☐ **Not given** ☐

---

❶ Don't talk to your grandparents because they can't remember anything.
True ☐ **False** ☐ **Not given** ☐

❷ It's a good idea to record what your family tells you.
True ☐ **False** ☐ **Not given** ☐

❸ Some types of family documents are more helpful than others.
True ☐ **False** ☐ **Not given** ☐

❹ Family documents can tell you when your ancestors married and died.
True ☐ **False** ☐ **Not given** ☐

❺ Censuses can tell you what jobs your ancestors did.
True ☐ **False** ☐ **Not given** ☐

❻ Don't make copies of old documents because that can damage them.
True ☐ **False** ☐ **Not given** ☐

❼ You have to do family history research alone.
True ☐ **False** ☐ **Not given** ☐

❽ Social media can help you find out where your nearest family history society is.
True ☐ **False** ☐ **Not given** ☐

13 Les habitudes et les états passés

Pour parler d'habitudes ou d'états du passé, vous pouvez utiliser « used to » ou « would ». L'anglais emploie souvent ces formes pour contraster le passé avec le présent.

⚙ **Grammaire** « Used to » et « would »

Aa **Vocabulaire** Les valeurs familiales

🧩 **Compétence** Contraster le passé avec le présent

⚙ **13.1 RÉCRIVEZ LES PHRASES EN CORRIGEANT LES ERREURS.**

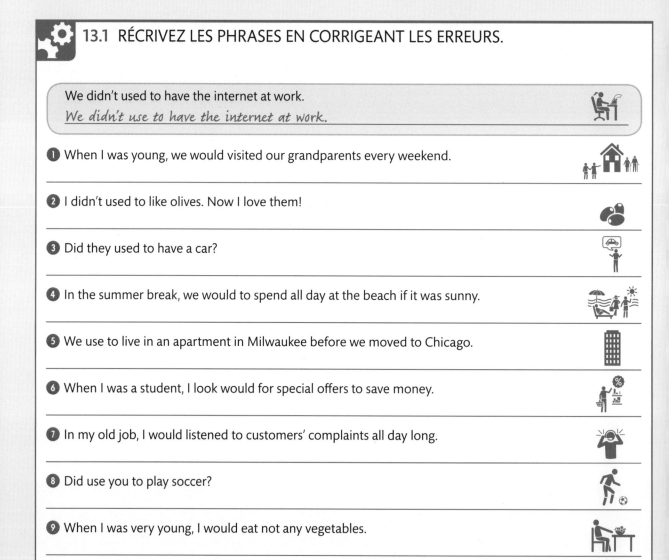

We didn't used to have the internet at work.
We didn't use to have the internet at work.

① When I was young, we would visited our grandparents every weekend.

② I didn't used to like olives. Now I love them!

③ Did they used to have a car?

④ In the summer break, we would to spend all day at the beach if it was sunny.

⑤ We use to live in an apartment in Milwaukee before we moved to Chicago.

⑥ When I was a student, I look would for special offers to save money.

⑦ In my old job, I would listened to customers' complaints all day long.

⑧ Did use you to play soccer?

⑨ When I was very young, I would eat not any vegetables.

⑩ At school, my best friend was Leo. We used do everything together.

⑪ My brother didn't use like to swimming. Now he loves it.

🔊

13.2 COCHEZ LES PHRASES CORRECTES.

When I was a kid, I used to hate doing homework. I would always hand it in late. ☑
When I was a kid, I use to hate doing homework. I would always hand it in late. ☐

1 Did you use to have a computer at home when you were a child? ☐
Did you used to have a computer at home when you were a child? ☐

2 I worked in Paris from 2005 to 2009. ☐
I used to work in Paris from 2005 to 2009. ☐

3 Liam would go to Los Angeles twice. ☐
Liam has been to Los Angeles twice. ☐

4 We didn't used to have to wear a school uniform at my school. ☐
We didn't use to have to wear a school uniform at my school. ☐

5 I used to ride a bicycle to school every day, even in the rain. ☐
I use to ride a bicycle to school every day, even in the rain. ☐

🔊

13.3 RÉCRIVEZ LES PASSAGES SURLIGNÉS EN CORRIGEANT LES ERREURS.

used to live

1 _____

2 _____

3 _____

4 _____

5 _____

6 _____

7 _____

BEACH LIFE
When I was 17, I got my first summer job. I worked at the beach near where I use to live. I would got up at 6am and I would cycling to the beach. Then I used spend an hour putting out sunbeds and umbrellas. For 12 hours a day, I would got money off the people who used them. I use to moan about my job endlessly. I used complain that I was tired, I was bored, it was hot...
Then one day, I had a revelation. I realized how lucky I really was working outdoors in the sunshine on the beach. I never use to complain after that!

@ Jack et sa mère discutent
des avantages d'Internet.

The woman has been doing online shopping.
True ☑ **False** ☐ **Not given** ☐

❸ Shopping took longer before the internet.
True ☐ **False** ☐ **Not given** ☐

❶ She has bought her husband a new phone.
True ☐ **False** ☐ **Not given** ☐

❹ Products on the internet are cheaper.
True ☐ **False** ☐ **Not given** ☐

❷ She thinks things were better before the internet.
True ☐ **False** ☐ **Not given** ☐

❺ She never had contact with her relatives before.
True ☐ **False** ☐ **Not given** ☐

🎧 **13.5 ÉCOUTEZ À NOUVEAU, PUIS COCHEZ LE RÉSUMÉ QUI CONVIENT LE MIEUX.**

❶ The son thinks the internet is a positive development, but his mom disagrees. ☐

❷ The mother does not agree with most of her relatives about the internet. ☐

❸ The mother has a positive attitude toward the benefits of the internet. ☐

❹ The mother and son both prefer shopping online to shopping at the mall. ☐

⚙️ **13.6 COMPLÉTEZ LES PHRASES AVEC LES MOTS DE LA LISTE.**

Please don't _____*interrupt*_____ me. I'm trying to make an important point.

❶ Janine has similar _____ to us. She loves animals and she's a vegetarian.

❷ Your dog is so _____ ! He's eaten a bowl of food and still wants more.

❸ I take _____ very seriously. I can't employ people who lie to me.

❹ These days there is greater _____ of people with differing points of view.

❺ The best thing about Philip's _____ is that he is so kind.

| acceptance | character | greedy | honesty | ~~interrupt~~ | values |

🔊

13.7 CORRIGEZ LES PHRASES, PUIS LISEZ-LES À VOIX HAUTE.

We used go the movie theater every weekend when I was a kid.

We used to go to the movie theater every weekend when I was a kid.

1 Did you used to go to dance classes when you were young?

2 I would do a lot of housework yesterday afternoon.

3 I didn't used to enjoy jogging, but now I do.

4 When I was young, my parents would taking us to the beach every summer.

13.8 RÉCRIVEZ CHAQUE PHRASE AVEC « WOULD » OU « USED TO ».

I would often have lunch at Rico's Café when I was working in Monterrey.

I often used to have lunch at Rico's Café when I was working in Monterrey.

1 When I was young, I didn't use to clean up my bedroom. It made my mom really angry!

_____

2 My brother and I used to play video games for hours when we were young.

_____

3 I wouldn't drink tea when I was little. Now I drink it all day long!

_____

4 In college, I often used to meet my friends for coffee after classes had finished for the day.

_____

14 Comparer et contraster

Employer « as... as » est une manière facile de faire des comparaisons. Vous pouvez l'utiliser pour comparer et contraster des quantités ou des qualités de personnes, d'objets, de situations et d'idées.

⚙ **Grammaire** Les comparaisons avec « as... as »
Aa Vocabulaire Les collocations adjectif-nom
🧩 **Compétence** Comparer et contraster

⚙ 14.1 COMPLÉTEZ LES PHRASES AVEC LES EXPRESSIONS DE LA LISTE.

CONSEIL
Vous devrez utiliser certaines expressions plus d'une fois.

🏆 Our chances of winning are even. We're _just as_ good a team as they are.

1. This train ticket is _____ expensive as that one because of the 50 percent discount.

2. He is _____ intelligent as his brother. They both got high grades.

3. Peter is _____ good at soccer as the others. He'll catch up quickly.

4. My new place is _____ big as my old one. It only has one bedroom instead of four.

5. The new album is _____ catchy as their old stuff. I liked their first album a little more.

6. My new computer is _____ fast as my old one. It's actually a little slower.

7. This new soft drink tastes _____ good as SodaUp, but it's not quite the same.

8. The car was _____ expensive as we'd thought. It was a real bargain.

9. They both worked hard. She deserved to win _____ much as he did.

| just as | nearly as | not quite as | half as | nowhere near as |

🔊

14.2 ÉCOUTEZ L'ENREGISTREMENT, PUIS COCHEZ LES BONNES RÉPONSES.

Deux cafés, Frank's et Morello's, sont comparés.

Which coffee shop has better coffee?
Morello's ☑ Frank's ☐ Neither ☐

❶ Which coffee shop is older?
Morello's ☐ Frank's ☐ Neither ☐

❷ Which coffee shop is bigger?
Morello's ☐ Frank's ☐ Neither ☐

❸ Which coffee shop has more staff?
Morello's ☐ Frank's ☐ Neither ☐

❹ Which coffee shop has more customers?
Morello's ☐ Frank's ☐ Neither ☐

❺ Which coffee shop provides a faster service?
Morello's ☐ Frank's ☐ Neither ☐

❻ Which shop sells a wider range of pastries?
Morello's ☐ Frank's ☐ Neither ☐

❼ Which coffee shop is closer to downtown?
Morello's ☐ Frank's ☐ Neither ☐

14.3 COCHEZ LES PHRASES CORRECTES.

She walks as silently as a mouse. ☑
She walks silently as a mouse. ☐

❶ This train isn't quite as fast as we'd thought. ☐
This train isn't not as fast as we'd thought. ☐

❷ He can't type quickly as she can. ☐
He can't type as quickly as she can. ☐

❸ It was nowhere near as good as I'd hoped. ☐
It wasn't as half good as I'd hoped. ☐

❹ It tasted just as good as it did last time. ☐
It tasted just as good it did last time. ☐

❺ She doesn't shop as much as she used to. ☐
She doesn't shop she used to. ☐

❻ They ran as quickly as they could. ☐
They ran quickly as they could. ☐

❼ The car was as nearly as fast as we thought. ☐
The car wasn't nearly as fast as we thought. ☐

❽ He told us to do it efficiently as possible. ☐
He told us to do it as efficiently as possible. ☐

❾ Cooking took half as long as usual today. ☐
Cooking took as half as long as usual today. ☐

❿ I wasn't as confident as I was before. ☐
I wasn't as confident I was before. ☐

⓫ These pastries are just good as Ann's. ☐
These pastries are just as good as Ann's. ☐

◀))

Aa 14.4 COMPLÉTEZ LES PHRASES AVEC LES COLLOCATIONS DE LA LISTE.

Louise always wears ear plugs in bed because she's such a [*light sleeper*] .

❶ Most people think that if a product has a [   ] , it must be good quality.

❷ My friend Robbie is a very [   ] . Nothing wakes him up!

❸ I was very pleased to hear that my teacher has a [   ] of me.

❹ After traveling for thirty hours with very little sleep, I needed some [   ] .

❺ Discount retailers like this one sell everything at a [   ] .

❻ Everyone leaves work at about 5pm, so there's always [   ] at that time.

❼ I like [   ] with lots of milk in it.

high price	low price	heavy sleeper	~~light sleeper~~
strong coffee	weak coffee	high opinion	heavy traffic

🔊

Aa 14.5 RELIEZ LE DÉBUT DE CHAQUE PHRASE À LA FIN QUI LUI CORRESPOND.

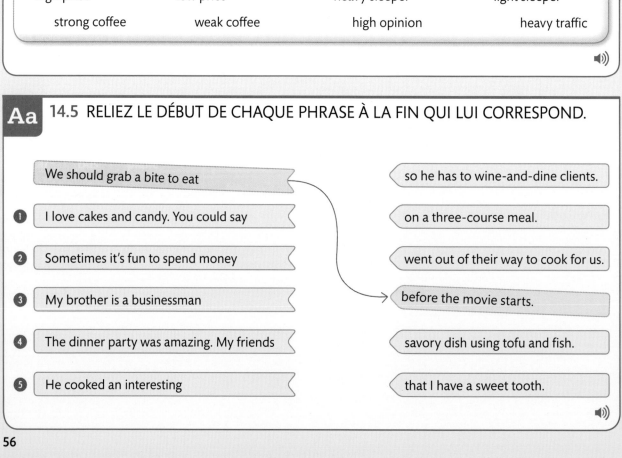

We should grab a bite to eat → before the movie starts.

so he has to wine-and-dine clients.

❶ I love cakes and candy. You could say

on a three-course meal.

❷ Sometimes it's fun to spend money

went out of their way to cook for us.

❸ My brother is a businessman

before the movie starts.

❹ The dinner party was amazing. My friends

savory dish using tofu and fish.

❺ He cooked an interesting

that I have a sweet tooth.

🔊

14.6 LISEZ LE BLOG, PUIS RÉPONDEZ AUX QUESTIONS.

CATHERINE'S BLOG

HOME | ENTRIES | ABOUT | CONTACT

 POSTED FRIDAY, 6:20PM

Going back to school...

I did just as well in college as my sister did. She had become a banker and was already earning nearly as much as my dad, who's a manager in a factory. I was not quite as enthusiastic about banking as my sister was, but I thought I'd give it a try. The work was nowhere near as interesting as I'd hoped and I was working about 80 hours a week. When I talked to friends about their jobs, I found out they were working about half as many hours as me. My mom told me she was really worried about me. My dad was just as worried.

In the end, I decided I was enjoying my job nowhere near as much as I should have been and I was really depressed. I quit my job and decided to go back to college to study photography. Studying was not quite as scary the second time around because I knew how everything worked and I loved every minute. I also met other older students who were just as happy to be there as I was. I didn't miss class nearly as often as I'd done before. I was always there. The major was just as interesting as I'd thought and it helped me to develop into a photographer and a much happier woman!

How did Catherine do in college?

Catherine did just as well as her sister in college.

❶ Who was more enthusiastic about a career in banking, Catherine or her sister?

_____

❷ How did Catherine's working hours compare to her friends' when she was a banker?

_____

❸ How did Catherine's parents feel about how much she was working?

_____

❹ How did Catherine's second experience of college life compare with her first?

_____

❺ How did the photography major compare with what Catherine had thought it would be like?

_____

15 Le double comparatif

Vous pouvez utiliser deux comparatifs dans une phrase pour montrer l'effet d'une action. Vous pouvez aussi les employer pour montrer que quelque chose est en train de changer.

⚙ **Grammaire** Le double comparatif
Aa **Vocabulaire** L'âge et la population
🧩 **Compétence** Exprimer la cause et l'effet

15.1 RELIEZ LE DÉBUT DE CHAQUE PHRASE À LA FIN QUI LUI CORRESPOND.

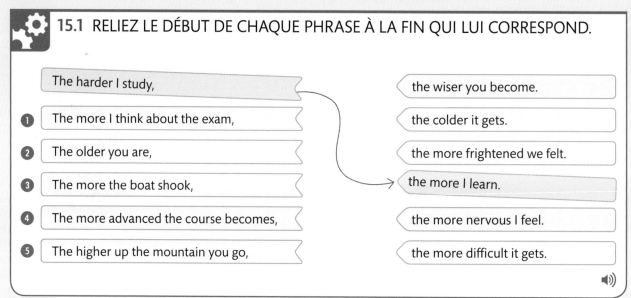

The harder I study,

1 The more I think about the exam,

2 The older you are,

3 The more the boat shook,

4 The more advanced the course becomes,

5 The higher up the mountain you go,

the wiser you become.

the colder it gets.

the more frightened we felt.

the more I learn.

the more nervous I feel.

the more difficult it gets.

15.2 ÉCRIVEZ LES MOTS SUIVANTS DANS LE BON ORDRE AFIN DE RECONSTITUER LES PHRASES.

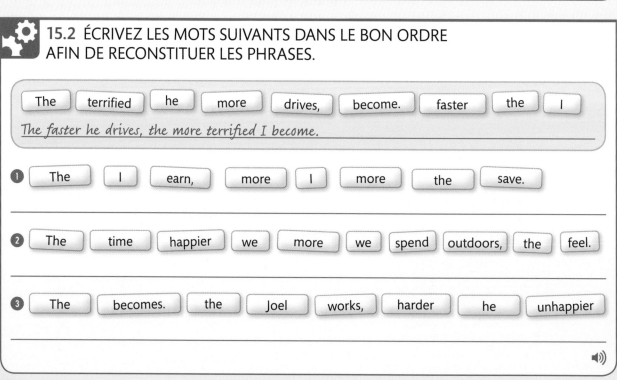

The | terrified | he | more | drives, | become. | faster | the | I

The faster he drives, the more terrified I become.

1 The | I | earn, | more | I | more | the | save.

2 The | time | happier | we | more | we | spend | outdoors, | the | feel.

3 The | becomes. | the | Joel | works, | harder | he | unhappier

15.3 RÉCRIVEZ LES PHRASES EN CORRIGEANT LES ERREURS.

Later I watch TV, more bad the shows become.
The later I watch TV, the worse the shows become.

1 The most difficult a challenge is, the most I enjoy it.

_____

2 The early you start working on the project, sooner you'll finish.

_____

3 Long an action film is, less I want to watch it.

_____

4 The hottest it is, thirstiest I become in the summer months.

_____

5 The more angry Peter gets, the lesser sure I become of how to react.

_____

6 More successful my sister becomes, more stressed she gets.

_____

7 The friendly a person is, the more popular they are at work.

_____

8 The more I study, the less certainer I become of what I know.

_____

9 The dangerous an adventure sport is, the more I like it.

_____

10 Further you swim in the mornings and evenings, fitter you'll become.

_____

11 The least junk food you eat in the day, the slimmest you'll get.

_____

12 More interviews with successful people I read, more I realize success is down to hard work.

_____

🔊

15.4 ÉCOUTEZ L'ENREGISTREMENT, PUIS COCHEZ LES BONNES RÉPONSES.

Linda tombe sur Chloe, une amie de longue date.
Elles parlent de leurs vies bien remplies.

Linda thinks that as you get older, time goes...

quicker and quicker ☑

quicker and longer ☐

quicker and slower ☐

3 Chloe's attitude toward going to bed is...

the later the better ☐

the earlier the better ☐

the quieter the better ☐

1 Chloe says her life is...

busier and busier ☐

easier and easier ☐

more and more interesting ☐

4 Dan's job is becoming more...

and more exciting ☐

and more stressful ☐

and more rewarding ☐

2 Chloe is feeling more...

and more depressed about life ☐

and more lonely ☐

and more tired ☐

5 Chloe's attitude towards her vacation is...

the more relaxing the better ☐

the hotter the better ☐

the sooner the better ☐

15.5 COMPLÉTEZ LES PHRASES AVEC LES DOUBLES COMPARATIFS DE LA LISTE.

The days in November and December become _____ *shorter and shorter.* _____

1 Because of climate change, temperatures on Earth are getting _____ .

2 In developed countries, people are getting _____ . Is this fair?

3 Ben practices the piano every day so he's getting _____ .

4 Every time I look at my baby daughter she seems _____ to me.

5 I waved as the boat got _____ away, and a tear slid down my cheek.

better and better   farther and farther   hotter and hotter

more and more beautiful   richer and richer   ~~shorter and shorter~~

Aa 16.1 **LES ÉTUDES** ÉCRIVEZ LES ESPRESSIONS DE LA LISTE SOUS LA DÉFINITION CORRESPONDANTE.

Consider and describe how things are alike

compare similarities

1 Register to start something

2 Go to lessons or lectures

3 Surprisingly not alike

4 Answer questions or perform actions to show how much you know about something

5 Consider and describe how things are different

6 Someone studying for a first degree at college or university

7 Finish something within a given time

8 A significant level of difference

9 Fail to finish something within a given time

10 Grading based on work done over a long period

11 Study carried out following graduation from a first degree

12 Provide comments and advice on how somebody is doing something

13 An obvious difference

---

clear distinction   give someone feedback on something   meet a deadline   compare similarities

undergraduate   attend classes   postgraduate   contrast differences   continuous assessment

take a test / take an exam   a world of difference   miss a deadline   strikingly different   enrol in

17 Prendre des notes

Les marqueurs rhétoriques peuvent aider l'auditeur
ou le lecteur à mieux comprendre votre message.
Ils sont très utiles lorsque l'on prend des notes.

⚙ **Grammaire** Organiser l'information
Aa **Vocabulaire** La vie universitaire
🧩 **Compétence** Prendre des notes

Aa 17.1 RELIEZ CHAQUE MARQUEUR RHÉTORIQUE À SON SYNONYME.

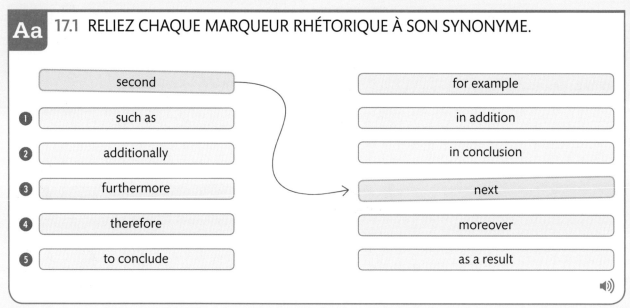

second		next
❶ such as		for example
❷ additionally		in addition
❸ furthermore		in conclusion
❹ therefore		moreover
❺ to conclude		as a result

⚙ 17.2 RELIEZ LE DÉBUT DE CHAQUE PHRASE À LA FIN QUI LUI CORRESPOND.

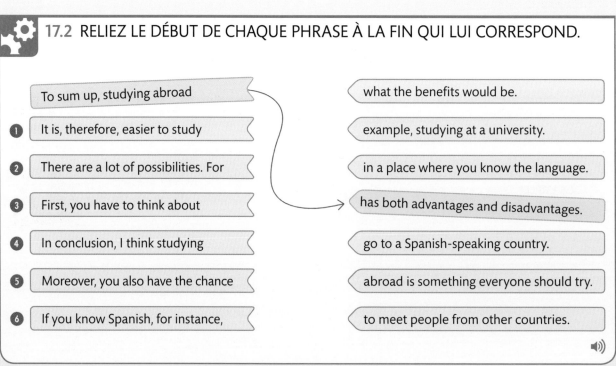

To sum up, studying abroad — has both advantages and disadvantages.

❶ It is, therefore, easier to study

❷ There are a lot of possibilities. For

❸ First, you have to think about

❹ In conclusion, I think studying

❺ Moreover, you also have the chance

❻ If you know Spanish, for instance,

what the benefits would be.

example, studying at a university.

in a place where you know the language.

go to a Spanish-speaking country.

abroad is something everyone should try.

to meet people from other countries.

17.3 ÉCOUTEZ L'ENREGISTREMENT, PUIS COCHEZ LES BONNES RÉPONSES.

Un professeur s'adresse à un groupe d'étudiants de première année qui vient de s'inscrire à l'université.

The speaker is talking to people who are studying English.	True ☑	False ☐
❶ Students can attend classes as and when they choose to do so.	True ☐	False ☐
❷ The first point she makes is the importance of speaking English in class.	True ☐	False ☐
❸ The last of her three points is the importance of studying outside of class.	True ☐	False ☐
❹ The teacher will never assign extra reading.	True ☐	False ☐
❺ Students have access to an online platform during their course.	True ☐	False ☐
❻ There is only one way that students can study outside of class.	True ☐	False ☐

17.4 LISEZ LE COURRIEL, PUIS PLACEZ LES MARQUEURS RHÉTORIQUES DANS LE BON ENCADRÉ.

SEQUENCING

first
_____
_____

ADDING

_____
_____

EXAMPLES

_____
_____
_____

CONCLUDING

_____
_____

To: Sam Jones
Subject: Re: Studying overseas

Hi Sam,

You're right. I noticed some differences between being a student in the UK and in France when I studied abroad. First, the days on campus were long. We had to be in class for six or eight hours every day, for example. Second, the classes were more like lessons than lectures. The teacher would give us homework, for instance, and this would be things such as exercises from a book. Third, the atmosphere at the university was much more relaxed. Additionally, there were a lot of clubs to get involved in. Overall it was a fantastic experience. Moreover, it helped me to improve my French a lot. In conclusion, I would recommend studying abroad to anyone.

Best wishes,
John

17.5 RÉCRIVEZ LES PHRASES AU PREMIER CONDITIONNEL EN CORRIGEANT LES ERREURS.

> Unless you write the essay by Friday, you have to leave the class.
> *Unless you write the essay by Friday, you will have to leave the class.*

1 If they will want to go on the trip, they'll need to sign up today.

_____

2 Unless we will get three more registrations, we won't be able to run the class.

_____

3 If he wants to join the Spanish class, he is needing to email me this evening.

_____

4 If you will join the committee, you will have to give up a lot of your free time.

_____

5 If you want to meet up for coffee later, I will be being in the library.

_____

6 I will having to cancel Tuesday's class unless we find another room.

_____

7 If they will want to find out more about our club, we are at the fair tomorrow.

_____

8 Unless we will hear from them in the next five minutes, we will start without them.

_____

9 If you will be biology student, you will need to buy a lab coat by Friday.

_____

10 If you are needing a study partner next semester, I might be available.

_____

11 If they will be able to come to the film night, it will be a great evening.

_____

🔊

17.6 RELIEZ LE DÉBUT DE CHAQUE PHRASE À LA FIN QUI LUI CORRESPOND.

If you register on the online platform,

I expect you to do it.

① If you sign up for this study group,

unless you work a lot harder.

② When you are a student ambassador,

if you have any further questions.

③ You will fail the exam

you can see the information there.

④ When I give you homework,

you have to come to weekly meetings.

⑤ Send me an email

you can apply to study abroad.

⑥ If you want to find a part-time job,

you are a representative of the university.

⑦ If you're interested in hiking,

don't take your library books back late.

⑧ Unless you can pay a big fine,

you can go to our career center.

⑨ When you go into the second year,

if you need someone to talk to.

⑩ I am always ready to listen

you can join the Expeditions Society.

⑪ If you want to study French,

you will not understand this subject.

⑫ Unless you attend classes regularly,

you should visit the language center.

🔊

17.7 ÉCOUTEZ L'ENREGISTREMENT, PUIS COCHEZ LE BON RÉSUMÉ.

Le conseiller d'une université informe les étudiants des options à leur disposition pour leur année à l'étranger.

① Only rich students can study during their year abroad. Everyone else will need to work. ☐

② The best option is to combine work experience and studying while you're abroad. ☐

③ Students can choose whichever of the three options for their year abroad they prefer. ☐

18 Exprimer l'approximation

La langue anglaise possède de nombreuses expressions utiles pour décrire des quantités et montants approximatifs. Vous pouvez les utiliser lorsqu'un chiffre n'est pas connu ou est approximatif.

⚙️ **Grammaire** La généralisation
Aa Vocabulaire Les expressions de quantités approximatives
🧩 **Compétence** Parler de nombres

Aa 18.1 RELIEZ CHAQUE IMAGE À LA DESCRIPTION CORRESPONDANTE.

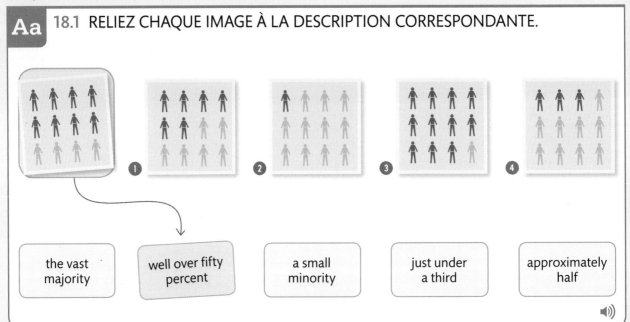

| the vast majority | well over fifty percent | a small minority | just under a third | approximately half |

18.2 BARREZ LES MOTS INCORRECTS DANS CHAQUE PHRASE.

52% Approximately / ~~Well over~~ half of the students in the college in the current year are male.

❶ **8%** In a few / the majority of cases students are asked to retake the year.

❷ **9%** In a number / approximately half of cases students drop out and leave college.

❸ **7%** In some / most cases students can ask to defer and start college a year later.

❹ **91%** In a majority / third of cases students make friends for life while in college.

❺ **95%** In a minority of / most cases students live on campus in their first year.

❻ **23%** Just under / Well over a quarter of students have part-time jobs.

18.3 LISEZ LE COURRIEL, PUIS COCHEZ LES BONNES RÉPONSES.

To: College Governors

Subject: Student numbers report

Dear Governors,

Please find below the latest figures on our student body this year.

Students: 1,672 undergraduates, 329 graduates. 54 percent female, 46 percent male. 89 international students (60 from Asia, three from South America, 26 from North America).

Campus: 320 acres, 15 minutes from Riverside city center. 98 percent of students live on campus.

Subjects: 32 different degree subjects in Arts (35 percent), Sciences (41 percent), Humanities (11 percent) and Engineering (13 percent).

Clubs: 47 different clubs ranging from skiing to chess to hot-air ballooning. Most students can find a club for something they are interested in.

Meet and Greet: Last year, 1,480 students attended the Meet and Greet. This year's Meet and Greet takes place at the Union Hall, 7pm on October 3.

The majority of students at the college are undergraduates.   True ☑   False ☐   Not given ☐

❶ Just under half of students are female.   True ☐   False ☐   Not given ☐

❷ There are some students from South America.   True ☐   False ☐   Not given ☐

❸ In most cases, international students are Asian.   True ☐   False ☐   Not given ☐

❹ The college campus is much bigger than at most colleges.   True ☐   False ☐   Not given ☐

❺ A vast majority of students live on campus.   True ☐   False ☐   Not given ☐

❻ Just under a third of students study an arts subject.   True ☐   False ☐   Not given ☐

❼ Biology is the most popular subject.   True ☐   False ☐   Not given ☐

❽ There are just under 50 different clubs.   True ☐   False ☐   Not given ☐

❾ In a few cases, students can't find a club that interests them.   True ☐   False ☐   Not given ☐

❿ You need lots of other students in order to start a club.   True ☐   False ☐   Not given ☐

⓫ Well over 2,000 students went to last year's Meet and Greet.   True ☐   False ☐   Not given ☐

18.4 COMPLÉTEZ LES PHRASES AVEC LES MOTS DE LA LISTE.

92% In ___*the majority of*___ cases, foreign language students study abroad for one year.

❶ 15% In a _____ cases, the company will hire candidates who do not have a degree.

❷ 67% Approximately _____ of students regularly buy fast food.

❸ $180 I'm not prepared to pay as _____ as $180 to go to a music festival.

❹ 20% In _____ cases, patients are asked to stay at home so they don't infect others.

❺ $30 The plane tickets are really cheap. They cost as _____ as $30.

❻ 90/120 Can you believe it? Out of 120 professors, as _____ as 90 can speak three languages.

❼ 96% _____ 90 percent of students complete their studies.

❽ 30% In a _____ of cases, students will have to find their own accommodation.

❾ 84% In _____ cases, you'll feel much better within a week.

❿ 3 The yoga class isn't very popular. There are as _____ as three people at most classes.

⓫ 23% _____ a quarter of students take more than a year to find a job.

⓬ 53% _____ half of students meet their future partner in college.

few	~~the majority of~~	Just over	Just under	little	Well over	many
minority		most	much	some	few	two-thirds

18.5 ÉCOUTEZ L'ENREGISTREMENT, PUIS COCHEZ LES BONNES RÉPONSES.

The majority of students at Jeremy's college join a sports club. **True** ☑ **False** ☐ **Not given** ☐

1 Most students who join a club have never tried the sport. **True** ☐ **False** ☐ **Not given** ☐

2 There are lots of female students in the soccer club. **True** ☐ **False** ☐ **Not given** ☐

3 In most cases, it costs no more than $5 per semester to join a club. **True** ☐ **False** ☐ **Not given** ☐

4 Students can choose from over 70 clubs. **True** ☐ **False** ☐ **Not given** ☐

5 In your first year, you can only join six clubs. **True** ☐ **False** ☐ **Not given** ☐

6 You have to apply for membership two weeks before you join. **True** ☐ **False** ☐ **Not given** ☐

18.6 COMPLÉTEZ LES RÉPONSES AUX QUESTIONS DE L'ENREGISTREMENT AVEC LES MOTS DE LA LISTE.

Most of the people who go to this college end up in really low-paid jobs.

Is that right? I heard completely _____ *the opposite.* _____

1 Unfortunately, the class sizes are really big.

Really? I heard that the class sizes are _____

2 The professors are really uninspiring and have nothing new to say.

Is that so? My experience is very _____ from that.

3 I've been told that the student accommodation is dirty and dark.

Is that right? I heard that it is _____

really small.   clean and comfortable.   ~~the opposite.~~   different

19 Changer l'emphase

Il y a de nombreuses manières de changer l'emphase en anglais : vous pouvez par exemple avoir recours à une construction grammaticale moins courante, comme la voix passive.

⚙ **Grammaire** La voix passive
Aa Vocabulaire L'apprentissage en ligne
🧩 **Compétence** Changer l'emphase de la phrase

 19.1 LISEZ LE BLOG, PUIS CHOISISSEZ LE RÉSUMÉ QUI CONVIENT LE MIEUX.

Young Entrepreneurs

HOME | ENTRIES | ABOUT | CONTACT

POSTED THURSDAY, 8.20AM
A piece of cake

More and more people are now using crowdfunding websites to set up their own businesses. Just post some information about your business idea online and people will transfer money to your account. We talked to Rachel from London, who started using a crowdfunding website a few years ago.

"I started my business, Tea and Cakes, after I graduated from college. I used my savings to buy some basic equipment and started off at small local events. It went well, so I decided to make the business into my full-time job."

That was when Rachel started using the internet where she read about a crowdfunding website she could use. Within about an hour of joining, eight people had offered to fund Rachel's business and within a week it was 200!

Rachel started to expand the business, but after a while she realized that she would need to find a funding model that is appropriate for a larger company. "That was when I found another site where you can get investment in return for shares in your business and some of the investors on there were interested in me! It was a bit scary because I had to write a proper business plan and send it to them."

Rachel is now going to open a tea shop of her own in London. Her advice to other entrepreneurs? "Don't be afraid to try crowdfunding," she says. "It worked for me."

❶ Entrepreneurs are being given training in how to set up their own businesses by crowdfunding websites. ☐

❷ Crowdfunding websites are being used by entrepreneurs like Rachel to raise funds for their business. ☐

❸ Crowdfunding is being used to raise large amounts of money for companies that are active on social media. ☐

❹ A business advisor helped Rachel to put together a business plan and find funding for her business online. ☐

19.2 BARREZ LES MOTS INCORRECTS DANS CHAQUE PHRASE.

Crowdfunding websites ~~are using~~ / are being used by more and more people today.

1 Money for setting up a new business can raise / can be raised through these websites.

2 Rachel had been selling / had been sold at local events before she decided to get serious.

3 Rachel found out that social media was using / was being used by other entrepreneurs.

4 Rachel set up / was set up her own website by using a simple web platform.

5 Within a week, Rachel had offered / had been offered funding by eight investors online.

6 Rachel took on / was taken on someone to work for her as her business grew.

7 Later Rachel found / was found another crowdfunding website.

8 Rachel's new tea shop will locate / will be located in London.

🔊

19.3 RÉCRIVEZ LES PHRASES EN UTILISANT LA VOIX PASSIVE.

Entrepreneurs set up new businesses.

New businesses _are set up by entrepreneurs._

1 They were selling their products at the baseball club last weekend.

Their products _____

2 Entrepreneurs can easily use social media to promote their businesses.

Social media _____

3 We will write our detailed business plan for the next 12 months this weekend.

Our detailed business plan _____

4 He had already sold his old catering business when he bought the hairdressing business.

His old catering business _____

5 Someone delivered all of the cooking equipment to our new shop yesterday.

All of the cooking equipment _____

🔊

CONSEIL

L'accentuation des noms formés à partir de verbes à particule est placée sur la première syllabe.

Here are the _____*login*_____ details you need to use this website.

1 _____ time at this hotel is 2pm. Your room won't be free until then.

2 Just put the _____ in the fridge. We'll have them for lunch tomorrow.

3 Don't forget to make a _____ of your files.

4 The police are looking for an _____ who may have seen the bank robbers.

5 Let me make it clear from the _____ what I expect from you.

6 In the first part of the lesson I'll give you a lot of _____ and then you'll be able to use it.

7 Getting angry with the boss in the boardroom was his _____. He'll never work here again.

8 The police have announced a _____ on bicycle thieves.

| downfall | onlooker | crackdown | backup | outset |
| input | leftovers | ~~login~~ | Check-in |

19.5 LISEZ L'ARTICLE, PUIS COCHEZ LES BONNES RÉPONSES.

All hotel guests are able to sleep in until noon before checking out.
True ☐ **False** ☑

❶ There are more budget hotels today than there were in the past.
True ☐ **False** ☐

❷ Guests at budget hotels have early check-in times.
True ☐ **False** ☐

❸ Budget hotels have had a negative effect on other hotels.
True ☐ **False** ☐

❹ A receptionist will always be there when you check into a budget hotel.
True ☐ **False** ☐

TRAVEL TIPS

The rise and rise of the budget hotel

The days when hotel guests could enjoy sleeping in until noon before checking out are gone. As the number of budget hotels rises, they are making stricter rules for their guests and one of them is earlier check-out times and later check-in times. Such hotels have been the downfall of some of the more expensive hotel chains, which are no longer attracting as many guests as they used to.

Budget hotels will provide you with the services you expect, but from the outset you will notice that they also do everything they can to ensure savings. If you arrive in the evening, for example, you might have to go to a computer terminal to check in. There usually won't be a receptionist there to do it for you. You may also find that your room isn't as clean as you would like it to be.

 19.6 RELIEZ LE DÉBUT DE CHAQUE PHRASE À LA FIN QUI LUI CORRESPOND.

From the outset, ——→ we were told about the challenges.

it's essential to have a backup.

❶ When my dad cooks,

on social media use during class.

❷ After losing my data, I know

to hold back onlookers.

❸ Never share your login

we were told about the challenges.

❹ There has been a crackdown

to make the journey easier.

❺ I always prefer an early check-in

with anyone for security reasons.

❻ The police put up a line

there are never any leftovers.

🔊

20 Cela pourrait arriver

Il y a plusieurs façons de parler de situations futures hypothétiques. Vous pouvez utiliser différentes constructions pour indiquer si vous pensez qu'une hypothèse est probable ou improbable.

⚙ **Grammaire** « What if », « suppose », « in case »

Aa Vocabulaire Examens et évaluations

🧩 **Compétence** Parler de situations hypothétiques

20.1 RELIEZ CHAQUE SITUATION À SA CONSÉQUENCE PROBABLE.

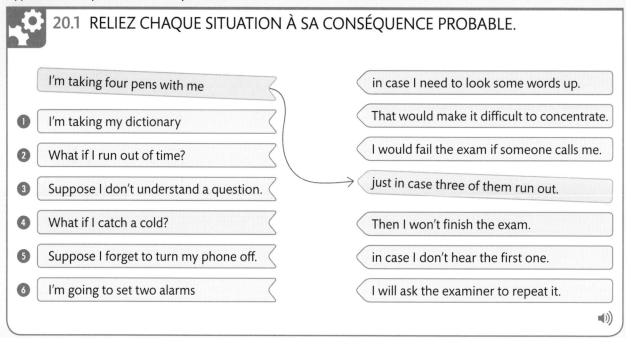

I'm taking four pens with me

1 I'm taking my dictionary

2 What if I run out of time?

3 Suppose I don't understand a question.

4 What if I catch a cold?

5 Suppose I forget to turn my phone off.

6 I'm going to set two alarms

in case I need to look some words up.

That would make it difficult to concentrate.

I would fail the exam if someone calls me.

just in case three of them run out.

Then I won't finish the exam.

in case I don't hear the first one.

I will ask the examiner to repeat it.

🔊

20.2 INDIQUEZ SI LE RÉSULTAT EST PROBABLE OU PEU PROBABLE.

Suppose I won the lottery? I could buy my own car.   **Likely** ☐   **Unlikely** ☑

1 What if we all fail the test? We'll have to take it again.   **Likely** ☐   **Unlikely** ☐

2 Suppose I wrote a book. I could become famous.   **Likely** ☐   **Unlikely** ☐

3 I'm taking two pens in case my old one stops working.   **Likely** ☐   **Unlikely** ☐

4 What if I misunderstood the road signs? I could get lost.   **Likely** ☐   **Unlikely** ☐

5 Suppose I got a job. I could move to a new house.   **Likely** ☐   **Unlikely** ☐

6 It's supposed to be rainy, so I'll get my raincoat.   **Likely** ☐   **Unlikely** ☐

20.3 BARREZ LA FORME VERBALE INCORRECTE DANS CHAQUE PHRASE.

What if you ask / ~~asked~~ the teacher for some help? He won't mind.

 ❶ I know it's not likely, but suppose I have / had an accident on the way to school.

 ❷ What if I help / helped you review, and you help me with my essay?

 ❸ Suppose we find / found a rat in our classroom and the test was delayed.

 ❹ You should ask if you can have more time just in case they say / said yes.

 ❺ Suppose another fire alarm goes / went off during the exam. Will they give us more time?

 ❻ What if we don't / didn't know the answers to any of the questions? What would we do?

20.4 COMPLÉTEZ LES PHRASES EN CONJUGUANT LES VERBES AU TEMPS QUI CONVIENT.

I would be surprised if that topic _____*was*_____ (be) in the exam. It seems unlikely.

❶ If you _____ (get) 100 percent in the biology exam on Monday, I would be amazed.

❷ We _____ (learn) much more quickly if we use an app to help us learn the words.

❸ What if it _____ (snow) and we couldn't get to school on the day of the exam?

❹ If my brother _____ (win) the prize for the best student, I would be shocked.

❺ My parents will be happy if I _____ (pass) the chemistry exam.

❻ If we bought a new car, we _____ (not be) late so often!

❼ She _____ (not finish) in time if she doesn't start her project soon.

❽ It would be so much less stressful if the teachers _____ (give) us some help.

20.5 RÉPONDEZ AUX QUESTIONS DE L'ENREGISTREMENT EN IMAGINANT CE QUI POURRAIT ARRIVER, PUIS LISEZ LES PHRASES À VOIX HAUTE.

Suppose you were a teacher. What subject would you teach?

I'd teach biology because that's my favorite subject.

1 Suppose you could decide how long the weekend was. How many days would it have?

2 Suppose you have some time to watch TV this evening. What will you watch?

3 If you could spend six months anywhere in the world, where would you go?

4 If you could have dinner with anyone, who would you choose?

5 Suppose you had the chance to study abroad. Where would you go?

6 If you won the lottery, what would be the first thing you'd buy?

7 Suppose you got two free tickets to a concert. Who would you go with?

Aa 21.1 LE TRAVAIL ÉCRIVEZ LES MOTS DE LA LISTE SOUS LA DÉFINITION CORRESPONDANTE.

Do more than you are required to do

go the extra mile

7 Deal with something directly

1 A position without many prospects

8 Suddenly begin to have more success

2 Aim to achieve a particular goal

9 A position with the lowest level of responsibility or compensation

3 The knowledge and skill gained through doing something yourself

10 A job with regular hours

4 Make more progress than others

11 Made to leave a job because there is not enough work available

5 Be forced to leave your job for doing something wrong

12 Compromise

6 Have too much work to do

13 The conditions in which you work

---

hands-on experience   bottom of the career ladder   be snowed under   nine-to-five

give and take   ~~go the extra mile~~   set your sights on something   get ahead   dead-end job

take off   tackle something head-on   be fired   working environment   laid off

22 Les demandes d'emploi

En anglais, les prépositions ne peuvent être suivies que d'un groupe nominal ou d'un gérondif. Cela est particulièrement important lorsque vous parlez de l'ordre dans lequel les événements ont eu lieu.

⚙ **Grammaire** Les prépositions et le gérondif
Aa Vocabulaire Les demandes d'emploi
🧩 **Compétence** Écrire un CV et une lettre de candidature

22.1 COMPLÉTEZ LES PHRASES AVEC LES MOTS DE LA LISTE.

Since _____*leaving*_____ my old job and going back to college, I've started a better-paid job.

1 After _____ my studies I decided to take a year off and go traveling.

2 _____ original and innovative products is something I'm particularly interested in.

3 _____ spending the summer having fun, I want to get a job and earn some money.

4 _____ attending a workshop on project management, I have a deeper understanding of this area.

5 I've applied _____ so many jobs, but I haven't had a single interview.

6 _____ starting my studies, I had earned very high grades at school.

7 While _____ at a school in Peru, I realized how much I enjoy helping other people.

8 _____ giving me a strong theoretical grounding, my degree also gave me practical skills.

9 _____ work at your company immediately would be perfect for me.

10 They're _____ doing interviews for the job, they're also asking people to take a test.

11 _____ completing my studies, I have gained some work experience in marketing.

12 After _____ the job ad, I knew this job was the one for me and I applied for it.

13 _____ working in human resources for 10 years, I wouldn't be able to take on this role.

14 Since _____ as a doctor, I've started working at a local hospital.

15 _____ out into the community to work with people has been very valuable.

Going	As well as	Before	Without	Since	seeing	After	completing
for	Instead of	not only	volunteering	Starting	Developing	qualifying	~~leaving~~

🔊

VACANCIES

Job opening

Digital Marketing Manager: Transvan logistics

We are looking for an experienced and enthusiastic individual to coordinate marketing activities across desktop and mobile digital platforms. With at least five years' experience in a similar position, you will be responsible for growing the number of visitors to our website. We are a logistics company, so any experience in the logistics industry would be particularly relevant and desirable.

About you: You will be happy to get involved with all aspects of our marketing activities. Ideally, we want someone who will stay with us for a long time and who will be an active part of the young, fun team we've built up.

Must haves:
• Five or more years' experience in digital marketing

• A Bachelor's degree or higher
• Perfect spoken and written English skills
• Excellent communication skills
• Previous experience working for a logistics company (desirable, not essential)
• A great eye for detail

How to apply: Please send a résumé and cover letter by March 26.

How much experience in digital marketing would the ideal candidate for this job have?

The ideal candidate would have at least 5 years' experience in digital marketing.

---

❶ Experience of which industry would be particularly desirable?

---

❷ What will the candidate be responsible for?

---

❸ How long would the ideal candidate stay with the company for?

---

❹ What academic qualifications do you need to have to apply for this job?

---

❺ Which language do you need to be able to speak and write perfectly?

---

❻ What do you have to send to the company if you want to apply for this job?

22.3 RÉCRIVEZ LES PHRASES EN CORRIGEANT LES ERREURS.

> I write to apply for the position of sales representative advertised on your website.
> *I'm writing to apply for the position of sales representative advertised on your website.*

1 I have recently completing a degree in mechanical engineering.

_____

2 This has prepared me very good for working in the area of product management.

_____

3 One course I made on brand design is particularly relevant to this position.

_____

4 I have a keen interest in follow developments in the food industry.

_____

5 Thank you for taking the time to consider my application and I look forward to hear from you.

_____

 22.4 COMPLÉTEZ LES PHRASES AVEC LES MOTS DE LA LISTE.

> I have been _____*responsible for*_____ teams of up to 10 people in my previous positions.

1 The contents of my degree course have prepared me very well for _____ .

2 I have a _____ in the energy sector and have work experience in this area.

3 You will find that I'm a fast and accurate writer with a keen _____ .

4 I would be able to _____ the responsibility that this position involves.

5 The experience I have gained in my previous jobs is _____ to this position.

eye for detail   particularly relevant   take on

strong interest   ~~responsible for~~   this position

A lot of the stuff I studied during my degree would be relevant to this job. ☐
A lot of the courses I did during my degree would be relevant to this job. ☑

① I can see myself being an awesome boss one day. ☐
I think I would make an excellent office supervisor at some point in the future. ☐

② My first job was a complete nightmare because my colleagues weren't very nice to me. ☐
In my old job I experienced some conflict with colleagues. ☐

③ I've organized lots of events like trade fairs and product launches. ☐
I've organized a lot of events such as trade fairs and product launches. ☐

④ Since graduating from college, I've gained a lot of experience in public relations. ☐
Since graduating from college, I've got loads of experience in PR. ☐

⑤ I may look to move into a managerial job in a few years' time. ☐
Maybe I'll move into a managerial job in a few years' time. ☐

⑥ I want to do stuff like organize marketing campaigns. ☐
I would like to be involved with the organization of marketing campaigns. ☐

⑦ As you can see, I have extensive work experience in the area of retail. ☐
As you can see, I have lots of work experience in retail. ☐

⑧ My skills are significantly superior to those of the average candidate. ☐
My skills are way better than the skills most people have. ☐

⑨ It would be great if you could look at my application. ☐
Thank you for taking the time to consider my application. ☐

⑩ My work experience is particularly relevant to this position. ☐
My work experience is really great for this position. ☐

⑪ I have an in-depth knowledge of product development processes. ☐
I know lots about product development processes. ☐

⑫ I've wanted to be an electrician for ages. ☐
I've wanted to be an electrician for a very long time. ☐

⑬ I very much look forward to hearing from you. ☐
I hope you'll write back to me soon. ☐

◀))

23 Poser des questions polies

En anglais, poser des questions directement peut être perçu comme impoli. Les anglophones posent donc couramment des questions de façon plus indirecte.

⚙ **Grammaire** Les questions directes et indirectes
Aa Vocabulaire Les entretiens d'embauche
🧩 **Compétence** Poser des questions poliment

⚙ **23.1 RÉCRIVEZ LES QUESTIONS DIRECTES EN QUESTIONS INDIRECTES.**

Do you have any weaknesses?
Could you tell me if _you have any weaknesses?_

❶ Do you have any relevant experience in this area?

Could you tell me if _____

❷ Are your studies relevant to this area?

I was wondering whether _____

❸ Have you applied for any other jobs?

We'd like to know whether _____

❹ Do you like working on a team?

I was wondering if _____

❺ Are you a good team player?

We'd like to know if _____

❻ What would you like to be doing in 10 years' time?

Do you have any idea what _____

❼ What are your weaknesses?

Could you tell me what _____

❽ Where did you work after completing your studies?

I was wondering where _____

❾ Where in China did you study?

I'm curious to know where _____

❿ Which area of our activities are you particularly interested in?

Could you tell us which _____

⓫ Have you ever worked abroad?

I'd like to know if _____

🔊

23.2 ÉCRIVEZ LES MOTS SUIVANTS DANS LE BON ORDRE AFIN DE RECONSTITUER LES QUESTIONS INDIRECTES.

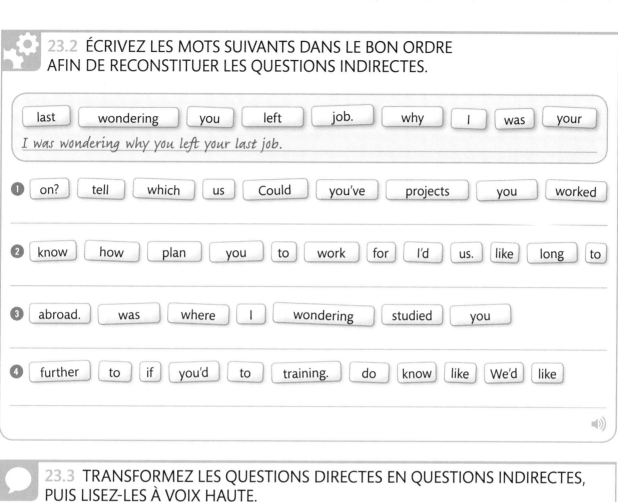

last | wondering | you | left | job. | why | I | was | your

I was wondering why you left your last job.

1 on? | tell | which | us | Could | you've | projects | you | worked

2 know | how | plan | you | to | work | for | I'd | us. | like | long | to

3 abroad. | was | where | I | wondering | studied | you

4 further | to | if | you'd | to | training. | do | know | like | We'd | like

23.3 TRANSFORMEZ LES QUESTIONS DIRECTES EN QUESTIONS INDIRECTES, PUIS LISEZ-LES À VOIX HAUTE.

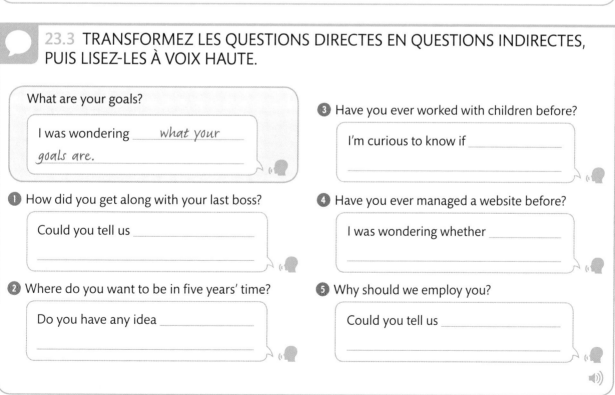

What are your goals?

I was wondering _____ *what your* _____ *goals are.*

1 How did you get along with your last boss?

Could you tell us _____

2 Where do you want to be in five years' time?

Do you have any idea _____

3 Have you ever worked with children before?

I'm curious to know if _____

4 Have you ever managed a website before?

I was wondering whether _____

5 Why should we employ you?

Could you tell us _____

23.4 RELIEZ CHAQUE QUESTION À SA RÉPONSE DILATOIRE.

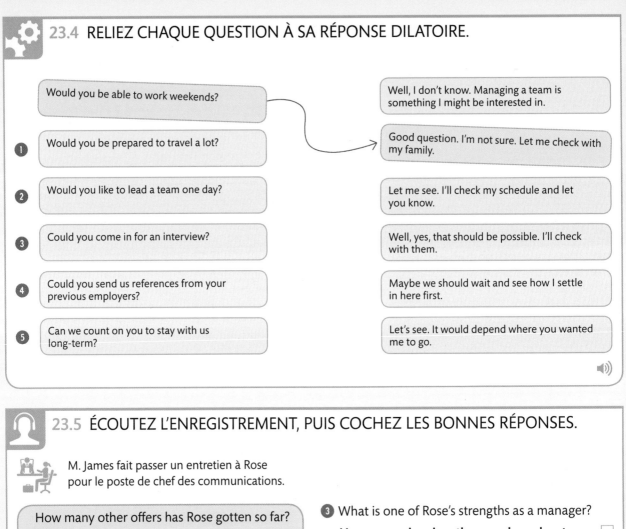

Would you be able to work weekends?	Well, I don't know. Managing a team is something I might be interested in.
1 Would you be prepared to travel a lot?	Good question. I'm not sure. Let me check with my family.
2 Would you like to lead a team one day?	Let me see. I'll check my schedule and let you know.
3 Could you come in for an interview?	Well, yes, that should be possible. I'll check with them.
4 Could you send us references from your previous employers?	Maybe we should wait and see how I settle in here first.
5 Can we count on you to stay with us long-term?	Let's see. It would depend where you wanted me to go.

23.5 ÉCOUTEZ L'ENREGISTREMENT, PUIS COCHEZ LES BONNES RÉPONSES.

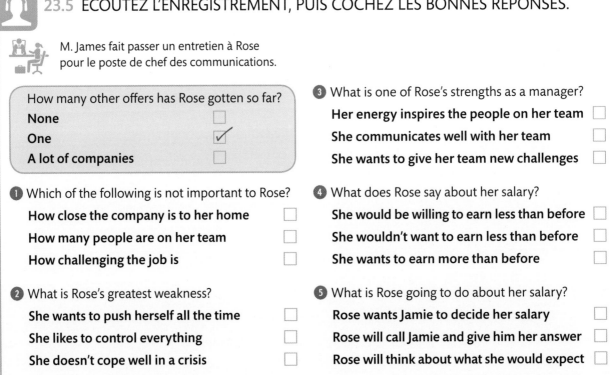

M. James fait passer un entretien à Rose pour le poste de chef des communications.

How many other offers has Rose gotten so far?
None ☐
One ☑
A lot of companies ☐

1 Which of the following is not important to Rose?
How close the company is to her home ☐
How many people are on her team ☐
How challenging the job is ☐

2 What is Rose's greatest weakness?
She wants to push herself all the time ☐
She likes to control everything ☐
She doesn't cope well in a crisis ☐

3 What is one of Rose's strengths as a manager?
Her energy inspires the people on her team ☐
She communicates well with her team ☐
She wants to give her team new challenges ☐

4 What does Rose say about her salary?
She would be willing to earn less than before ☐
She wouldn't want to earn less than before ☐
She wants to earn more than before ☐

5 What is Rose going to do about her salary?
Rose wants Jamie to decide her salary ☐
Rose will call Jamie and give him her answer ☐
Rose will think about what she would expect ☐

23.6 RÉPONDEZ AUX QUESTIONS EN UTILISANT LES EXPRESSIONS DILATOIRES QUI CONVIENNENT, PUIS LISEZ LES PHRASES À VOIX HAUTE.

Is this the only job you've applied for?

Well, to be honest with you, I have applied for a few other jobs, too.

❶ Could you tell us something about yourself?

_____ I'm a dedicated worker and a great communicator.

❷ Where do you want to be in 10 years' time?

_____ I'd like to have a position in management.

❸ How do you feel about working as part of a team?

_____ it's something that I enjoy and would like to continue doing.

❹ Could you tell me what your strengths are?

_____ I have a keen eye for detail and I always give 100 percent.

❺ Do you have any experience of holding a leadership role?

_____ I did once take over from my boss while he was on vacation.

❻ Would you be able to do overtime if we needed you to?

_____ It would depend how much you needed me to do.

❼ How soon would you be able to start if we offer you the job?

_____ I could start next month.

| Yes, where to start? | ~~Well, to be honest~~ | Let's see. I suppose | Let me see. |
| I'm not sure. | Oh, let me see. | Well, | Good question, let me see. |

24 Les schémas complexes de verbes

Les verbes peuvent suivre différents schémas, et être suivis par un infinitif ou un gérondif.

Grammaire Verbe + infinitif / gérondif
Aa Vocabulaire Le monde du travail
Compétence Utiliser des schémas complexes de verbes

24.1 RÉCRIVEZ LES PHRASES EN CORRIGEANT LES ERREURS.

> She hates people to make decisions without consulting her.
> *She hates people making decisions without consulting her.*

1 She finally managed cutting down the number of hours she works from 40 to 35.

2 I think our manager should allow us leaving work a bit earlier on Friday afternoon.

3 This new piece of software enables me to making updates very quickly.

4 Sam threatened leaving if the boss doesn't find a new employee to help him.

5 I'm the person in my office who always volunteering to stay late.

6 This is the first time that a colleague has invited me having dinner at their home.

7 The merger deal we completed last month has caused our profits increase.

8 He doesn't like people to tell him what to do while he's at work.

9 The boss has offered sending me on a training course to improve my computer skills.

10 He enjoys to play the role of the hot-shot manager when visitors come.

24.2 BARREZ LES MOTS INCORRECTS DANS CHAQUE PHRASE.

> I was glad that I managed ~~finishing~~ / to finish all my work on Friday afternoon. Now I can relax.

1 My colleague enjoys hearing / to hear from satisfied customers.

2 My new smartphone enabling / enables me to stay connected with my office wherever I am.

3 She hates her colleagues telling / to tell her what she should do in her department.

4 We like our customers giving / to give us feedback on the services we provide them.

5 My boss has offered / offered to give me an office of my own next year.

24.3 LISEZ L'ARTICLE, PUIS COCHEZ LES BONNES RÉPONSES.

EMPLOYEES AND EMPLOYERS

Why people quit jobs

Rudeness and work/life balance are the top factors

Companies are advised to hold on to their employees for as long as possible. Losing employees is expensive and threatens to lower the morale on the teams that the employees leave behind. According to a recent survey, the thing that causes the largest number of employees to resign is rudeness. People just don't like their colleagues being rude to them. Another reason given by a lot of people is having a job that doesn't enable them to have a good work/life balance. Some people are being forced to do two people's jobs and, as a result, they have to work long hours and weekends.

Companies should try to keep employees as long as they can.	True ✓	False ☐	Not given ☐
1 It doesn't cost companies much money when employees leave.	True ☐	False ☐	Not given ☐
2 Other employees' morale might be lower when a colleague leaves.	True ☐	False ☐	Not given ☐
3 More than 80 percent of people resign because of rudeness.	True ☐	False ☐	Not given ☐
4 Having a good work/life balance is important to a lot of people.	True ☐	False ☐	Not given ☐
5 Some people volunteer to do two people's jobs.	True ☐	False ☐	Not given ☐

24.4 COMPLÉTEZ LES PHRASES AVEC LES MOTS DE LA LISTE.

I was surprised when my daughter told me she would like ___to study___ in Canada next year.

1. She always stops _____ at what's on at the movie theater when we walk past it.

2. I remember _____ that movie with Brian Owen, but it was a very long time ago.

3. She reminded him _____ to the supermarket after work, but he still forgot!

4. I wish they would stop _____ at us like that. They're making me nervous.

5. He finally remembered _____ me some flowers for my birthday. He usually forgets.

6. When I was a child, my mother always encouraged me _____ fruit and vegetables.

7. The turbulence caused the airplane _____ from side to side for about 10 minutes.

8. He knew that we weren't interested in what he had to say, but he still went on _____ .

9. I would advise you _____ an aspirin for your headache.

10. Did you see Donald volunteering _____ the office party this year?

11. He tried _____ the table through the door of our new living room, but it was too big.

12. The boss threatened _____ us work all weekend if we didn't finish the project by Friday.

to move	to take	watching	to eat	looking	to buy
to organize	to look	to go	to push	talking	~~to study~~	to make

88

24.5 COCHEZ LES PHRASES CORRECTES.

I forgot to tell something important to my boss at the meeting. ☐
I forgot to tell my boss something important at the meeting. ☑

1 Jade remembered giving that doll me as a birthday present when I was a child. ☐
Jade remembered giving me that doll as a birthday present when I was a child. ☐

2 The inspector advised us to change our safety procedures in the factory. ☐
The inspector advised us changing our safety procedures in the factory. ☐

3 She likes people talking about how great she is. She has a very big ego! ☐
She likes people talk about how great she is. She has a very big ego! ☐

4 The loan we got from the bank enabled us to build an extension on our house. ☐
The loan we got from the bank enabled us building an extension on our house. ☐

5 I'll write a note to remind myself to bring that book with me next week. ☐
I'll write a note to remind myself bringing that book with me next week. ☐

🔊

24.6 LISEZ LE COURRIEL, PUIS RÉPONDEZ AUX QUESTIONS.

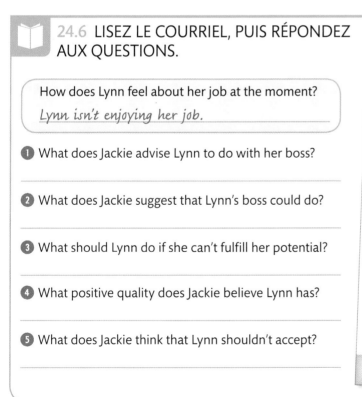

How does Lynn feel about her job at the moment?

Lynn isn't enjoying her job.

1 What does Jackie advise Lynn to do with her boss?

2 What does Jackie suggest that Lynn's boss could do?

3 What should Lynn do if she can't fulfill her potential?

4 What positive quality does Jackie believe Lynn has?

5 What does Jackie think that Lynn shouldn't accept?

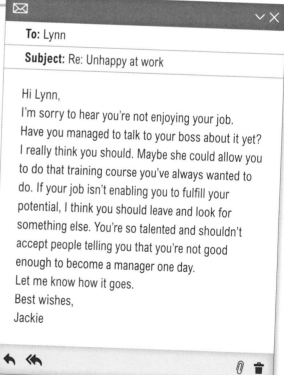

✉ ⌄ ✕

To: Lynn

Subject: Re: Unhappy at work

Hi Lynn,
I'm sorry to hear you're not enjoying your job.
Have you managed to talk to your boss about it yet?
I really think you should. Maybe she could allow you
to do that training course you've always wanted to
do. If your job isn't enabling you to fulfill your
potential, I think you should leave and look for
something else. You're so talented and shouldn't
accept people telling you that you're not good
enough to become a manager one day.
Let me know how it goes.
Best wishes,
Jackie

↩ ↩↩ 📎 🗑

25 Les verbes à double objet

Certains verbes peuvent être suivis soit par un complément d'objet direct, soit par un complément d'objet indirect. Les phrases qui utilisent ces verbes peuvent être ordonnées de plusieurs façons.

⚙ **Grammaire** Les verbes à double objet
Aa Vocabulaire Les nouvelles activités
🧩 **Compétence** Parler de créer une entreprise

25.1 RÉCRIVEZ LES PHRASES EN CORRIGEANT L'ORDRE DES MOTS.

He bought a new book his daughter.
He bought his daughter a new book.

1 Jake lent a pencil me.

2 The teacher offered some help me.

3 She borrowed from Liz a book.

4 Susanne sent a postcard from her vacation me.

5 We donated to the families some old clothes.

6 They paid for the book 20 dollars.

7 John sent an email me yesterday.

8 I'm sure she told the truth you.

9 We gave some biscuits the dog.

10 He brought to her house his computer.

11 Joanne gave her notes him.

12 She lent to her son her car.

13 They bought some chocolates the teacher.

14 Brian the message passed on to Fiona for me.

15 Richard lent his pen me.

16 She always gives a ride to work me.

17 The teacher gave to those students bad grades.

18 Jason passed to me a note in class.

19 Kathryn lent some money her son.

20 They brought to the discussion a lot of energy.

21 He sold to the neighbor his old car.

22 They gave some candy her.

23 She gave to them some books she didn't need.

🔊

25.2 ÉCRIVEZ LES MOTS SUIVANTS DANS LE BON ORDRE AFIN DE RECONSTITUER LES PHRASES.

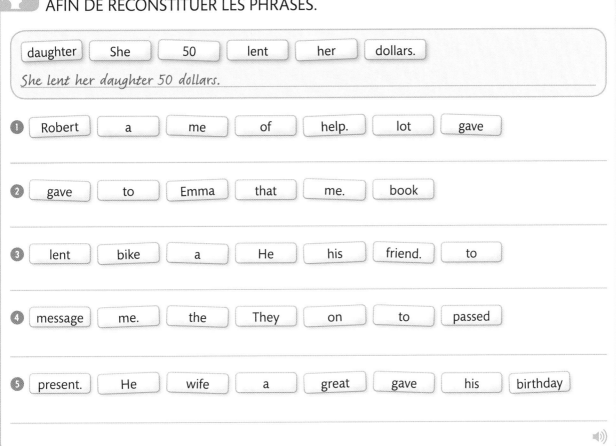

daughter | She | 50 | lent | her | dollars.

She lent her daughter 50 dollars.

1. Robert | a | me | of | help. | lot | gave

2. gave | to | Emma | that | me. | book

3. lent | bike | a | He | his | friend. | to

4. message | me. | the | They | on | to | passed

5. present. | He | wife | a | great | gave | his | birthday

25.3 RELIEZ LES PHRASES QUI DÉCRIVENT LE MÊME ÉVÉNEMENT.

The students received a lot of homework. | They donated money to the charity.

1. Another student bought his books. | I sent him an email.

2. The daughter received a car. | He lent some money to his son.

3. She received a message from him. | The teacher gave them a lot of homework.

4. The charity received money from them. | He sold his books to another student.

5. He borrowed some money from his dad. | He passed the message on to her.

6. He received an email from me. | She bought a car for her daughter.

25.4 LISEZ LE BLOG, PUIS COCHEZ LES BONNES RÉPONSES.

The Neighbor Network is a supermarket chain.
True ☐ **False** ☐ **Not given** ☑

❶ *The Neighbor Network* is a new company.
True ☐ **False** ☐ **Not given** ☐

❷ *The Neighbor Network* was set up by two entrepreneurs.
True ☐ **False** ☐ **Not given** ☐

❸ You access *The Neighbor Network* through the internet.
True ☐ **False** ☐ **Not given** ☐

❹ You use *The Neighbor Network* to contact neighbors.
True ☐ **False** ☐ **Not given** ☐

❺ You can borrow things through *The Neighbor Network*.
True ☐ **False** ☐ **Not given** ☐

❻ There is a monthly charge for using the site.
True ☐ **False** ☐ **Not given** ☐

What's new

HOME | ENTRIES | ABOUT | CONTACT

POSTED FRIDAY, 1:45PM
THE SAVIOR

Run out of milk? Need to borrow a ladder from someone? The Neighbor Network is a social media start-up which helps you solve all these problems.

Ted used *The Neighbor Network* to get in touch with Isabelle who lent some books to him. Isabelle borrowed a light bulb from another neighbor she met on the site.

More connections in your community are just one click of a mouse away.

25.5 COMPLÉTEZ LES PHRASES AVEC LES EXPRESSIONS DE LA LISTE.

At first I was worried about all of the ___red tape___ I would have to deal with.

❶ However, I thought _____ and I decided to just go for it anyway.

❷ Things really took off when I met an angel investor who basically wrote me a _____ .

❸ Her faith in my abilities was the _____ that gave me an edge over the competition.

❹ As a result, I was able to _____ and everyone was coming to me.

❺ I had really _____ there.

cornered the market	~~red tape~~	ace up my sleeve	blank check

nothing ventured, nothing gained　　　　hit the ground running

26 Vocabulaire

Aa **26.1 LES RÉUNIONS ET LES PRÉSENTATIONS** ÉCRIVEZ LES SYNTAGMES DE LA LISTE SOUS LA DÉFINITION CORRESPONDANTE.

Arrive at a point of agreement

reach a consensus

❶ Write a record of what was said during a meeting

❷ Present a formal talk for a group of people

❸ Listen to and answer questions

❹ Start working or doing something that you have to do

❺ Conclude

❻ A vote performed by raising hands to show agreement to a proposal

❼ Arrange a date in the future

❽ Have no time left for something

❾ Included on the list of things to discuss

❿ A group of people who manage a business or organization

⓫ Go to a meeting

⓬ A telephone call with a number of people at the same time

⓭ Not present

---

get down to business   show of hands   take minutes   absent

~~reach a consensus~~   attend a meeting   take questions   on the agenda   conference call

give a presentation   board of directors   run out of time   sum up   set a date

27 Les pronoms réfléchis

Les pronoms réfléchis indiquent que le sujet d'un verbe est le même que son objet. Ils peuvent aussi être utilisés dans d'autres situations pour plus d'emphase.

⚙️ **Grammaire** Les pronoms réfléchis
Aa **Vocabulaire** Le langage du milieu du travail
🧩 **Compétence** Parler de problèmes au travail

 27.1 COMPLÉTEZ LES PHRASES AVEC UN PRONOM RÉFLÉCHI.

The company director ___*himself*___ came to our team meeting.

❶ Anna, you're welcome to help _____ to tea or coffee and cookies.

❷ I taught _____ to use this computer program.

❸ He is very proud of _____ for getting the highest grade in his class.

❹ You can all sit _____ down anywhere you like.

❺ We helped _____ to the free food at the staff party.

❻ I'm annoyed with _____ for not thinking about that.

❼ She accidentally cut _____ while she was cooking.

❽ The members of the team argued among _____ for about half an hour.

❾ They're very pleased with _____ because their boss praised their work.

❿ I often ask _____ why I decided to leave the country and move to the city.

⓫ He felt that he had let _____ down.

🔊

27.2 BARREZ LE PRONOM RÉFLÉCHI INCORRECT DANS CHAQUE PHRASE.

I've emailed the presentation to ~~me~~ / myself so I don't forget to look at it.

1 My grandparents are 90 years old, but they can still do everything for them / themselves.

2 He prides him / himself on his honesty and integrity.

3 Ramona is really busy today. Could you take this package to the post office for her / herself?

4 You don't need to translate that for me. I can do it for me / myself.

5 They got the contract because they worked much harder than us / ourselves.

6 You are all very welcome. Please make yourself / yourselves at home here.

7 Our neighbors were shouting at each other / themselves until 10 o'clock last night.

27.3 COMPLÉTEZ LES PHRASES AVEC LE PRONOM RÉFLÉCHI QUI CONVIENT, PUIS LISEZ-LES À VOIX HAUTE.

I bought a book and the author _____*herself*_____ signed it! She was really sweet.

1 We want you to prepare the presentations _____ .

2 The CEO _____ mentioned me during his annual speech.

3 I am very proud! I repaired the bike _____ .

4 We should be proud that we've achieved all of this by _____ .

5 Food _____ is changing and so are our eating habits.

6 They congratulated _____ on a job well done.

7 The shop manager _____ came down to apologize to me for her mistake.

27.4 COMPLÉTEZ LES PHRASES AVEC LES PRONOMS RÉFLÉCHIS DE LA LISTE.

The winners of the competition will be able to enjoy *themselves* at this luxury hotel in the Caribbean.

❶ I'm glad that we were able to do it _____ without asking the boss for help.

❷ The presentation _____ went well, but the meeting afterwards went badly.

❸ All of the children behaved _____ really well during the flight.

❹ The president's wife _____ came to shake my hand and give me the award.

❺ I felt very pleased with _____ when I found out that my painting had won the prize.

❻ This is the first time that he's been able to walk by _____ since the accident.

❼ I'm looking forward to having the house to _____ while my parents are away.

❽ You should all help _____ to any books on my bookcase that you're interested in.

❾ Your mother isn't going to wash your clothes anymore. You'll have to do it _____ .

himself	ourselves	~~themselves~~	yourselves	herself
myself	yourself	myself	itself	themselves

27.5 RELIEZ LE DÉBUT DE CHAQUE PHRASE À LA FIN QUI LUI CORRESPOND.

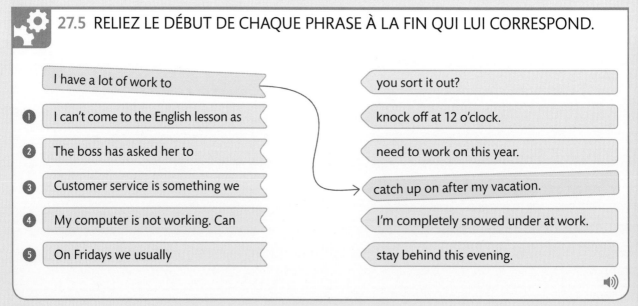

I have a lot of work to — catch up on after my vacation.

❶ I can't come to the English lesson as — you sort it out?

❷ The boss has asked her to — knock off at 12 o'clock.

❸ Customer service is something we — need to work on this year.

❹ My computer is not working. Can — I'm completely snowed under at work.

❺ On Fridays we usually — stay behind this evening.

96

27.6 RÉCRIVEZ LES PHRASES EN CORRIGEANT LES ERREURS.

> It's so busy that I think I'll have to stay after at work this evening.
> _It's so busy that I think I'll have to stay behind at work this evening._

1 Sometimes, I'm so snowed over at work that I don't have time to eat my lunch.

_____

2 I need to sort up these customer queries.

_____

3 She allowed her enough time to drive to the bank and park her car before the meeting.

_____

4 Our project manager has given ourselves more responsibility.

_____

5 I'm still trying to catch off with the work I should have done last week.

_____

6 We can't tear him up from the video game he's playing for more than 10 minutes.

_____

7 I think I have taken under too much work. I'm absolutely exhausted!

_____

8 I always ask for challenging projects, but my boss never lets myself do them.

_____

9 Here's the safety information for working in this building. Could you all familiarize itself with it?

_____

10 I'm sorry, but I'll have to ask Jason to deal with this. I'm completely snowed on at the moment.

_____

11 When students fail their exams, they usually don't blame themself.

_____

12 When I take my children on the train, I bring some toys that they can occupy them with.

_____

🔊

28 Les réunions et la planification

De nombreux verbes peuvent être suivis d'un autre verbe. Celui-ci peut être un infinitif en « to » (« want to eat ») ou un gérondif (« enjoy cooking »).

⚙ **Grammaire** Combiner les verbes
Aa Vocabulaire Les tâches de bureau
🧩 **Compétence** Participer à des réunions

28.1 COMPLÉTEZ LES PHRASES AVEC LES VERBES DE LA LISTE.

I hate _traveling_ by train. There are always delays and the seats usually aren't very clean.

1. He can't stand _____ for people. He doesn't understand why people can't be on time.

2. I have to say that I prefer _____ for myself to eating out. I can eat whatever I want then.

3. I hate _____ , but fresh flowers make a new house feel more like home.

4. How would you propose _____ the big problems that we have?

5. Your flight had such a long delay that I began _____ if you would ever make it back home.

6. He likes _____ to a concert or the opera once a month or even more frequently if he can.

7. You continued _____ my concerns even after you had seen the negative effects yourself.

8. I love _____ outdoors in a lake or in the ocean, even if the water's quite cold.

9. We started _____ our wedding last year as we knew it would take a long time.

to wonder	waiting	to plan	solving	to ignore
cooking	to go	moving	~~traveling~~	swimming

🔊

28.2 RELIEZ LE DÉBUT DE CHAQUE PHRASE À LA FIN QUI LUI CORRESPOND.

When we were young we **started** → collecting stamps and now we have 5,000!

1 In our family we usually **prefer** — walking in the countryside.

2 The design department **proposed** — making some changes to the sizes.

3 Despite being tired, he **continued** — to run for the last six miles.

4 We've always really **loved** — beach vacations to city breaks.

5 When I was younger I **hated** — getting up early, but now I like it.

6 I have to say I **can't stand** — hearing music from people's phones.

7 The music was so good that I **started** — dancing along to it.

8 Ten years ago he **began** — saving money so he could buy a house.

9 Marjorie **proposed** — putting more time between our meetings.

to run for the last six miles.

getting up early, but now I like it.

walking in the countryside.

collecting stamps and now we have 5,000!

saving money so he could buy a house.

beach vacations to city breaks.

putting more time between our meetings.

making some changes to the sizes.

dancing along to it.

hearing music from people's phones.

28.3 BARREZ LE MOT INCORRECT DANS CHAQUE PHRASE.

I'll never forget ~~to see~~ / seeing my daughter receive her degree certificate. I felt so proud of her.

1 Now I regret to ask / asking him about his family. I had no idea what had happened to them.

2 He graduated at the top of his class and we think that he will go on to be / being a successful lawyer.

3 We regret to inform / informing you that on this occasion your application was not successful.

4 I remember to put / putting my car keys on the table, but then someone must have moved them.

5 Don't worry, he won't forget to call / calling you when he arrives in Australia.

6 After our success this season, we're sure the hotel will go on to be / being popular next season.

7 Please remember to write / writing to catering and ask if they can cater for 80 instead of 60.

8 Can we stop to buy / buying some snacks and get coffee at the next service station we get to?

28.4 RELIEZ CHAQUE DÉFINITION AU VERBE EN COULEUR QUI LUI CORRESPOND.

proceed to do something in the future

1. stop doing something to do something else
2. not forget to do something
3. wish you hadn't done something
4. have no memory of having done something
5. continue doing something
6. no longer do something
7. not remember to do something
8. feel bad about having to do something
9. have a memory of having done something

They **went on** celebrating until 2am.

I **remembered** to buy her a present.

Did you **forget** going to Paris with me?

She'll **go on** to be a great teacher.

I **regret** to inform you about the changes.

We **stopped** to get coffee.

I **remember** visiting you when I was a child.

I **regret** telling him that.

I **stopped** going to the gym in February.

Sometimes I **forget** to charge my phone.

28.5 COCHEZ LES PHRASES CORRECTES.

I stopped to smoke cigarettes last year. I live much more healthily nowadays. ☐
I stopped smoking cigarettes last year. I live much more healthily nowadays. ☑

1. I forgot to ask Valerie if she wanted to join us for dinner this evening. ☐
   I forgot asking Valerie if she wanted to join us for dinner this evening. ☐

2. I always remember to close all of the windows when I leave the house. ☐
   I always remember closing all of the windows when I leave the house. ☐

3. Who would have thought he would go on to be such a successful ballet dancer in the future? ☐
   Who would have thought he would go on being such a successful ballet dancer in the future? ☐

4. The views along the coast road were so beautiful we decided to stop to take photos. ☐
   The views along the coast road were so beautiful we decided to stop taking photos. ☐

5. I regret to say that he doesn't work as hard as everyone else. He hasn't spoken to me since. ☐
   I regret saying that he doesn't work as hard as everyone else. He hasn't spoken to me since. ☐

28.6 ÉCRIVEZ LES MOTS SUIVANTS DANS LE BON ORDRE AFIN DE RECONSTITUER LES PHRASES.

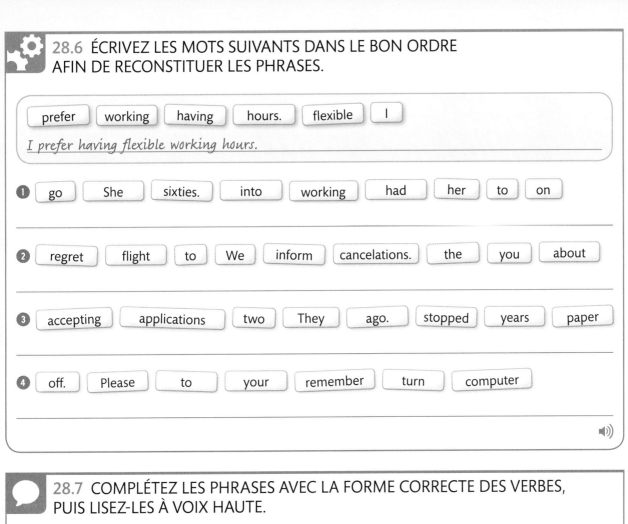

prefer | working | having | hours. | flexible | I

I prefer having flexible working hours.

1. go | She | sixties. | into | working | had | her | to | on

2. regret | flight | to | We | inform | cancelations. | the | you | about

3. accepting | applications | two | They | ago. | stopped | years | paper

4. off. | Please | to | your | remember | turn | computer

28.7 COMPLÉTEZ LES PHRASES AVEC LA FORME CORRECTE DES VERBES, PUIS LISEZ-LES À VOIX HAUTE.

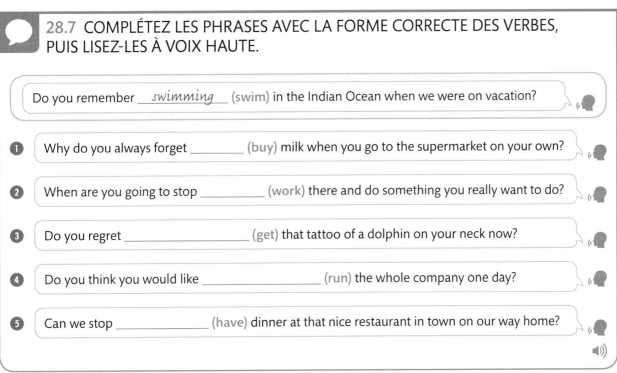

Do you remember ___*swimming*___ (swim) in the Indian Ocean when we were on vacation?

1. Why do you always forget _____ (buy) milk when you go to the supermarket on your own?

2. When are you going to stop _____ (work) there and do something you really want to do?

3. Do you regret _____ (get) that tattoo of a dolphin on your neck now?

4. Do you think you would like _____ (run) the whole company one day?

5. Can we stop _____ (have) dinner at that nice restaurant in town on our way home?

29 Les descriptions qualificatives

Il existe plusieurs façons de qualifier ou d'ajouter des détails aux adjectifs. Certains types d'adjectifs ne peuvent être modifiés que de certaines manières.

⚙ **Grammaire** Les adjectifs non gradables
Aa Vocabulaire Les mots qualificatifs
🧩 **Compétence** Ajouter des détails aux descriptions

⚙ **29.1 COMPLÉTEZ LES PHRASES AVEC LES MOTS DE LA LISTE.**

 The concert venue was _____*enormous*_____ . Seventy thousand people could fit in there.

1 She's a _____ scientist. I'm sure she'll win the Nobel Prize for physics one day.

2 The fact that smoking can damage your health was _____ to most people until the 1970s.

3 It's amazing that such a _____ chip can contain so much data.

4 This scarf was handmade in Malaysia and the design is completely _____ .

5 Could you please send me this document in a _____ format? I can then upload it to our site.

6 The weather was _____ last weekend. It wouldn't stop raining and it was really cold, too.

7 I think it's _____ that there's so much bacteria on our phones.

8 She tries to avoid using cosmetic products that have too many _____ ingredients in them.

9 We're very proud of our _____ heritage, such as these 19th-century factory buildings.

| brilliant | awful | disgusting | unique | ~~enormous~~ |
| chemical | industrial | unknown | tiny | digital |

🔊

29.2 COCHEZ LES PHRASES CORRECTES.

> It's not very economical to leave the lights on all night. Your electricity bill will be high! ☑
> It's not completely economical to leave the lights on all night. Your electricity bill will be high! ☐

1. They had a very fantastic trip to South Africa. They're already planning their next trip. ☐
   They had an absolutely fantastic trip to South Africa. They're already planning their next trip. ☐

2. He's absolutely fascinated by trains so we decided to buy him a train set for his birthday. ☐
   He's very fascinated by trains so we decided to buy him a train set for his birthday. ☐

3. The delegates at the conference were very European with a few North Americans. ☐
   The delegates at the conference were largely European with a few North Americans. ☐

4. We wanted to create a very digital product for today's young people. ☐
   We wanted to create a completely digital product for today's young people. ☐

5. It's very impossible to put this table together. I'll never be able to do it. ☐
   It's completely impossible to put this table together. I'll never be able to do it. ☐

🔊

29.3 BARREZ LE MOT INCORRECT DANS CHAQUE PHRASE.

> If you use our new heating system, you'll be very / ~~completely~~ hot even on cold winter nights.

1. It's hugely / absolutely important that as many people as possible see these billboards.

2. This product is totally / extremely useful if you don't have very much time to spend on housework.

3. We think that our customer base will be rather / perfectly interested in this new feature.

4. Our competitors' products are extremely / wholly inadequate to deal with these challenges.

5. The first design was absolutely / slightly awful, so we had to get rid of it and create a new one.

6. The coffee machine has a totally / very unique feature that enables you to make hot or cold milk.

7. I'm utterly / rather exhausted after putting so much effort into the product launch last week.

8. The CEO can speak slightly / quite good English, but he's much better at Spanish or Portuguese.

9. Have you noticed that our new packaging designer is completely / really talented?

🔊

29.4 COMPLÉTEZ LES PHRASES AVEC LES MOTS DE LA LISTE, PUIS LISEZ-LES À VOIX HAUTE.

How would you feel if you got a hundred percent on an English test?

I'd feel _____*extremely happy*_____ if I got a hundred percent on an English test.

① What did you think of the film?

I loved it! I thought it was _____ and very funny.

② How would you feel about giving a presentation in front of a thousand people?

I'm shy, so I'd feel _____ if I had to do that.

③ How would you feel if you lost your cell phone?

It would be so inconvenient! I'd be _____ .

absolutely terrified   thoroughly enjoyable   utterly miserable   ~~extremely happy~~

29.5 RELIEZ LE DÉBUT DE CHAQUE PHRASE À LA FIN QUI LUI CORRESPOND.

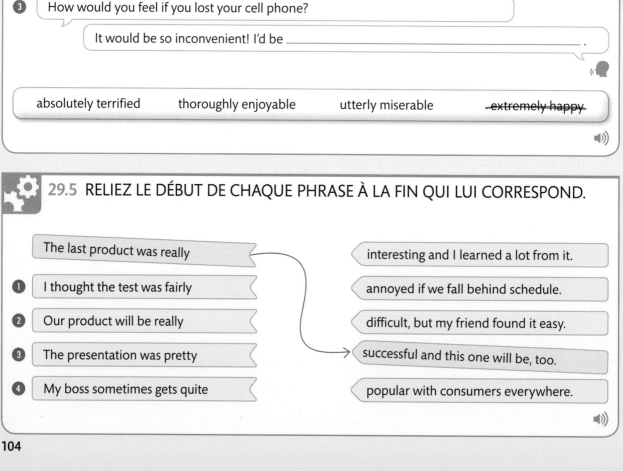

The last product was really ——→ successful and this one will be, too.

interesting and I learned a lot from it.

① I thought the test was fairly

annoyed if we fall behind schedule.

② Our product will be really

difficult, but my friend found it easy.

③ The presentation was pretty

popular with consumers everywhere.

④ My boss sometimes gets quite

29.6 LISEZ LA DESCRIPTION DU PRODUIT, PUIS COCHEZ LES BONNES RÉPONSES.

TurboTravel XS

The travel accessory that will change your flying experience

The TurboTravel XS is a brand new product for business travelers that packs several essential travel accessories inside a comfortable cushion. We're fairly sure that you've never seen a product quite like this before.

What makes the TurboTravel XS completely unique is its extra features, such as a phone charger, light, and pen. The technology it uses is relatively low-tech, but it gives business travelers exactly what they need.

A cable enables you to connect the cushion to your phone and charge it up using an electrical power pack inside the cushion. The light and pen enable you to fill in customs forms really easily.

When it comes to price, the TurboTravel retails at $69.99 so it's quite an expensive, high-end product. However, tests with consumer groups have shown that it's also an extremely reliable travel accessory. To sum up, the TurboTravel XS is a product worth investing in for any business traveler looking for a wholly innovative new combination of comfort and convenience.

The TurboTravel XS is a completely new product.	**True** ✓ **False** ☐	**Not given** ☐

① Its makers are absolutely sure you've never seen a product like it.   **True** ☐   **False** ☐   **Not given** ☐

② It has features that no other product of its type has.   **True** ☐   **False** ☐   **Not given** ☐

③ One of its extra features is an eye mask.   **True** ☐   **False** ☐   **Not given** ☐

④ The technology it uses it fairly low-tech.   **True** ☐   **False** ☐   **Not given** ☐

⑤ The light and pen make it easy to fill in forms.   **True** ☐   **False** ☐   **Not given** ☐

⑥ It's quite an expensive, high-end product.   **True** ☐   **False** ☐   **Not given** ☐

⑦ It's available for business travelers to buy online.   **True** ☐   **False** ☐   **Not given** ☐

⑧ It's already been on sale for a long time.   **True** ☐   **False** ☐   **Not given** ☐

⑨ Consumers think the product is not reliable.   **True** ☐   **False** ☐   **Not given** ☐

⑩ It's perfectly acceptable to use it at work.   **True** ☐   **False** ☐   **Not given** ☐

30 Exprimer le but

Il y a plusieurs façons d'exprimer le but, ou la raison, d'une action. Diverses expressions permettent de décrire la fonction d'un objet.

⚙ **Grammaire** « In order to » et « so that »
Aa Vocabulaire Les mots pour s'excuser
🧩 **Compétence** Exprimer le but

30.1 RELIEZ LE DÉBUT DE CHAQUE PHRASE À LA FIN QUI LUI CORRESPOND.

We organized a training course

1 He wrote a bad review of the movie

2 She took the toaster back

3 I looked everywhere in the store

4 The store gave them a voucher

5 He called the restaurant manager

6 She raised her voice

7 We called the airline

8 You need to fill in this form

9 I called our internet provider

10 I talked to our neighbors

11 Now we check all of the pallets

12 He looked for the company online

13 I called the HR department

14 He asked to speak to the chef

15 She talked to the salon manager

16 I covered the goods in shrink wrap

in order to find the items I needed.

to complain about a rude waiter.

to find out when they will connect us.

to let everyone know about safety.

in order to get your money back.

to let everyone know it's terrible.

so as to keep their business.

not to get a new one, but to get a refund.

to let them know they're being too noisy.

so that everyone would hear her.

to find out about vacancies.

to ask them to cancel our flights.

in order to complain about her haircut.

to find out what others think about it.

to ensure the goods in them aren't broken.

in order to protect them.

to compliment his cooking.

🔊

30.2 RÉCRIVEZ LES PHRASES EN LES LIANT AVEC « SO THAT ».

He decided to advertise his business online. He wanted more people to know what he does.
He decided to advertise his business online so that more people would know what he does.

1 She took her car to the garage. She needed the mechanics to fix it.

_____

2 We use RFID technology. This enables us to track the goods.

_____

3 He wrote a positive review of the hotel. He wanted other people to know how good it is.

_____

4 I usually get up at 5am. I like to go running before I go to work.

_____

5 She spent a lot of time planning her presentation. She wanted to be well-prepared.

_____

◄))

30.3 COMPLÉTEZ LES PHRASES AVEC « FOR » OU « TO ».

This device is _____ *for* _____ monitoring your heartbeat.

1 Our products are made _____ withstand all temperatures.

2 Our career website is _____ busy professional people.

3 You can use this little USB stick _____ connect to the internet in any location.

4 This headset is _____ video-chatting and web-conferencing.

5 This hi-fi system is only _____ serious music fans, as it's very expensive.

◄))

30.4 CHOISISSEZ LE MOT QUI CONVIENT, PUIS LISEZ LES PHRASES À VOIX HAUTE.

I'm calling to complain / ~~complaining~~ about the service I received at this store yesterday.

1 Can we offer you a voucher to show / showing we are sorry for the inconvenience caused.

2 I will be making a complain / complaint about your airline as soon as I get home.

3 I'm not very satisfied for / with the product I received from the company two days ago.

4 Could you let / tell me know when the basket of fruit that I ordered last week will arrive?

5 These workers are employed to / for pick and pack the goods in the factory outside the city.

6 Thank you for your prompt assist / assistance with the ongoing matter of delayed product delivery.

7 You can use this device to / for cleaning the windows in your house quickly and effectively.

8 I recently delivered / ordered a pair of running shoes from you as a gift for my sister.

9 I need a replace / replacement for this kettle as soon as possible, or else I will require a refund.

10 I look forward to hear / to hearing from you about the meeting next week.

31 Vocabulaire

Aa 31.1 L'ENVIRONNEMENT ÉCRIVEZ LES SYNTAGMES DE LA LISTE SOUS LA DÉFINITION CORRESPONDANTE.

Gases that cause the greenhouse effect, heating up the Earth
greenhouse gases

7 At risk of extinction

_____

1 No longer existing

_____

8 Equipment needed to turn sunlight into electricity

_____

2 Causing damage to the environment

_____

9 The act of damaging something so badly that it cannot survive or be repaired

_____

3 A place with many turbines for generating wind power

_____

10 Changes in the Earth's weather patterns

_____

4 Use a supply of something, such as fuel or energy

_____

11 Lower the level of carbon dioxide produced by your actions

_____

5 Fuels based on oil, coal, and gas

_____

12 The increase in the Earth's temperature

_____

6 Energy from sources that do not run out

_____

13 Energy that does not use fossil fuels

_____

harmful to the environment   renewable energy   climate change   endangered
~~greenhouse gases~~   extinct   global warming   reduce your carbon footprint   consume
solar panel   alternative energy   destruction   fossil fuels   wind farm

32 Les conditionnels

Vous pouvez utiliser le troisième conditionnel pour décrire un passé irréel ou des événements qui n'ont pas eu lieu. Ce temps est utile pour parler de regrets que vous avez concernant le passé.

⚙ **Grammaire** Le troisième conditionnel
Aa Vocabulaire Les menaces environnementales
🧩 **Compétence** Parler d'un passé irréel

32.1 COMPLÉTEZ LES PHRASES EN CONJUGUANT LES VERBES AU TEMPS QUI CONVIENT POUR FAIRE DES PHRASES AU TROISIÈME CONDITIONNEL.

If I _had been_ (be) in London yesterday, I _would have seen_ (would / see) the parade.

1 If I _____ (know) it was raining, I _____ (would / bring) my umbrella.

2 I _____ (would / not know) the party was canceled if he _____ (not tell) me.

3 If I _____ (arrive) at the station earlier, I _____ (would not / miss) the train.

4 If they _____ (study) more, they _____ (might / pass) the exam.

5 If I _____ (know) you didn't like onions, I _____ (would / not use) them.

6 If I _____ (not go) to college, I _____ (might / take) a gap year.

7 We _____ (would / not put) the box there if we _____ (know) that it would fall.

8 If I _____ (realize) he was unhappy, I _____ (could / talk) to him about it.

9 I _____ (would / wear) a suit if I _____ (know) the CEO was coming to visit us.

10 If we _____ (give) out more samples, we _____ (would / sell) more products.

11 If she _____ (know) there was a test, she _____ (would / prepare) .

🔊

110

32.2 ÉCRIVEZ LA FORME CONTRACTÉE DES PHRASES, PUIS LISEZ-LES À VOIX HAUTE.

If we had known the play was that bad, we would not have gone to see it.

If we'd known the play was that bad, we wouldn't have gone to see it.

❷ If I had not gone to that party, I would not have met my husband.

❶ If we had known there was a train strike on, we would have driven there.

❸ If I had worked harder, I might have been promoted last year.

32.3 RÉCRIVEZ LES PHRASES EN CORRIGEANT LES ERREURS.

If you hadn't come to this school, where would you study?

If you hadn't come to this school, where would you have studied?

❶ I would have called you if I had knew you were in town.

❷ If we had taken a taxi, we won't have missed our flight.

❸ If I would have left the house at nine, I would not have been late for the interview.

❹ I would made it home by 7 o'clock if my train had left on time.

❺ If we had known the movie was that good, we should have gone to see it.

32.4 LISEZ L'ARTICLE, PUIS COCHEZ LES BONNES RÉPONSES.

TIMELY RESCUE

Pete Falconer recounts his harrowing experience in California

Pete Falconer has been mountain climbing since he was seven years old. The 32 year old thought that he had seen everything and was prepared for any situation, but one day that all changed. It was a hot August day in California and Pete was out climbing with a group of friends. "That day started just like any other. If you'd have told me what was going to happen later on, I would never have believed you," Pete told us. He decided to move ahead of the rest of the group and started climbing up the face of a mountain known as The Antelope. If he'd stayed with the others, they would have been able to reach him faster or even catch hold of him to stop him falling, but Pete was out there all alone when he lost his footing and fell down into a canyon. "I knew right away that my leg was broken," Pete continued. "And even if I hadn't been injured, I don't think I would have been able to climb out of that narrow canyon." Pete called out to his friends for help, but they were still a hundred meters away. "After what felt like an hour, but was probably only about 15 minutes, I heard footsteps overhead and called out for help again. My friends quickly realized what had happened and called the emergency services. If I'd been out there on my own, with no reception on my cell phone, I doubt I would have made it out of there alive, but the emergency services came in a helicopter and used specialist equipment to get me out of there. I was so grateful to be alive and I decided that from now on, I'll always stay close to the group when I go out climbing."

Pete is an experienced climber.   **True** ☑ **False** ☐ **Not given** ☐

❶ Pete knew that day was going to be different right from the start.   **True** ☐ **False** ☐ **Not given** ☐

❷ Pete was using the latest climbing equipment.   **True** ☐ **False** ☐ **Not given** ☐

❸ Pete was climbing a mountain called The Deer.   **True** ☐ **False** ☐ **Not given** ☐

❹ Pete could have called the emergency services himself.   **True** ☐ **False** ☐ **Not given** ☐

❺ Pete realized his leg was broken as soon as he fell.   **True** ☐ **False** ☐ **Not given** ☐

❻ Pete's friends found him after four hours.   **True** ☐ **False** ☐ **Not given** ☐

❼ Pete has decided to stay with other climbers in future.   **True** ☐ **False** ☐ **Not given** ☐

32.5 BARREZ LES MOTS INCORRECTS DANS CHAQUE PHRASE.

> I wish we **had stayed** / ~~stayed~~ somewhere closer to downtown. It would've been easier to get around.

1 If only we **had asked** / **asked** for a room on the second or third floor. It wouldn't have been so noisy.

2 I wish we had been able to spend more time at that museum. It **would be** / **was** really interesting.

3 If only we had been there in summer. We **could have taken** / **could take** a boat trip on the river.

4 I wish we **had gone** / **went** to the Eiffel Tower earlier. We might not have had to wait so long.

5 I wish we **had read** / **read** the reviews of that restaurant before we decided to eat there.

6 I love that band. If only we **had known** / **knew** they were doing a concert down the road from the hotel.

7 If only we had taken the train to the airport. We **would have arrived** / **had arrived** there faster.

32.6 COMPLÉTEZ LES PHRASES AVEC « I WISH » ET « IF ONLY ».

> I find this subject so difficult! I wish ___*I'd studied more*___ (study / more).

1 My brother always makes fun of me. If only _____ (have / a sister instead)!

2 Why didn't I take your advice? I wish _____ (listen / to you).

3 I left my wallet on the train. I wish _____ (not forget /it).

4 My presentation was awful. If only _____ (practice / more).

5 I got soaked outside. If only _____ (bring /my umbrella).

6 I'm so bored at work. I wish _____ (take / time off).

7 I hate walking. If only _____ (not crash / my car).

33 Les regrets

Vous pouvez utiliser « should have » et « ought to have » pour parler d'erreurs passées. Ces deux tournures indiquent que vous souhaiteriez avoir fait quelque chose différemment dans le passé.

⚙ **Grammaire** « Should have » et « ought to have »
Aa Vocabulaire Les marqueurs temporels
🧩 **Compétence** Exprimer des regrets

 33.1 COMPLÉTEZ LES PHRASES AVEC « SHOULD », « SHOULD NOT » OU « OUGHT ».

> Your company _____ *should* _____ have reduced its pollution levels.

CONSEIL
« Ought not to... » n'est pas incorrect, mais n'est pas couramment utilisé.

1 You _____ have separated your waste for recycling.

2 We _____ to have bought fair trade chocolate.

3 She _____ have wasted so much paper.

4 The company _____ have dumped their waste in the river.

5 They _____ have used wood from sustainable forests.

6 We _____ have found out about the risks beforehand.

7 You _____ have changed to energy-saving light bulbs.

8 He _____ have turned the lights off when he left.

9 They _____ to have reduced the amount of traveling their employees do.

10 We _____ have cut down so much of the rainforest.

11 You _____ to have drunk tap water instead of bottled water.

12 She _____ have showered for so long. She's wasting water!

13 They _____ have flown the goods halfway across the world.

14 We _____ to have talked to the local community about this.

15 Governments _____ have made a law to stop this happening.

16 We _____ have buried the waste in that landfill.

17 He _____ to have turned his computer off at night.

18 You _____ have stopped using new plastic bags every time you go shopping.

🔊

33.2 RELIEZ CHAQUE IMAGE À LA PHRASE QUI LUI CORRESPOND.

We should not have dumped the waste in the river.

We ought to have dealt with the causes of climate change earlier.

1

2

We ought to have switched to greener cars sooner.

3

We should have protected the wildlife from the oil spill.

4

We should not have overfished the oceans.

5

We should not have used so many pesticides in these fields.

6

We should have thought about the effects of the mine on the river.

33.3 ÉCRIVEZ LES MOTS SUIVANTS DANS LE BON ORDRE AFIN DE RECONSTITUER LES PHRASES.

stopped · oil · the · that · into · should · We · have · sea. · all · leaking

We should have stopped all that oil leaking into the sea.

1 built · there. · dam · should · We · the · not · have

_____

2 ought · started · renewable · earlier. · using · We · to · energy · have

_____

3 recycled · They · have · waste · all · materials. · should · their

_____

4 it · We · left · the · as · island · to · was. · ought · have

_____

5 orangutans' · not · destroyed · the · habitat. · We · should · have

_____

6 impact · have · They · thought · should · the · fish · on · supplies. · about

_____

7 said. · ignored · should · We · not · what · the · have · protesters

_____

8 stored · more · those · chemicals · We · to · carefully. · ought · have

_____

9 the · controls · have · more · had · We · at · power · should · plant.

_____

🔊

Aa 33.4 LISEZ LES INDICES, PUIS ÉCRIVEZ LES MOTS DE LA LISTE AU BON ENDROIT DANS LA GRILLE.

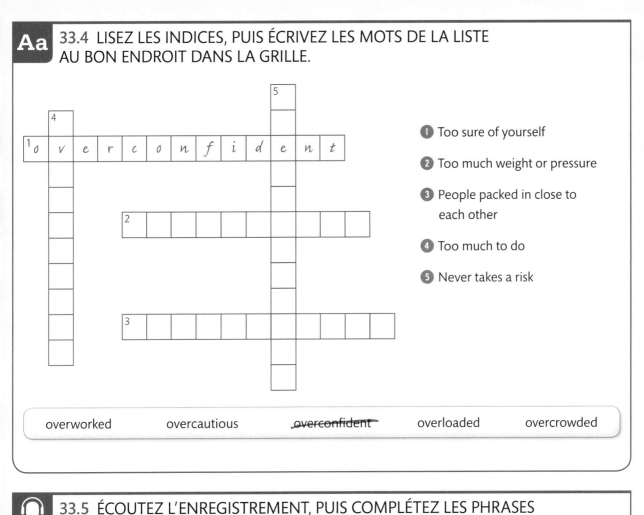

1. Too sure of yourself
2. Too much weight or pressure
3. People packed in close to each other
4. Too much to do
5. Never takes a risk

1 o v e r c o n f i d e n t

overworked   overcautious   ~~overconfident~~   overloaded   overcrowded

33.5 ÉCOUTEZ L'ENREGISTREMENT, PUIS COMPLÉTEZ LES PHRASES EN UTILISANT LES MOTS DE LA LISTE.

_____*Initially*_____ , it was just the one rig in the Gulf of Mexico that was contaminated.

1. However, _____ the original explosion, a large oil leak was discovered.

2. It is estimated that oil was flowing into the sea at a rate of 62,000 gallons a day _____ .

3. Oil continued to flow into the ocean at this rate _____ the next six weeks.

4. Efforts were made to stop the flow of oil _____ that time, but none of them proved successful.

5. _____ , the oil spill has become known as one of the worst manmade disasters in recent history.

Since then   by that time   throughout   ~~Initially~~   following   during

34 Les actions et les conséquences

Contrairement à de nombreuses parties du discours, les prépositions ont souvent peu de sens en elles-mêmes, mais elles permettent de modifier le sens des mots qui les entourent.

⚙ **Grammaire** Les prépositions dépendantes
Aa Vocabulaire Les actions et les conséquences
🧩 **Compétence** Changer l'accentuation de la phrase

Aa 34.1 COMPLÉTEZ LES PHRASES AVEC LES LOCUTIONS DE LA LISTE.

Is he a famous scientist? I've never _____ *heard of* _____ him before.

1 I'm _____ getting trapped in an elevator, so I always take the stairs.

2 In recent years, there's been a huge _____ smartphone ownership.

3 My children sometimes _____ who gets to watch TV.

4 I always _____ a window seat when I fly so I can look out the window.

5 We'll never _____ how to raise children.

6 I think he'll win. All of the signs _____ his direction.

7 There's been a _____ the number of letters people have written in the last decade.

8 The economic situation had the _____ pushing house prices down.

9 There's a _____ interest in the project among the people in my team.

10 I'm afraid I'm going to be _____ our appointment this morning.

11 They're really _____ all of the opportunities they've been given.

12 We _____ my previous work experience and career goals.

13 There's been a _____ the number of people watching live television in recent years.

14 When I call my sister, we _____ absolutely everything that's been going on in my life.

talked about	~~heard of~~	increase in	talk about	effect of
afraid of	late for	decline in	argue about	decline in
lack of	point in	agree about	grateful for	ask for

🔊

34.2 COMPLÉTEZ CHAQUE PHRASE AVEC LA PRÉPOSITION QUI CONVIENT.

There's been a massive increase _____*in*_____ the number of people using social media.

1 My husband and I sometimes argue _____ whose turn it is to do the dishes.

2 Frank is never late _____ any meetings in the office.

3 The course was canceled due to a lack _____ interest by students.

4 I know a lot of people who are afraid _____ spiders and snakes.

5 She's very grateful _____ the chance to study medicine in the US.

6 Marlon will talk _____ his travels in the Amazon rainforest this evening.

7 I'm so grateful _____ the opportunity you have given me.

◀))

34.3 LISEZ LE BLOG, PUIS COCHEZ LES BONNES RÉPONSES.

Linda went to Costa Rica this year.
True ☐ **False** ☐ **Not given** ☑

1 Ecotourism is an option for people traveling alone.
True ☐ **False** ☐ **Not given** ☐

2 Linda found out about ecotourism online.
True ☐ **False** ☐ **Not given** ☐

3 Linda usually doesn't like being high up.
True ☐ **False** ☐ **Not given** ☐

4 Linda's family wanted to go bird watching in Costa Rica.
True ☐ **False** ☐ **Not given** ☐

5 Ecotourism has become more popular in recent years.
True ☐ **False** ☐ **Not given** ☐

6 Evidence suggests that ecotourism has a positive impact.
True ☐ **False** ☐ **Not given** ☐

Travel Blog

HOME | ENTRIES | ABOUT | CONTACT

POSTED MONDAY, 12:25AM
ECOTOURISM

My name's Linda and last year my family and I went to Costa Rica, where we discovered ecotourism. It's suitable for solo travelers, couples, and families.

When deciding on our vacation last year, we all agreed that we wanted to trek through rainforests and see animals living in the wild. Our travel agent then suggested ecotourism in Costa Rica, which is about visiting parts of the world where you can experience interesting or unique wildlife and cultural heritage while having a minimal impact on the natural environment and the local culture. It's popularity has increased in recent years, as more people are realizing the importance of responsible travel.

34.4 BARREZ LES PRÉPOSITIONS INCORRECTES.

 There's no doubt that an increase in fuel consumption leads to / in higher pollution levels.

1 We are currently searching for / about a suitable location for a new offshore wind farm.

2 The Prime Minister apologized to / for the public for not giving them all of the facts.

3 I'm so bored about / with news stories about how the Earth is getting hotter. It's freezing today!

4 If we reduce the amount of packaging we use, that will result to / in us having less waste.

34.5 SOULIGNEZ LES MOTS QUE VOUS DEVEZ ACCENTUER, PUIS LISEZ CHAQUE PHRASE À VOIX HAUTE.

We <u>can't undo</u> what humans have already done to the environment.

[It's not possible to change this.]

1 Environmentally-friendly farming practices help farmers grow more food.

[Other farming practices don't.]

2 This government isn't going to stand by and do nothing about climate change.

[Other governments have.]

3 What changes can you make in your everyday life to make it a healthier one?

[I'm just interested in what you can do and your life.]

4 There isn't a future for the nuclear power industry in this country.

[I know you think there is.]

YOUR FOOD

Food security

Explaining food security and related concepts

One of the big issues facing governments around the world this century is food security. Just in case you've never heard for it before, when we talk over food security, we mean a state where everyone has access to an amount of food that is suitable of their needs. Those of us lucky enough to be food secure should be grateful over it because a lot of people live in a state of food insecurity and this number is set to grow. Long-term food insecurity leads in hunger and large-scale food-insecurity becomes famine when it has the effect at forcing more than 20 percent of a country's population to live without the food they need.

Experts can't agree for exactly how many people worldwide are food insecure, but the evidence points at the direction of it being over 1.2 billion and we're likely to see an increase of that number in the years to come.

The expression "food desert" refers to places with limited access to healthy, nutritious food. "Food deserts" tend to be low-income areas and are found in developed as well as developing countries. People living in "food deserts" become used to this lack in choice and, even when there is an option, they're more likely to ask of a burger and chips than a fresh salad at a restaurant. It's almost as if they're afraid over healthy eating. The results are high obesity levels as people eat large amount of high-fat and high-sugar foods with little nutritional value. Social factors may be to blame in developed countries and especially the decline of the number of families who sit down together to eat a home-cooked meal.

Politicians have argued on what the best way to deal with food security is, but they haven't reached a consensus on what action to take yet.

heard of _____

7 _____

1 _____

8 _____

2 _____

9 _____

3 _____

10 _____

4 _____

11 _____

5 _____

12 _____

6 _____

13 _____

35 « Few » ou « little » ?

Le choix des mots utilisés pour décrire des quantités dépend de nombreux facteurs, notamment s'il s'agit de quelque chose de dénombrable ou d'indénombrable.

⚙ **Grammaire** « Few », « little », « fewer », « less »
Aa Vocabulaire La nature et l'environnement
🧩 **Compétence** Décrire des quantités

⚙ **35.1 BARREZ LES MOTS INCORRECTS DANS CHAQUE PHRASE.**

 I'm so excited. I've got ~~few~~ / a few hours to explore the city tonight.

1 I'm not rich, but I try to donate little / a little money to charity every month.

2 Sadly, there are few / a few Sumatran tigers left in the world today.

3 I have little / a little patience for people who are always late. I'm always on time!

4 There are very few / a few people I would lend money to. But my brother is one of them.

5 Little / A little can be done to completely stop climate change in our time.

6 Do you need some help to finish that report? I have little / a little time I can spare.

7 There are few / a few paintings in the museum I haven't seen. Can we stay a bit longer?

8 There's little / a little point in explaining it to Jen. She never listens to what I say.

9 I know you're on a diet, but would you like little / a little bit of chocolate?

10 There are very few / a few old buildings left in this city. It's sad that we've lost so much history.

11 I don't have lots of friends, but I've got few / a few that I'm really close to.

🔊

35.2 RELIEZ LE DÉBUT DE CHAQUE PHRASE À LA FIN QUI LUI CORRESPOND.

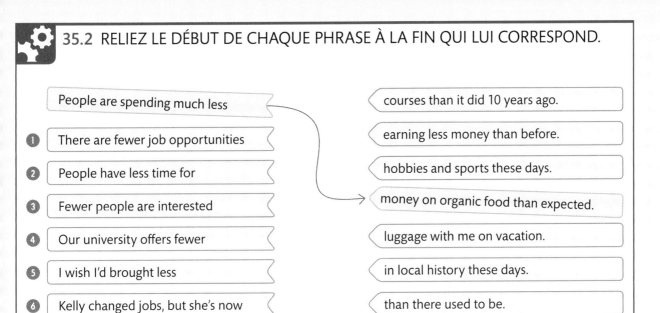

People are spending much less

1. There are fewer job opportunities

2. People have less time for

3. Fewer people are interested

4. Our university offers fewer

5. I wish I'd brought less

6. Kelly changed jobs, but she's now

courses than it did 10 years ago.

earning less money than before.

hobbies and sports these days.

money on organic food than expected.

luggage with me on vacation.

in local history these days.

than there used to be.

35.3 COCHEZ LES PHRASES CORRECTES.

There are fewer whales in the ocean. ☑
There are less whales in the ocean. ☐

1. Fewer money is spent on care for the elderly. ☐
   Less money is spent on care for the elderly. ☐

2. We all need to use fewer electricity. ☐
   We all need to use less electricity. ☐

3. Fewer people are worried about pollution. ☐
   Less people are worried about pollution. ☐

4. I wish I had fewer work to do. ☐
   I wish I had less work to do. ☐

5. People are having fewer children. ☐
   People are having less children. ☐

6. Fewer people enjoy gardening nowadays. ☐
   Less people enjoy gardening nowadays. ☐

35.4 ÉCOUTEZ L'ENREGISTREMENT, PUIS COCHEZ LES BONNES RÉPONSES.

Stuart Brookes se bat pour sauver l'écureuil roux, une espèce menacée.

Stuart Brookes began his fight 15 years ago.
True ☑ **False** ☐

1. The planned road was not close to his home.
   True ☐ **False** ☐

2. The road would have helped protect the squirrel.
   True ☐ **False** ☐

3. There are 2.5 million gray squirrels in the UK.
   True ☐ **False** ☐

4. There are just 140,000 red squirrels in the UK.
   True ☐ **False** ☐

5. The initial group had fewer than five members.
   True ☐ **False** ☐

35.5 COMPLÉTEZ LES PHRASES EN UTILISANT « FEW » OU « BIT ».

I have quite a _____*few*_____ questions.

1 She has been working for quite a _____ years.

2 I've earned quite a _____ of money.

3 Amal has quite a _____ of work experience.

4 There are quite a _____ students in this class.

5 I've spent quite a _____ of time on this report.

6 Jo has made quite a _____ friends at university.

7 There's quite a _____ of rice left over.

8 There are quite a _____ things I have to do.

9 It took quite a _____ of effort to finish the race.

10 I've got quite a _____ pairs of sneakers.

11 We've got quite a _____ vacations planned.

12 She gave me quite a _____ of useful advice.

13 There's quite a _____ of garbage on the floor.

35.6 BARREZ LES MOTS INCORRECTS DANS CHAQUE PHRASE.

We go on holiday to France in ~~fewer than~~ / less than four weeks.

1 The park is empty. There must be fewer than / less than 10 people here.

2 My daughter's school is tiny. It has fewer than / less than five teachers.

3 Seattle is fewer than / less than 20 miles from here. It won't take long to drive there.

4 Applicants should supply no fewer than / less than two references.

5 The plane leaves in fewer than / less than half an hour. We'd better hurry!

6 I've got fewer than / less than $2 in cash. Could you lend me some money, please?

7 The company had to cut some jobs, so we now have fewer than / less than 15 employees.

8 It's fewer than / less than 10 minutes until the game starts. I'm so excited!

9 I'm afraid the course is canceled because fewer than / less than 10 people signed up.

10 Jeremy is being paid fewer than / less than all his friends. He wants a new job.

11 I always pack light. My suitcase weighs fewer than / less than 12 pounds.

12 It's very disappointing that fewer than / less than eight countries signed the agreement.

Aa 36.1 **LES TRADITIONS ET LES SUPERSTITIONS** ÉCRIVEZ LES SYNTAGMES DE LA LISTE SOUS LA DÉFINITION CORRESPONDANTE.

A single piece of good fortune

a stroke of luck

1 Hope for something to happen

2 A group of values

3 Have strong feelings that something is not right

4 A positive / negative sign about something that will happen

5 Talk about other people, often in a negative way

6 Information or news transmitted by people telling other people

7 Say something indirectly

8 Good fortune with no skill involved

9 Stories, sayings, and traditions from a certain area or culture

10 A modern story which is untrue but believed by many

11 Have good fortune the first time you do something

12 To start / continue saying things that may or may not be true

13 Think that something exists or is true

---

gossip   make a wish   beginner's luck   have serious misgivings / doubts   pure luck

a stroke of luck   start / spread a rumor   word of mouth   drop a hint   folklore

set of beliefs   urban myth   good / bad omen   believe in something

125

37 Les possibilités passées

Vous pouvez utiliser divers modaux pour parler d'événements possibles dans le passé et pour indiquer si vous êtes d'accord ou pas avec des hypothèses émises.

⚙ **Grammaire** « Might/may/could » dans le passé
Aa Vocabulaire Les légendes urbaines
🧩 **Compétence** Parler de possibilités passées

 37.1 BARREZ LES MOTS INCORRECTS DANS CHAQUE PHRASE.

> I feel a bit sick. I **might** / ~~may not~~ / ~~could not~~ have eaten something bad earlier.

1 Chris hasn't turned up for training. He **might** / **might not** / **could not** have realized it was today.

2 Your phone **may** / **might not** / **could not** have been stolen. Have you checked in your desk?

3 I found a wallet. It **might** / **might not** / **could not** have been dropped by someone walking to the station.

4 Liz isn't answering her emails. She **may** / **may not** / **could not** have gone away.

5 I **may** / **might not** / **could not** have forgotten to send Lola a birthday card. I'm not sure.

6 That strange noise **could** / **may not** / **could not** have been a fox outside. There are a lot of them in this area.

7 I'm sure Les **may** / **might not** / **could not** have sent such a rude message. He's usually such a gentleman.

8 Jen and Will are late. They **might** / **might not** / **could not** have missed the train.

9 Helena **may** / **might not** / **could not** have grown 20 inches last year. That's too much in 12 months!

10 That bag is a fake. You **might** / **might not** / **could not** have bought a real one. It was far too cheap.

11 You **may** / **might not** / **could not** have caught the flu. It might just be a bad cold.

12 I **may** / **may not** / **could not** have left my glasses at work. I can't find them.

13 You **might** / **might not** / **could not** need an operation. You might just need to take some medicine.

14 You **could** / **might not** / **could not** have seen Sally in town yesterday. She's in China.

15 It **might** / **might not** / **could not** have been Sally I saw in town. But it was someone who looks like her.

16 Your purse **could** / **may not** / **could not** have been stolen when you were waiting in line at the market.

17 We **may** / **may not** / **could not** have bought the right ingredients for the cake. I'm not sure. Let's check.

🔊

37.2 RELIEZ CHAQUE IMAGE À LA PHRASE QUI LUI CORRESPOND.

They may have forgotten to turn down the hob.

1

They might have forgotten to turn the iron off.

2

They may not have remembered to close the window.

3

She couldn't have gone out. All her clothes are dirty!

4

Anyone could have left the freezer door open.

5

They might have made a big dinner for lots of people.

6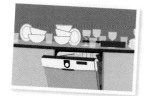

They may have had a party.

37.3 COCHEZ LES PHRASES CORRECTES.

My arm is red and itchy. I might have been bitten by a mosquito. ☑
My arm is red and itchy. I could not have been bitten by a mosquito. ☐

1 My car has a scratch on it. Someone could reverse into it in the parking lot. ☐
My car has a scratch on it. Someone could have reversed into it in the parking lot. ☐

2 Your email could have gone into my junk folder. I'll check again. ☐
Your email could gone into my junk folder. I'll check again. ☐

3 You may have visited my old school. It was turned into an office in 2012. ☐
You could not have visited my old school. It was turned into an office in 2012. ☐

4 You might have spoken to Jill on the phone. She's flying to Brazil right now. ☐
You could not have spoken to Jill on the phone. She's flying to Brazil right now. ☐

5 I might have said the right thing to Annabel. She looked a bit upset. ☐
I might not have said the right thing to Annabel. She looked a bit upset. ☐

37.4 RÉCRIVEZ LES PHRASES AU DISCOURS INDIRECT.

I saw it with my own eyes! (tell) = He _told me that he had seen it with his own eyes._

1 We couldn't believe what we were seeing. (say) = They _____

2 I'm not lying. (say) = She _____

3 I don't believe in things like ghosts. (tell) = She _____

4 I heard a terrible scream last night. (say) = He _____

5 I'll never stay in a castle ever again. (say) = She _____

6 I took a photo and there is a ghost in it. (say) = She _____

7 We had a lot of fun on Halloween. (tell) = He _____

8 We were so scared that we couldn't move. (tell) = They _____

128

37.5 RÉCRIVEZ LES QUESTIONS AU STYLE INDIRECT AVEC « I ASKED ».

What are you doing tonight? (she)
I asked her what she was doing tonight.

❶ How much was your new jacket? (he)

❷ Do you feel tired? (he)

❸ Are they going to get married? (she)

❹ What did you do last weekend? (he)

❺ Is Carina good enough to play for the team? (she)

❻ Are you busy right now? (he)

❼ Where did you go on vacation? (he)

❽ Will you call me back when you're free? (she)

❾ Is Robert the new office manager? (she)

37.6 ÉCRIVEZ LES QUESTIONS RAPPORTÉES QUI CORRESPONDENT AUX RÉPONSES.

She said she was looking for her husband.

I asked her what she was doing.

❶ She said her favorite food was pasta.

❷ He told me he was nervous about the exam.

❸ He said he played tennis at the sports center.

❹ He told me she wasn't easy to talk to.

❺ She said they weren't a difficult team to play.

❻ They told me they were away next week.

❼ He said he was sad because his cat was missing.

38 Les hypothèses et les déductions

Vous pouvez utiliser des verbes modaux pour décrire des événements passés avec différents degrés de certitude. Ces constructions sont utiles pour évoquer des événements dont vous n'avez pas été témoin.

 Grammaire Les autres emplois des verbes modaux

Aa Vocabulaire Les verbes à particule avec « out »

Compétence Émettre des hypothèses et déduire

38.1 RÉCRIVEZ LES PHRASES EN CORRIGEANT LES ERREURS.

> They can have been serious. There's no such thing as the Loch Ness monster.
> _They can't have been serious. There's no such thing as the Loch Ness monster._

① Someone could have took my coat because they thought it was theirs.

② They could have already left. That's the only explanation.

③ He couldn't have wrote such a good essay without any help from his teachers.

④ There must have been an accident, but I'm not really sure.

⑤ I know it's unlikely, but someone must have found the money and handed it in.

⑥ He might have gave me the wrong directions. He doesn't know this town very well.

⑦ He couldn't known that they would ask him a question about that. That's unfair.

⑧ It can't have be a ghost. They don't really exist!

⑨ She must have be imagining it. There's nobody upstairs.

38.2 RELIEZ LES PHRASES CORRESPONDANTES.

It's twenty past two now.	That's why our letters keep being returned.
1 Have you checked your phone?	Nobody called Sheila lives here.
2 He's not answering the door.	Is there anything on the arrivals board?
3 I still can't get through to her.	He must have forgotten about our meeting.
4 They must have changed their address.	She could have tried to call you.
5 Have you looked in the top drawer?	They must be here somewhere.
6 Their plane might have been delayed.	She might have left her phone at home.
7 You must have dialled the wrong number.	He might have left already.
8 We may have lost James and Katie.	He might have left the keys there.
9 He can't have thrown the tickets away!	They're no longer following behind us.

◀))

38.3 BARREZ LES MOTS INCORRECTS DANS CHAQUE PHRASE.

We ~~can't~~ / ~~couldn't~~ / may have stayed too long. I think they were glad when we left.

1 I can't / couldn't / might have won the competition if my entry had arrived in time.

2 They can't / may / might have lost their way. They know this area very well.

3 I can't / couldn't / must have done something to upset her. She's not speaking to me.

4 She couldn't / may / must have opened that door. She doesn't have a key for it.

5 They can't / couldn't / may have destroyed those documents. We haven't found them.

◀))

38.4 COMPLÉTEZ LES PHRASES EN CONJUGUANT LES VERBES À LA BONNE FORME.

He couldn't _____*have been*_____ (be) at that meeting because he was in France at the time.

① You must _____ (deal with) a lot of customers over the last 20 years.

② Mom and Dad might _____ (hide) our presents in this cupboard.

③ He can't _____ (leave) without saying goodbye. He must still be here.

④ The children might _____ (outgrow) these toys. They prefer video games now.

⑤ They must _____ (run) very fast to finish the race in such good time.

⑥ They can't _____ (tell) you everything. There's a lot more that you need to know.

⑦ The students might _____ (go) to the classroom we were in last semester instead.

🔊

38.5 ÉCOUTEZ L'ENREGISTREMENT, PUIS COCHEZ LE BON RÉSUMÉ.

Jason et Valerie parlent de leur collègue Richard qui a disparu du bureau.

Valerie thinks Richard couldn't have gone to the cafeteria.
True ☐ **False** ☑

① Jason says Richard may have gone to see a client.
True ☐ **False** ☐

② Valerie thinks Richard may have gone home early.
True ☐ **False** ☐

③ Valerie says Richard must have gone to buy a present for his wife.
True ☐ **False** ☐

④ Valerie says Richard couldn't have left a note for Jason on his desk.
True ☐ **False** ☐

⑤ Jason thinks Richard might have forgotten their meeting.
True ☐ **False** ☐

39 Les conditionnels mixtes

Vous pouvez utiliser différents types de déclarations au conditionnel pour parler de situations hypothétiques. Les conditionnels mixtes comprennent plus d'une de ces déclarations dans une même phrase.

⚙ **Grammaire** Les conditionnels mixtes
Aa Vocabulaire Les traits de caractère
🧩 **Compétence** Parler de situations hypothétiques

⚙ **39.1 COMPLÉTEZ LES PHRASES AVEC LES VERBES DE LA LISTE.**

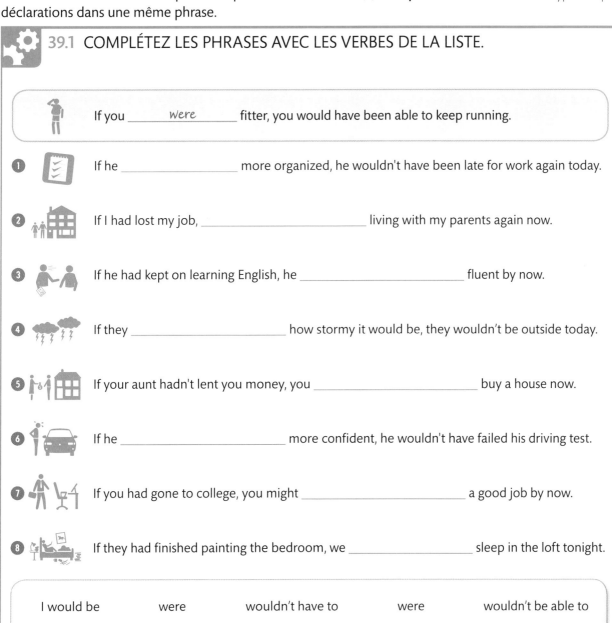

If you _____ were _____ fitter, you would have been able to keep running.

1 If he _____ more organized, he wouldn't have been late for work again today.

2 If I had lost my job, _____ living with my parents again now.

3 If he had kept on learning English, he _____ fluent by now.

4 If they _____ how stormy it would be, they wouldn't be outside today.

5 If your aunt hadn't lent you money, you _____ buy a house now.

6 If he _____ more confident, he wouldn't have failed his driving test.

7 If you had gone to college, you might _____ a good job by now.

8 If they had finished painting the bedroom, we _____ sleep in the loft tonight.

I would be	were	wouldn't have to	were	wouldn't be able to
~~were~~	have	would be	had known	

🔊

39.2 RELIEZ LE DÉBUT DE CHAQUE PHRASE À LA FIN QUI LUI CORRESPOND.

He wouldn't be so good at swimming

if his Dad had shown him how to do it.

① I would wear my coat

you would not be where you are today.

② If we had saved more money,

you wouldn't think that the test was easy.

③ If you had believed what they said,

if he hadn't trained so hard over the years.

④ He wouldn't be so bad at cooking

if she had bought herself a new watch.

⑤ He might be more patient

we wouldn't have to be so thrifty now.

⑥ If he had reserved a seat on the train,

if I hadn't forgotten it.

⑦ She wouldn't always be late

he wouldn't have to stand for two hours.

⑧ If you had read all of the questions,

if he hadn't already been waiting so long.

39.3 COMPLÉTEZ LES PHRASES EN CONJUGUANT LES VERBES DE LA LISTE AU TEMPS QUI CONVIENT.

You could be a professional violin player today if you had _____*practiced*_____ more as a child.

① He would feel better if he had _____ a little more last night.

② If you had _____ for the interview properly, you wouldn't be so nervous now.

③ You wouldn't be stuck here if you had _____ the hotel staff about the problem.

④ If you had _____ off earlier, you wouldn't have to rush so much now.

⑤ He would be less stressed if he had _____ more time out to relax.

⑥ If they hadn't _____ our luggage to the wrong terminal, we would be home by now.

⑦ She might not be such a good typist if she hadn't _____ so much time at the computer.

| sleep | set | spend | take | ~~practice~~ | send | tell | prepare |

39.4 RÉCRIVEZ LES PHRASES AVEC DES CONDITIONNELS MIXTES EN CORRIGEANT LES ERREURS EN VERT.

> If you **had be** there, you would have a Christmas present, too.
> *If you had been there, you would have a Christmas present, too.*

1 If he **have told** me how upset he was, I would still be there comforting him.

2 If I were a good cook, I **would invited** you to lunch at our place by now.

3 He **would have stroke** Fido if he wasn't so scared of dogs.

4 If they weren't going to France tomorrow, they **would have went** to your party.

5 We **could have go** to the theater if we weren't busy tonight.

6 I would be surprised if Katherine **had want** me to go to the ball with her.

7 If the teacher were here, she **would have tell** you all to be quiet.

8 If I **had move** to America, I might be rich and happy now.

9 I would be happy to help you if I **haven't already agreed** to help Jack.

10 If they **had learn** to ski, they could go on a skiing vacation next year.

11 If we **had look** at the map earlier, we wouldn't be so lost!

12 If I had taken that job, I **would been** earning a lot more money now.

40 Ajouter « -ever » aux mots interrogatifs

Ajouter « -ever » aux mots interrogatifs change leur sens.
Ce suffixe signifie « no matter » ou « it doesn't matter ».

 Grammaire Les mots avec « -ever »

Aa Vocabulaire Les expressions liées à la météo et à la chance

Compétence Lier une proposition à une phrase

40.1 COMPLÉTEZ LES PHRASES AVEC LES MOTS DE LA LISTE.

Whoever James marries will be a very lucky lady. He's handsome, intelligent, and charming.

① I can't remember what we decided about the color, but I'm sure it'll be bright, _____ it is.

② _____ I go on vacation abroad, I always try the dishes that are typical for that country.

③ I'm sure the new boss will do a good job and treat everyone fairly, _____ he or she is.

④ They always believe that they will win the lottery one day, _____ small the chances are.

⑤ She always ignores any criticism she gets, _____ anyone says about her.

⑥ _____ I fly, I always make sure that I get to the airport two hours before my flight time.

⑦ I don't think I'll be able to find the answer to this math problem, _____ hard I try.

⑧ We could talk about this on the phone or I could arrange a meeting, _____ you prefer.

⑨ He always finds the time to call and say goodnight to me _____ he is in the world.

whoever	Whenever	whichever	however	wherever
whatever	however	Whenever	whatever	~~Whoever~~

🔊

136

40.2 BARREZ LE MOT INCORRECT DANS CHAQUE PHRASE.

Whatever / ~~Whichever~~ you decide, you can be sure that we'll support you.

1 Whoever / However completes the questionnaire first will win an exciting prize.

2 We always stay in touch by text message or email whenever / wherever we're apart.

3 I won't give up until I reach the top of the mountain, whichever / however hard it gets.

4 I can pick you up at the airport or you can take the train, whichever / whoever you prefer.

5 I'm not going to put up with this kind of behavior from him, whatever / whoever he is.

6 We can have Chinese or Italian food or something else, whatever / wherever you want to do.

7 I always take a little first aid kit with me whenever / whatever I go on vacation.

8 I'm sure she'll look beautiful in her dress, whichever / whatever one she chooses.

9 She's determined to change his mind about the Nigeria project, however / whatever long it takes.

🔊

40.3 RELIEZ LE DÉBUT DE CHAQUE PHRASE À LA FIN QUI LUI CORRESPOND.

Let's meet on Friday the 13th or the next day,

however often they prove to be false.

I give them something blue for luck.

1 I always fear I'm going to have a bad day

however strange it looks.

2 Whatever happens in my life,

whichever you prefer.

3 Whoever told you that

4 My mother believes in superstitions

she thinks that it'll bring her bad luck.

5 Whenever a family member gets married,

whenever I walk under a ladder.

6 This horse shoe will bring me luck

my superstitions bring me comfort.

7 She always wears that ring,

must be very superstitious.

8 Whenever she sees a black cat,

however difficult life gets.

🔊

137

Aa 40.4 RELIEZ CHAQUE DÉFINITION À L'EXPRESSION QUI LUI CORRESPOND.

decline an invitation until a later date

right as rain

① no matter what happens

throw caution to the wind

② behave recklessly

take a rain check

③ extremely happy

a bolt from the blue

④ something sudden and unexpected

come rain or shine

⑤ do something before someone else does it

on cloud nine

⑥ healthy or well

steal someone's thunder

40.5 RÉCRIVEZ LES PHRASES EN CORRIGEANT LES ERREURS.

I'm going to go to the festival this weekend, come rain and shine.
I'm going to go to the festival this weekend, come rain or shine.

① That's a bolt of the blue. I had no idea she was planning to leave the country.

_____

② I'm going to throwing caution to the wind and just buy that expensive car!

_____

③ My daughter was ill with the flu last week, but she's right than rain now.

_____

④ I'm afraid I'll have to make a rain check on that. I'm really busy this week.

_____

⑤ Whenever I give a sales presentation, Maureen always tries to steel my thunder.

_____

41 Vocabulaire

Aa 41.1 **LES MÉDIAS ET LES CÉLÉBRITÉS** ÉCRIVEZ LES MOTS DE LA LISTE SOUS LA DÉFINITION CORRESPONDANTE.

An interview that no other source has obtained
exclusive interview

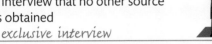

7 Become a famous person

1 Be known by most people

8 A show based on or around real-life events

2 Something designed to get your attention quickly

9 A very rapid rise, often in a career

3 The first night of a show or film

10 Make something more dramatic or exciting than it is

4 A carpet for important guests to walk or stand on at an event

11 The popular culture which surrounds famous people

5 Photographers who take pictures of famous people

12 News that is widely reported

6 A competition with performances by entertainers showcasing their skills

13 The large text at the top of a a newspaper page

---

celebrity culture   become a celebrity   paparazzi   newspaper headline   red carpet

talent show   ~~exclusive interview~~   opening night   sensationalize   attention-grabbing

headline news   be a household name   reality show   meteoric rise

42 Rapporter avec le passif

Une façon de se distancier des faits est d'utiliser la voix passive et des verbes rapporteurs. Cette technique est couramment utilisée par les journalistes.

 Grammaire Rapporter avec la voix passive
Aa Vocabulaire Les mots pour rapporter des faits
Compétence Se distancier des faits

42.1 COMPLÉTEZ LES PHRASES AVEC LES PARTICIPES PASSÉS DE LA LISTE.

It has been ___*claimed*___ that eating processed meat is as dangerous as smoking.

❶ These items have been _____ in our new factory.

❷ It has been _____ that a hurricane will hit the coast this evening.

❸ Those tests have been _____ out in our new laboratory next door.

❹ Following the meeting, it has been _____ that we will increase our prices.

❺ He has been _____ by the pharmaceutical company as their new CEO.

❻ Our products have been _____ all over the world since 1995.

❼ The proposal has been _____ by all the members of the board.

❽ There are _____ to have been a series of crimes committed by this gang.

❾ It has long been _____ that money isn't his main motivation.

reported	produced	exported	carried	rejected
believed	~~claimed~~	alleged	named	decided

140

42.2 RELIEZ LE DÉBUT DE CHAQUE PHRASE À LA FIN QUI LUI CORRESPOND.

She is understood to have been → working in Ethiopia for the last six months.

there will be massive job cuts.

would recall its latest products.

some nice walking trails around here.

1. It is understood that there

2. Our organization is thought to

3. It has been reported that

4. It was announced that the company

5. He is thought to have been

6. There are said to be

7. It is hoped that the next generation

8. Norway is believed to be

be a trailblazer in the area we work in.

have been many flight cancelations.

among the most beautiful countries.

the most successful CEO we ever had.

will continue the work we've been doing.

🔊

42.3 BARREZ LES MOTS INCORRECTS DANS CHAQUE PHRASE.

Safety glasses must ~~worn~~ / **be worn** at all times in the laboratory.

1. This essay **should have been** / **should be** handed in two weeks ago!

2. Unfortunately, the project couldn't **completed** / **be completed** on time.

3. It must **have taken** / **be taken** us four hours to get here because of all the traffic jams.

4. She must **have thought** / **be thought** that the meeting started at 11am instead of 10am.

5. Any feedback you may have should **sent** / **be sent** to our administrator.

6. The machine may **have broken down** / **have broke down** because there was some dust in it.

7. Traffic could **been redirected** / **be redirected** here during the festival.

8. Free samples can **obtained** / **be obtained** from our store on the first floor.

9. The booking should **have been made** / **be made** earlier. Then we would have better seats.

🔊

42.4 COCHEZ LES PHRASES CORRECTES.

It was hoped that we could resolve the differences between them without any arguments. ☑
There was hoped that we could resolve the differences between them without any arguments. ☐

❶ The bell must have rang 10 times, but he still didn't come to the door. ☐
The bell must have rung 10 times, but he still didn't come to the door. ☐

❷ There has been understood to be a car accident on Station Road this evening. ☐
There is understood to have been a car accident on Station Road this evening. ☐

❸ All of the books we sent should have been delivered to the venue by now. ☐
All of the books we sent should be delivered to the venue by now. ☐

❹ It was announced yesterday that students can now apply for scholarships for next year. ☐
It has been announced yesterday that students can now apply for scholarships for next year. ☐

❺ The driver is thought to have lost his way while driving from the airport back to the city. ☐
The driver is thought to have lose his way while driving from the airport back to the city. ☐

🔊

42.5 ÉCOUTEZ L'ENREGISTREMENT, PUIS COCHEZ LES BONNES RÉPONSES.

Une chaîne d'informations financières aborde le sujet
des dernières subventions annoncées par le gouvernement.

Who will receive these new series of grants?
The government ☐
Young entrepreneurs ☑
Students ☐

❸ When will the government start awarding grants?
Today ☐
The start of next year ☐
This isn't clear yet ☐

❶ When did the government agree to this measure?
Today ☐
Yesterday ☐
Last year ☐

❹ How do entrepreneurs feel about this measure?
They welcome it ☐
They're not sure about it ☐
They will see what happens ☐

❷ Who set up hundreds of companies last year?
Young people ☐
Established businessmen ☐
The government ☐

❺ How will this measure affect business growth?
Negatively ☐
Positively ☐
It will remain unchanged ☐

42.6 RÉCRIVEZ LES PHRASES EN UTILISANT LA VOIX PASSIVE.

> He has extensively rewritten the text to make it a lot clearer.
>
> The text _has been extensively rewritten to make it a lot clearer._

1 We bottled a million gallons of water at this plant last year.

A million gallons of water _____

2 Business travelers rent our cars at the airport.

Our cars _____

3 We could organize another conference for next September.

Another conference _____

4 Our chefs make all of our dishes by hand.

All of our dishes _____

5 They hope that the supplier will accept the new terms and conditions.

It is hoped _____

6 According to reports, the government will change traffic laws this year.

It is reported _____

7 We service all of the company cars in this garage.

All of the company cars _____

8 A Spanish company installed the solar panels on our roof last month.

The solar panels on our roof _____

9 Everyone agrees that he would make an excellent team leader.

It is agreed _____

10 They could have unloaded the trucks in half the time that they actually took.

The trucks _____

11 She announced that she would be stepping down from the committee.

It was announced _____

12 Some students claimed that they didn't get enough help from their teachers.

It was claimed _____

🔊

43 Formuler des énoncés indirects

Vous voudrez parfois éviter de formuler des faits établis ou des opinions personnelles. On appelle cette technique « hedging » (éluder) en anglais. Certains mots et énoncés indirects peuvent vous y aider.

⚙ Grammaire Les énoncés indirects
Aa Vocabulaire Les mots élusifs
🧩 Compétence Exprimer l'incertitude

43.1 COMPLÉTEZ LES PHRASES EN UTILISANT LES MOTS DE LA LISTE.

_____ *Often* _____ people use hedging language if they do not have exact figures.

① _____ 40,000 spectators watched the game at the national stadium.

② The figures _____ that our population is aging rapidly.

③ Harris Mode is _____ the most handsome man alive today.

④ To _____ , we can all do more to improve the state of our health.

⑤ _____ that unless we stop climate change, the ice caps will melt.

⑥ It has been _____ that the witness lied during the trial.

⑦ People who purchase violent video games _____ to be young men.

⑧ _____ like we've missed the bus. We're going to be late again.

⑨ It _____ that the jewelry had been stolen in the early hours of the morning.

| appeared | tend | arguably | indicate | It looks |
| Often | suggested | Approximately | some extent | It has been said |

🔊

43.2 RELIEZ LE DÉBUT DE CHAQUE PHRASE À LA FIN QUI LUI CORRESPOND.

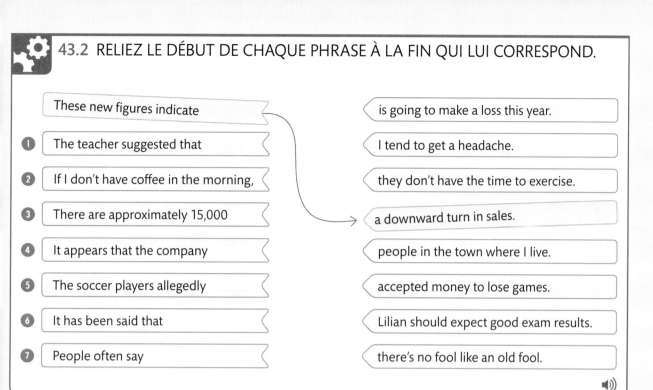

These new figures indicate — a downward turn in sales.

1. The teacher suggested that — Lilian should expect good exam results.
2. If I don't have coffee in the morning, — I tend to get a headache.
3. There are approximately 15,000 — people in the town where I live.
4. It appears that the company — is going to make a loss this year.
5. The soccer players allegedly — accepted money to lose games.
6. It has been said that — there's no fool like an old fool.
7. People often say — they don't have the time to exercise.

43.3 BARREZ LES MOTS INCORRECTS, PUIS LISEZ LES PHRASES À VOIX HAUTE.

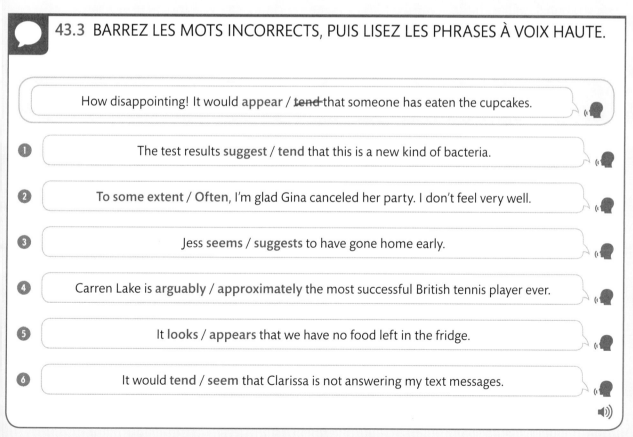

How disappointing! It would **appear** / ~~tend~~ that someone has eaten the cupcakes.

1. The test results **suggest** / **tend** that this is a new kind of bacteria.

2. **To some extent** / **Often**, I'm glad Gina canceled her party. I don't feel very well.

3. Jess **seems** / **suggests** to have gone home early.

4. Carren Lake is **arguably** / **approximately** the most successful British tennis player ever.

5. It **looks** / **appears** that we have no food left in the fridge.

6. It would **tend** / **seem** that Clarissa is not answering my text messages.

145

58 **CITY TODAY**

OH, DEER!

The curious incident of a deer that walked into a hospital

News stations in Banff have been reporting the story of arguably the smartest deer in Canada. Medical staff at Banff General Hospital were surprised to see what appeared to be a deer walking into the Emergency Room yesterday. It was indeed a deer, who seemed to have been injured in an accident on the roads. The deer must have walked approximately 10 kilometers from the scene of the accident to get to the hospital. Medical staff were at hand to pick him up and take him to a nearby vet, who said it looked like the animal would make a full recovery.

What is the story that the news stations have been reporting?

The news stations have been reporting about a deer that walked into a hospital.

❶ Where did the incident take place?

_____

❷ What surprised the medical staff at the hospital?

_____

❸ What seemed to be the reason for the deer's injury?

_____

❹ How many kilometers must the deer have walked to get to the hospital?

_____

❺ What did the medical staff do once the deer got to the hospital?

_____

❻ What did the vet say about the animal's condition?

_____

43.5 ÉCOUTEZ L'ENREGISTREMENT, PUIS COCHEZ LES BONNES RÉPONSES.

Une émission de radio évoque une erreur stupide commise par un criminel.

Alfie Richardson was found guilty of forging paintings.	True ☐ False ☐ Not given ☑

1 He committed a robbery about once every six months.   True ☐ False ☐ Not given ☐

2 Richardson's mistake seems to be that he got lazy.   True ☐ False ☐ Not given ☐

3 There were approximately 20 customers in the post office.   True ☐ False ☐ Not given ☐

4 Richardson erased everything on the phone before he used it.   True ☐ False ☐ Not given ☐

5 The selfies Richardson took were uploaded to an online account.   True ☐ False ☐ Not given ☐

6 The photos led the police to Alfie Richardson.   True ☐ False ☐ Not given ☐

43.6 RÉCRIVEZ LES PHRASES EN CORRIGEANT LES ERREURS.

There are approximate 25 students in my class.
There are approximately 25 students in my class.

1 To some extents, the project we worked on last month was a waste of time.

_____

2 It would seem than someone has hacked into our database.

_____

3 He has alleged stolen $2 million from his employer.

_____

4 It has been say that absence makes the heart grow fonder.

_____

5 It appear that you have forgotten to pay your bill.

_____

44 Ajouter de l'emphase

Vous pouvez ajouter de l'emphase, ou même un sens du drame, à une déclaration au travers de la grammaire et de la prononciation. L'inversion est une manière efficace d'y parvenir.

⚙ **Grammaire** L'inversion après les locutions adverbiales
Aa **Vocabulaire** Les médias et les célébrités
🧩 **Compétence** Ajouter de l'emphase aux déclarations

44.1 BARREZ LES MOTS INCORRECTS DANS CHAQUE PHRASE.

 Not ~~when~~ / until I was 18 did I start to cook for myself.

① Only after trying to reach the summit three times **he did** / **did he** give up.

② Little **she does** / **does she** know that we're planning a surprise party for her.

③ Only **when** / **until** it starts to snow do I stop gardening.

④ Not since the 1980s **the team has** / **has the team** won a major trophy.

🔊

44.2 RELIEZ LE DÉBUT DE CHAQUE PHRASE À LA FIN QUI LUI CORRESPOND.

Not only is the hotel luxurious, ——————— but it's also in a great location.

① Only after living there for five years — did he understand how it worked.

② Not only is she a great mother, — that they were in for a big surprise.

③ Little did they realize — did she realize how well they can write.

④ Only when she read their stories — did he master the Spanish language.

⑤ Not since his childhood — but she's also a top business executive.

⑥ Only after studying the instructions — had he ridden a skateboard.

🔊

44.3 COCHEZ LES PHRASES CORRECTES.

Only when she moved away from home did she become independent. ✓
Only when she moved away from home she did become independent. ☐

1. Little I did know that I would meet my future husband that evening. ☐
   Little did I know that I would meet my future husband that evening. ☐

2. Not only is he a talented pianist, is he also a writer. ☐
   Not only is he a talented pianist, he is also a writer. ☐

3. Only until he came on stage did the fans start to scream. ☐
   Only when he came on stage did the fans start to scream. ☐

4. Only after living there for six months they did talk to the neighbors. ☐
   Only after living there for six months did they talk to the neighbors. ☐

5. The movie was also entertaining, not only informative. ☐
   Not only was the movie informative, but it was also entertaining. ☐

44.4 RÉCRIVEZ LES PHRASES POUR TRANSFÉRER L'EMPHASE À PARTIR DES AMORCES..

I trained for nine months and then I felt ready to run the marathon. [only after]
Only after training for nine months did I feel ready to run the marathon.

1. My son asked me to help him with his homework the moment I arrived home. [no sooner]

_____

2. She didn't know that she would stay for 40 years when she started working there. [little]

_____

3. This is the first time that people from both communities have worked together. [never before]

_____

4. The last time I cried this much at a film was when I went to see *Sally's Song*. [not since]

_____

5. You don't often see a dog and cat that get along with each other so well. [rarely]

_____

44.5 COMPLÉTEZ LES PHRASES AVEC LES MOTS DE LA LISTE.

Not only ___do we___ have a buffet, you can also order from the menu.

❶ _____ have I seen so many people running together.

❷ Little _____ know that we would end up living in Italy.

❸ _____ had I reached the station than the train arrived.

❹ Not since 1988 _____ had such a hot summer.

❺ _____ did she know that she would win an award that evening.

❻ Never before _____ a child who loves reading as much as she does.

❼ Only when I'd had time to recover _____ realize what a lucky escape I'd had.

❽ Only after experiencing it ourselves _____ understand how difficult it is.

❾ _____ preparing for six months did they feel ready to take the exam.

❿ _____ my teenage years have I been so excited about a concert.

⓫ _____ had he started to speak when someone interrupted him.

⓬ _____ do we produce these dolls here, but we make them all by hand.

Only after	~~do we~~	Rarely	Little	did I	could we	have I seen
did we	Hardly	No sooner	Not only	Not since	have we

150

44.6 ÉCOUTEZ L'ENREGISTREMENT, PUIS COCHEZ LES BONNES RÉPONSES.

 Une station de radio annonce
un incendie qui s'est déclaré lors
d'une cérémonie de remise des prix.

More people attended the ceremony this year than ever before.	True ☑	False ☐ Not given ☐

1 The guests were able to go into the auditorium at 6pm.   True ☐   False ☐   Not given ☐

2 The fire started in the middle of the ceremony.   True ☐   False ☐   Not given ☐

3 About 5,000 people were evacuated from the building.   True ☐   False ☐   Not given ☐

4 It's unusual to see so many famous people waiting around outside.   True ☐   False ☐   Not given ☐

5 Everyone was allowed back inside once the firefighters had left.   True ☐   False ☐   Not given ☐

⚙ 44.7 ÉCRIVEZ LES MOTS SUIVANTS DANS LE BON ORDRE
AFIN DE RECONSTITUER LES PHRASES.

after	yes.	did	thought	say	it	giving	I	Only	some

Only after giving it some thought did I say yes.

1 | we | pitched | Hardly | rain. | to | our | had | it | when | tent | began |

_____

2 | as | I | when | feel | alone. | as | Rarely | I'm | do | happy |

_____

3 | was | girl | a | I | young | Not | since | danced. | I | have |

_____

4 | up. | after | times | calling | five | pick | him | he | Only | did |

_____

🔊

45 Déplacer la focalisation

En anglais, vous pouvez ajouter de l'emphase sur une partie de la phrase en séparant celle-ci en deux propositions. Cela permet d'attirer l'attention sur l'information nouvelle ou importante.

⚙ **Grammaire** Mettre en relief avec des propositions
Aa Vocabulaire Les expressions de l'emphase
🧩 **Compétence** Déplacer la focalisation

45.1 RÉCRIVEZ LES PHRASES EN UTILISANT DES PROPOSITIONS AVEC « WHAT » POUR DÉPLACER LA FOCALISATION.

I dislike people who put their bags on available seats in trains.
What I dislike is people who put their bags on available seats in trains.

① I would prefer to take the train to the international airport.
_____

② I really want to hike the Inca Trail in Peru with my friends this year.
_____

③ I would really appreciate some help with using the software to sort data.
_____

④ She was most surprised by the party they threw for her birthday yesterday.
_____

⑤ We really need some more time to get the booth ready for the annual fair.
_____

⑥ I hate it when people play music on their phones without using headphones.
_____

⑦ I really enjoyed the day we spent at the local spa last weekend.
_____

⑧ He realized that he didn't want to do that boring job for the rest of his life.
_____

⑨ I understood that they aren't very happy about the sudden changes we're making.
_____

🔊

45.2 COMPLÉTEZ LES PHRASES AVEC LES MOTS DE LA LISTE.

The _____country_____ I'd most like to visit is Japan because it really fascinates me.

1. The _____ I'd most like to go back to is Ancient Rome so I could visit the Colosseum.

2. The _____ that I enjoy making the most is spaghetti carbonara. It's quick and easy.

3. The _____ I liked the most at school was science, so I became a science teacher.

4. The _____ that I'll always remember is my twenty-first, when I had a huge party.

5. The _____ that I like the most is winter. I love walking in the snow.

6. The _____ I'd most like to have met is Alasdair Rove. I love his music and his style.

7. The _____ who influenced me the most is probably Mr. Lucas, my English teacher.

8. The _____ that reminds me the most of my childhood is *Little Tim*. I loved it!

9. The _____ that always gets me up and dancing at a party is *Dancing Bells* by Claude Robert.

famous person	time	~~country~~	birthday	teacher
song	subject	season	meal	movie

🔊

45.3 BARREZ LES MOTS INCORRECTS DANS CHAQUE PHRASE.

~~Where~~ / The city I enjoyed visiting the most on the cruise was Venice.

1. Why / The reason do you always take on more than you can actually do in a day?

2. Where / The place that I would most like to be right now is a Caribbean beach.

3. Who / The person I most admire and look up to is probably Shakespeare.

4. What / The thing he absolutely hates is people who talk while they're eating.

5. Where / The school is Jonathan doing his Master's degree?

6. The time of day / When I like the most is first thing in the morning when I'm alone.

🔊

45.4 RELIEZ LE DÉBUT DE CHAQUE PHRASE À LA FIN QUI LUI CORRESPOND.

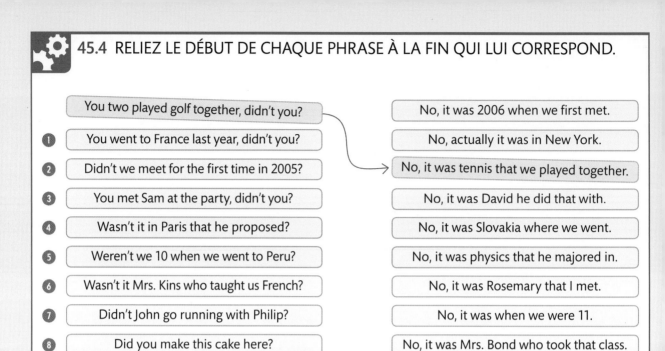

You two played golf together, didn't you? → No, it was tennis that we played together.

1. You went to France last year, didn't you?
2. Didn't we meet for the first time in 2005?
3. You met Sam at the party, didn't you?
4. Wasn't it in Paris that he proposed?
5. Weren't we 10 when we went to Peru?
6. Wasn't it Mrs. Kins who taught us French?
7. Didn't John go running with Philip?
8. Did you make this cake here?
9. He majored in history in college, didn't he?

No, it was 2006 when we first met.

No, actually it was in New York.

No, it was tennis that we played together.

No, it was David he did that with.

No, it was Slovakia where we went.

No, it was physics that he majored in.

No, it was Rosemary that I met.

No, it was when we were 11.

No, it was Mrs. Bond who took that class.

No, it was Joanne who made that one.

45.5 COCHEZ LES PHRASES CORRECTES.

That was the strawberry farmer it was that we talked to on the way home. ☐
It was the strawberry farmer that we talked to on the way home. ☑

1. It was the young man at the visitor center which helped us a lot in New York. ☐
It was the young man at the visitor center that helped us a lot in New York. ☐

2. It was an old lady helped us find the way when we were lost in that Greek village. ☐
It was an old lady that helped us find the way when we were lost in that Greek village. ☐

3. It was your colleague Charles that I met at the Christmas party last year. ☐
It was your colleague Charles where I met at the Christmas party last year. ☐

4. It was at a restaurant in Florence where we ate the delicious steak by the river. ☐
It was a restaurant in Florence where we ate the delicious steak by the river. ☐

5. I think it was our second year in college when the two of us first met. ☐
I think it was our second year in college where the two of us first met. ☐

46 Vocabulaire

Aa 46.1 **LA CRIMINALITÉ ET LE DROIT** ÉCRIVEZ LES MOTS DE LA LISTE SOUS LA DÉFINITION CORRESPONDANTE.

Financial, nonviolent crime

white-collar crime

❶ (Without) uncertainty about somebody's guilt

❷ Find somebody guilty of a crime

❸ A lot of crimes happening suddenly in the same area

❹ Say that you know nothing about something or somebody

❺ Use the power of the law to take and question somebody

❻ The people who decide whether a person is guilty of a crime

❼ Crime committed in a public space

❽ Break the law

❾ Say what punishment a criminal will have

❿ A list of crimes a person has committed

⓫ Come to a decision about somebody's guilt or innocence

⓬ Request that an insurance company pays you money

⓭ Be covered by insurance

jury   commit a crime   criminal record   reach a verdict   arrest
white-collar crime   convict a criminal   pass sentence   deny all knowledge
be insured   street crime   make a claim   crime wave   (beyond) reasonable doubt

47 Les propositions relatives

Les propositions relatives sont des parties de phrase qui apportent un complément d'information sur un nom dans l'énoncé principal. Elles peuvent être définissantes ou non définissantes.

⚙ Grammaire Les propositions relatives
Aa Vocabulaire La criminalité et les criminels
🧩 Compétence Préciser et détailler

 47.1 INDIQUEZ SI LE PRONOM RELATIF EST LE SUJET OU L'OBJET DE LA PROPOSITION RELATIVE.

> I'm writing about people **who** have been to prison for theft and robbery.   **Subject** ☑ **Object** ☐

❶ There's the woman **who** called the police.   **Subject** ☐ **Object** ☐

❷ The diamond necklace **which** they stole belonged to my grandmother.   **Subject** ☐ **Object** ☐

❸ The website **which** stole people's identities is based abroad.   **Subject** ☐ **Object** ☐

❹ The woman **who** I used to live next door to has been sent to prison for theft.   **Subject** ☐ **Object** ☐

❺ The men **who** solved the crime are fraud experts.   **Subject** ☐ **Object** ☐

🔊

 47.2 BARREZ LE PRONOM RELATIF INCORRECT DANS CHAQUE PHRASE.

>   The cat **that** / ~~who~~ I found belongs to a friend of mine.

❶   The dog **who** / **which** is standing outside the police station is a drug-detection dog.

❷   The woman **that** / **which** was crying had been robbed by two men on a motorcycle.

❸   The man **who** / **which** was sent to prison had stolen hundreds of credit cards.

❹   The man **who** / **which** is talking to the police officer had his car stolen.

❺   The job **who** / **which** I'd like to do after my graduation is in crime prevention.

🔊

47.3 COMPLÉTEZ LES PHRASES AVEC LE PRONOM RELATIF CORRECT.

The new sports car _____*that*_____ I recently bought is extremely expensive.

1. The old man _____ got lost in the city is 98 years old.

2. The lion _____ was born in captivity was released into the wild.

3. The crime _____ we reported is being broadcast on TV!

4. The woman _____ found Samantha's purse is a cleaner.

5. The cat _____ I recently adopted is black and white.

6. The woman _____ I introduced you to last Wednesday is a model.

🔊

47.4 RELIEZ LES TROIS PARTIES DE LA MÊME PHRASE.

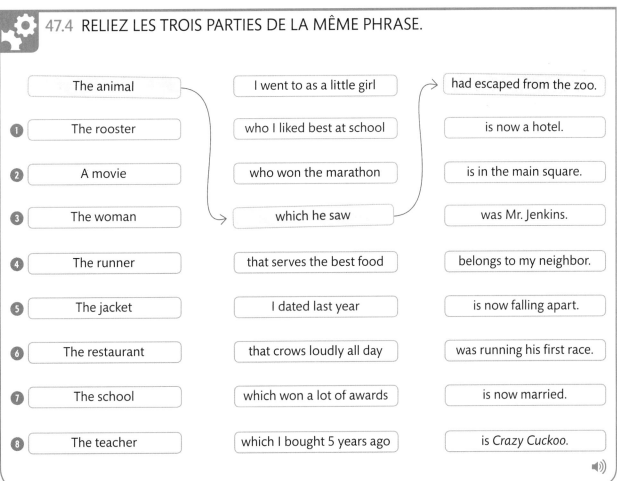

The animal	I went to as a little girl	had escaped from the zoo.
1. The rooster	who I liked best at school	is now a hotel.
2. A movie	who won the marathon	is in the main square.
3. The woman	which he saw	was Mr. Jenkins.
4. The runner	that serves the best food	belongs to my neighbor.
5. The jacket	I dated last year	is now falling apart.
6. The restaurant	that crows loudly all day	was running his first race.
7. The school	which won a lot of awards	is now married.
8. The teacher	which I bought 5 years ago	is *Crazy Cuckoo*.

🔊

157

47.5 RÉCRIVEZ LES PHRASES EN AJOUTANT DES VIRGULES SI NÉCESSAIRE.

My friend Sarah who I met at school is coming to visit.

My friend Sarah, who I met at school, is coming to visit.

❶ The stolen goods which were extremely valuable were found by the police.

❷ My little brother who is only six is always getting into trouble at school.

❸ The robbers who were all from Southampton were caught as they tried to leave the crime scene.

❹ My house which I moved into two months ago has been burgled.

47.6 CORRIGEZ LES ERREURS, PUIS LISEZ LES PHRASES À VOIX HAUTE.

My new car, who I'd only just bought last week, was scratched today.

My new car, which I'd only just bought last week, was scratched today.

❶ The robber, which left his fingerprints behind, was easily caught by the police.

❷ My wallet, who was in my bag, was stolen while we were in the market.

❸ Mr. Townsend, that is a suspect in a murder inquiry, has fled the country.

❹ My credit card details, who I'd used for an online purchase, were stolen.

31 CITY BEAT

LET'S FIGHT CRIME

Exhibition highlights new products that fight crime

Anybody concerned about safety should pay a visit to the Crime Aware Exhibition, which opened yesterday at the Millennium Conference Center.

The companies that are taking part are experts in the field of crime prevention, and many of them are launching new products at the show.

One standout product in the exhibition is the Digital Peephole. This product, which has been in development for two years, attaches to your front door. Usually when you use a peephole, the person who is on the other side of the door is very difficult to see. However, the Digital Peephole links to an LCD screen. The visitor, who you may or may not know, can be clearly seen.

The Crime Aware Exhibition, which is now in its twelfth year, runs from April 2 to April 7.

The Crime Aware Exhibition is only open to police officers.   True ☐ False ☐ Not given ☑

1 You have to pay to go into the Millennium Conference Center.   True ☐ False ☐ Not given ☐

2 There are crime prevention companies at the exhibition.   True ☐ False ☐ Not given ☐

3 You can see brand-new products at the exhibition.   True ☐ False ☐ Not given ☐

4 It took three years to make the Digital Peephole.   True ☐ False ☐ Not given ☐

5 The Digital Peephole is not expensive.   True ☐ False ☐ Not given ☐

6 The Digital Peephole allows you to identify visitors.   True ☐ False ☐ Not given ☐

7 The Digital Peephole allows you to talk to visitors via a screen.   True ☐ False ☐ Not given ☐

8 The first Crime Aware Exhibition was 20 years ago.   True ☐ False ☐ Not given ☐

9 You can visit the exhibition on April 3.   True ☐ False ☐ Not given ☐

48 Plus de propositions relatives

Les mots relatifs définissent ou décrivent un nom d'une partie principale de la phrase. On utilise des mots relatifs différents en fonction des noms auxquels ils se rapportent.

⚙ **Grammaire** « Where », « when », « whereby » et « whose »
Aa Vocabulaire Les expressions du tribunal
🧩 **Compétence** Utiliser des mots relatifs

⚙ **48.1 BARREZ LES MOTS INCORRECTS DANS CHAQUE PHRASE.**

 Let me tell you about the process ~~when~~ / ~~where~~ / whereby the sugar is dissolved in the water.

❶ That's the restaurant **when** / **where** / **whereby** we ate that excellent chicken curry.

❷ There was an agreement **when** / **where** / **whereby** both sides decided to support each other.

❸ This is the church **when** / **where** / **whereby** my parents got married 30 years ago.

❹ He's thinking about the time **when** / **where** / **whereby** we went to Barcelona for the weekend.

❺ We use an application procedure **when** / **where** / **whereby** everything is done electronically.

❻ The director talked about the area **when** / **where** / **whereby** the film was shot.

❼ That's the office **when** / **where** / **whereby** my colleagues Jessica and Peter work.

❽ We're now in the packing area **when** / **where** / **whereby** all of the items are packed.

❾ Heat treatment is a process **when** / **where** / **whereby** heat is applied to metals.

❿ This photo is from the semester **when** / **where** / **whereby** we lived in the dorm.

⓫ We provide a system **when** / **where** / **whereby** companies can find talented people.

🔊

48.2 COMPLÉTEZ LES PHRASES AVEC LES MOTS DE LA LISTE
ET « WHERE », « WHEN » OU « WHEREBY ».

We've set up ___*an exchange program whereby*___ our employees can work abroad for a short time.

1 The kitchen is _____ I most enjoy spending my time. I just love cooking.

2 Early morning is _____ I'm by myself and can have some peace and quiet.

3 Spring is _____ we most enjoy going out for walks in the country.

4 Photosynthesis is _____ plants convert sunlight into energy.

5 This is _____ the last annual trade fair for construction systems was held.

the time of day	the exhibition hall	the room
~~an exchange program~~	the season	the process

 48.3 RÉCRIVEZ LES PHRASES EN CORRIGEANT LES ERREURS.

That was the hotel when we found those insects in the bed. It was absolutely disgusting!
That was the hotel where we found those insects in the bed. It was absolutely disgusting!

1 The TV program gave us a lot of information about the process where cheese is produced.

_____

2 That was the big museum in New York when they have those wonderful Picasso masterpieces.

_____

3 That was the time where the car broke down and we had to wait hours before someone came to help.

_____

4 I'm just waiting for the moment whereby everyone goes quiet so I can start speaking.

_____

5 We're looking at the process where fuel is burned to create the steam that drives the turbine.

_____

1 A woman went to a beauty salon where she had a manicure that she wasn't happy with. ☐

2 A woman went to a beauty salon where she had a skin cleansing treatment she wasn't happy with. ☐

3 A woman went to a beauty salon to have a skin cleansing treatment that made her ill. ☐

4 A woman went to a beauty salon where she had a manicure that made all of her fingers bright red. ☐

48.5 RÉCRIVEZ LES PHRASES AVEC « WHOSE ».

Richard is doing as much overtime as he can. His son starts college this year.
Richard, whose son starts college this year, is doing as much overtime as he can.

1 Fiona always walks in the park in the morning. She has a large and energetic dog.

_____

2 ZFF is a company that is starting to work in China. Its CEO gave an interview on TV last night.

_____

3 Jack is learning to play the trumpet. His school has received more money for music classes.

_____

4 Francesca is really stressed out right now. Her computer has just crashed.

_____

5 Mandy took some time off work last week. Her mother has suddenly become ill.

_____

6 The company has innovative HR policies. Its employees now have unlimited time off.

_____

7 The tennis club is expanding every year. Its tennis courts are located on the outskirts of the town.

_____

🔊

48.6 LISEZ L'ARTICLE, PUIS RÉPONDEZ AUX QUESTIONS.

Smoke, smoke everywhere

An apartment building caught fire

Yesterday, there was a fire in the apartment building where I live. Everything was normal when I got home from work that evening, but then after a while I started to notice the smell of smoke.

I didn't think any more of it, but then suddenly, the smell of smoke became much stronger and it was impossible to ignore. I opened the front door to my apartment and saw that the smoke was coming from across the hall where Mr. Jerome lives.

I called the fire department and, just as the smoke was really starting to build up, they arrived. The firefighters organized a procedure whereby some of them entered the apartment from the balcony while some others tried to break down the door and get in that way. Fortunately, nobody was hurt and there wasn't too much damage to the apartment where the fire started.

Where did the fire happen?

The fire happened in the apartment building where the writer lives.

---

1 Did the writer notice anything unusual when he got home from work that day?

---

2 Where did the writer find out that the smoke was coming from?

---

3 Who called the fire department and when did it arrive at the building?

---

4 What procedure did the firefighters organize to save the person in the apartment?

---

5 What were the effects on the apartment where the fire started?

---

6 How many people were hurt in the fire?

---

49 Les verbes modaux au futur

Certains verbes modaux changent de forme lorsqu'on les utilise pour parler du futur. D'autres ne peuvent pas être utilisés au futur et doivent être remplacés par d'autres modaux ou syntagmes.

⚙ **Grammaire** « Will be able to » et « will have to »
Aa Vocabulaire Les termes juridiques
🧩 **Compétence** Exprimer des capacités et des obligations futures

49.1 RÉCRIVEZ LES PHRASES AU FUTUR.

> We can't go on vacation this year because we don't have enough money.
> _We won't be able to go on vacation this year because we don't have enough money._

❶ Unfortunately, I have to cancel our meeting because I can't make it.

❷ Can you pay the fine if you park your car in this restricted zone?

❸ I can't get to sleep if my neighbors are making a lot of noise.

❹ Do you have to stay in and study for your final exams?

❺ We have to get a good night's sleep tonight because we have an early start.

❻ Do you have to take all six exams this semester?

❼ We cannot meet our deadlines because the company hasn't delivered on time.

❽ Can you help me translate this text from Portuguese to English?

❾ I can't help you with the translation because I'm really busy at the moment.

🔊

49.2 ÉCRIVEZ LES MOTS SUIVANTS DANS LE BON ORDRE AFIN DE RECONSTITUER LES PHRASES.

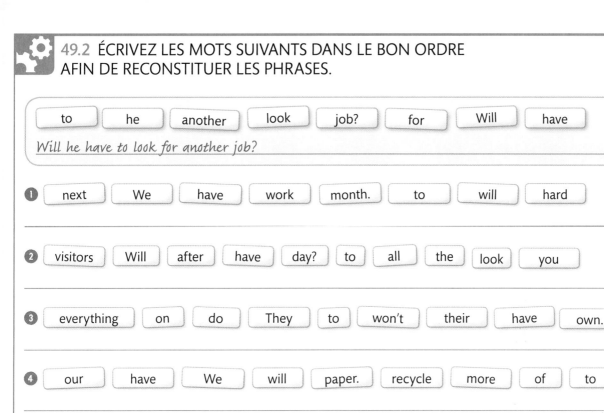

to   he   another   look   job?   for   Will   have

Will he have to look for another job?

① next   We   have   work   month.   to   will   hard

② visitors   Will   after   have   day?   to   all   the   look   you

③ everything   on   do   They   to   won't   their   have   own.

④ our   have   We   will   paper.   recycle   more   of   to

49.3 COMPLÉTEZ LES PHRASES AVEC LE FUTUR.

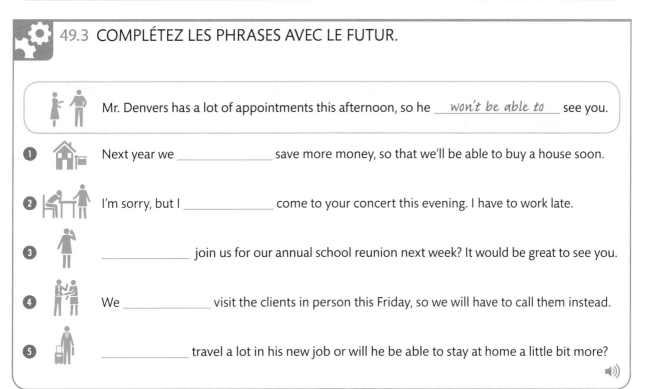

Mr. Denvers has a lot of appointments this afternoon, so he _won't be able to_ see you.

① Next year we _____ save more money, so that we'll be able to buy a house soon.

② I'm sorry, but I _____ come to your concert this evening. I have to work late.

③ _____ join us for our annual school reunion next week? It would be great to see you.

④ We _____ visit the clients in person this Friday, so we will have to call them instead.

⑤ _____ travel a lot in his new job or will he be able to stay at home a little bit more?

49.4 BARREZ LES MOTS INCORRECTS DANS CHAQUE PHRASE.

> Now we've got the boss's approval, we **will be able to** / ~~will have to~~ get started with the project.

1 According to the weather forecast, it will snow tomorrow, so we **will be able to** / **will have to** go skiing.

2 He **won't be able to** / **won't have to** take the course he wanted to do because it's been canceled.

3 I hope that one day every person **will be able to** / **will have to** realize their full potential.

4 When we turn the next corner, you **will be able to** / **will have to** see the beach and the ocean.

5 She's so happy that she **won't be able to** / **won't have to** wear braces on her teeth any more.

6 If you want to come to the party, you **will be able to** / **will have to** let me know by Friday at the latest.

7 If anyone would like a signed copy of the book, you **will be able to** / **will can to** buy one later.

8 You **won't be able to** / **won't have to** do so much paperwork now that you've got a secretary.

49.5 ÉCOUTEZ L'ENREGISTREMENT, PUIS RÉPONDEZ AUX QUESTIONS.

M. Hall parle à Mme Cooper
des résulats scolaires de son fils.

> Why has Peter been having problems at school recently?
> _Peter's been having problems at school recently because he hasn't been able to concentrate._

1 If Peter continues like this, what grades will he be able to get?

_____

2 According to Mr. Hall, what is Peter able to do?

_____

3 What will Peter have to do if he doesn't pass his exams?

_____

4 Will Peter be able to get some extra support over the next few months?

_____

45 GOVERNMENT WATCH

PUBLIC SMOKING BANNED

Government passes law banning smoking in public

The government has passed a law which will ban smoking in all public places. The politicians told us they felt they should pass the law because we are all much more aware of the dangers of passive smoking now. They thought they could be doing more to protect the public. Smokers will only be permitted to smoke on private property from next April when we will have to start observing the law. Some have suggested that the law could be difficult to enforce, but law enforcement agencies are hopeful that businesses will cooperate with them. There's no chance of anyone being arrested for smoking in public places, but offenders will be given an on-the-spot fine if someone reports them.

NO SMOKING AREA

The article tells us about a new law that the police have passed. **True** ☐ **False** ☑ **Not given** ☐

① Under the new law, people will not be permitted to smoke in public. **True** ☐ **False** ☐ **Not given** ☐

② The law was passed to protect people from passive smoking. **True** ☐ **False** ☐ **Not given** ☐

③ Smokers will be permitted to smoke in their own homes. **True** ☐ **False** ☐ **Not given** ☐

④ The law will be enforced from April 14 next year. **True** ☐ **False** ☐ **Not given** ☐

⑤ Everyone thinks it will be easy to enforce the law. **True** ☐ **False** ☐ **Not given** ☐

⑥ Smokers' groups have complained about the law. **True** ☐ **False** ☐ **Not given** ☐

⑦ The police think businesses will work with them to enforce the law. **True** ☐ **False** ☐ **Not given** ☐

⑧ Some people could be arrested for smoking in public places. **True** ☐ **False** ☐ **Not given** ☐

⑨ You will have to pay money if you're caught smoking in public. **True** ☐ **False** ☐ **Not given** ☐

50 Vue d'ensemble des verbes modaux

Les verbes modaux permettent de parler de probabilité, de capacité, de permission et d'obligation. Ils font souvent référence à des situations hypothétiques.

 Grammaire Utiliser les verbes modaux
Aa Vocabulaire Les verbes modaux
Compétence Demander, offrir et prédire

50.1 COMPLÉTEZ LES PHRASES AVEC LES VERBES MODAUX DE LA LISTE.

I keep telling him that he _____*shouldn't*_____ work so much. He'll make himself ill.

1. He's a great runner. He _____ run twelve miles in two hours.

2. _____ I have another piece of cake? It's delicious.

3. That _____ be Dominic at the door because he's in Spain at the moment.

4. When I was younger, I _____ party all night, but now I'm older I can't.

5. _____ we have lunch together on Thursday? It would be great to catch up.

6. Don't worry, I _____ make sure that everything's ready on time.

7. _____ you go down to reception and meet the visitors for me?

8. Joanna said she _____ join us, but she probably wouldn't be able to make it.

9. You've had that cough for two weeks now. You _____ go to the doctor.

May	will	should	can't	might
Shall	Would	could	can	~~shouldn't~~

50.2 BARREZ LES MOTS INCORRECTS DANS CHAQUE PHRASE.

> You ~~may~~ / ought to / ~~must~~ get a present for her. She would really appreciate that.

1 You **can** / **might** / **must** take your laptop out of your bag before you go through security control.

2 You **will** / **should** / **may** stay here as long as you want. Just remember to lock the door when you leave.

3 **Shall** / **Will** / **Might** I give you a ride home afterward? I'll be in the area at that time anyway.

4 **Would** / **May** / **Will** I help you carry your suitcase up the stairs?

5 When I was a child I **couldn't** / **can't** / **shouldn't** do a handstand, but now I can!

6 **Must** / **Should** / **Will** you help me prepare the training course for our Spanish colleagues?

7 If that doesn't work, you **might** / **could** / **must** call Edward and ask him if he knows what to do.

8 Since he had his operation, he **can't** / **couldn't** / **won't** walk more than 10 steps.

50.3 RELIEZ LE DÉBUT DE CHAQUE PHRASE À LA FIN QUI LUI CORRESPOND.

You could fly to Barcelona,	so you don't have so much to do?
1 Don't put your fingers so close to the pan.	They taste delicious!
2 Should I help you move those boxes,	get a decent haircut for a change.
3 Will you check that the door	but there's also a good train connection.
4 You must go to reception to register	if it's OK for us to arrive a little later?
5 May I have another cookie?	You could burn yourself.
6 I can't speak French very well,	is locked when you leave?
7 He ought to go to the hairdresser and	but I can understand a lot.
8 Would you call and ask	before you can go to the meeting room.

50.4 COCHEZ LES PHRASES CORRECTES.

We had to left early yesterday so we can get the last train home. ☐
We had to leave early yesterday so we could get the last train home. ☑

1. You should have asked your boss to pay you for the overtime you did. ☐
   You should have ask your boss to pay you for the overtime you did. ☐

2. He lost his voice, so he couldn't teach his classes last week. ☐
   He lost his voice, so he can't teach his classes last week. ☐

3. I can't find my keys anywhere. I must left them at home. ☐
   I can't find my keys anywhere. I must have left them at home. ☐

4. She should have asked me for advice. I would have been able to help. ☐
   She should ask me for advice. I would have been able to help. ☐

5. Could you visit the museum when you were on vacation, or was it closed? ☐
   Can you visit the museum when you were on vacation, or was it closed? ☐

50.5 RÉCRIVEZ LES PHRASES EN CORRIGEANT LES ERREURS.

I'm sure someone must found my wallet and handed it in.
I'm sure someone must have found my wallet and handed it in.

1. You should have bring your laptop to the meeting. Sarah reminded you yesterday.

_____

2. They ought to had more respect for the neighbors when they have a party.

_____

3. Why didn't you ask? I would shared a taxi from the airport to the hotel with you.

_____

4. I know what happened. We must take a wrong turn just after we left the hotel.

_____

Aa 51.1 LES COUTUMES ET LES CULTURES ÉCRIVEZ LES MOTS DE LA LISTE SOUS LA DÉFINITION CORRESPONDANTE.

Part of old customs or beliefs

traditional

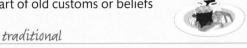

7 Range or variety

1 The principles and beliefs that somebody holds

8 Get used to an environment, surroundings, or culture

2 Something wrong that you do regularly

9 Polite or accepted social behavior

3 The way a person leads their life

10 Do something that upsets others

4 A fixed, often incorrect, idea about what a person or thing is like

11 People from a nation with a shared culture and language

5 Something that is done locally as part of a tradition

12 The increasing similarity between different cultures across the world

6 Look or seem similar to the surrounding place or people

13 The way that a language is spoken in a certain area

---

lifestyle	diversity	acclimate	manners
~~traditional~~	cause offence	dialect	bad habit	values
blend in	stereotype	nationality	local custom	globalization

Vous voudrez peut-être parfois parler de groupes de personnes ou de nationalités différentes de manière générale. Il est important de connaître la façon correcte de le faire.

⚙ **Grammaire** Utiliser des adjectifs comme noms

Aa **Vocabulaire** Les pays et les nationalités

🧩 **Compétence** Généraliser poliment

52.1 ÉCRIVEZ LE NOM APPROPRIÉ DE CHAQUE NATIONALITÉ.

Chinese = _The Chinese_

1 Dutch = _____

2 Kenyan = _____

3 Swiss = _____

4 Vietnamese = _____

5 Australian = _____

6 Egyptian = _____

7 Argentinian = _____

8 Korean = _____

9 Spanish = _____

10 Greek = _____

11 Japanese = _____

12 Brazilian = _____

13 British = _____

🔊

52.2 RELIEZ LE DÉBUT DE CHAQUE PHRASE À LA FIN QUI LUI CORRESPOND.

Canadians are famous for

1 We're looking for ways of helping

2 The young often have a reputation

3 The British are known for their love of

4 Some people believe that the rich

5 Pets are seen as excellent companions

6 We have started distributing food

7 The injured were airlifted to the hospital

fish and chips.

should pay a much higher level of tax.

to the poor.

their love of winter sports.

for being wild and irresponsible.

immediately after the accident.

for the elderly.

the homeless find accommodation.

🔊

52.3 COMPLÉTEZ LES PHRASES AVEC LES MOTS OU LES NOMS DE LA LISTE.

When we went to Beijing last month, we realized how hospitable _the Chinese_ are.

1. We've built these ramps and put in these rails to help _____ access the building.

2. I think that _____ should give away more of their money to people who are in need.

3. The emergency services have given _____ all of the medical attention they need.

4. _____ are the group who are likely to spend the most time using social media.

5. In Nairobi, _____ live on the edges of the city in homes they've built themselves.

6. Ancient _____ worshipped cats.

7. We offer accommodation for _____ who can no longer live alone.

8. _____ are known throughout the world for making clocks and chocolate.

9. We don't want _____ to come into contact with infectious diseases.

10. If you'd like to help _____ who live on our streets, come along to our soup kitchen.

11. _____ sometimes aren't offered very much help with finding a new job.

12. He decided to become a doctor because he wanted to help _____ .

the rich　　the poor　　The young　　the elderly　　the injured　　the homeless　　the disabled

the sick　　The unemployed　　the healthy　　The Swiss　　Egyptians　　the Chinese

52.4 COCHEZ LES PHRASES CORRECTES.

> The government has been spending a lot of money on services for the elderly in recent years. ✓
> The government has been spending a lot of money on services for elderly in recent years. ☐

1. The unemployed people are welcome to come and volunteer at the library if they want to. ☐
   Unemployed people are welcome to come and volunteer at the library if they want to. ☐

2. Our charity was set up to help the elderly by organizing a weekly social meet-up for them. ☐
   Our charity was set up to help elderly by organizing a weekly social meet-up for them. ☐

3. The majority of Germans were in support of the decision. ☐
   The majority of German were in support of the decision. ☐

4. Our first priority is to help the injured. Then we can talk to journalists about what's happened. ☐
   Our first priority is to help injured. Then we can talk to journalists about what's happened. ☐

5. This fort was built by the Dutch in the late 1600s. ☐
   This fort was built by Dutch in the late 1600s. ☐

6. The government wants to introduce a new law, which will make the rich pay more in taxes. ☐
   The government wants to introduce a new law, which will make rich pay more in taxes. ☐

7. These parking spaces are only for the disabled. Can you please park somewhere else? ☐
   These parking spaces are only for disabled. Can you please park somewhere else? ☐

8. Most Brazilians are taught English at school. ☐
   Most the Brazilians are taught English at school. ☐

9. Homeless are sometimes seen as dangerous, but this is far from the truth. ☐
   The homeless are sometimes seen as dangerous, but this is far from the truth. ☐

10. The British are coming over here to learn more about our processes and how we do things. ☐
    British are coming over here to learn more about our processes and how we do things. ☐

11. I decided to become a nurse because I really wanted to be able to help the sick. ☐
    I decided to become a nurse because I really wanted to be able to help sick. ☐

12. The French are known for being very relaxed and this is also something I've noticed. ☐
    French are known for being very relaxed and this is also something I've noticed. ☐

What is done in your country to make sure older people are looked after?

The elderly *are given a bus pass so that they can travel easily.*

1 How are people with less money treated in your country?

The poor _____

2 Are people with illnesses comfortable going to see a doctor?

The sick _____

3 Is there good access for people in wheelchairs in your town?

The disabled _____

4 What kind of support is there for people who can't find work?

The unemployed _____

5 How do you think the media portrays young people?

The young _____

6 Is anything done to help homeless people in your country?

The homeless _____

7 What do you and your friends think about rich people?

The rich _____

Les situations passées et nouvelles

Les situations nouvelles peuvent parfois sembler étranges, mais elles deviennent familières avec le temps. Vous pouvez dans ce cas utiliser des phrases contenant « be used to » et « get used to ».

⚙ **Grammaire** « Be used to » et « get used to »

Aa Vocabulaire S'installer et vivre à l'étranger

Compétence Parler de situations passées et nouvelles

53.1 BARREZ LES MOTS INCORRECTS DANS CHAQUE PHRASE.

 I **am** / **get** used to running the department on my own, so it's not a problem for me.

 It took me a while to **get** / **be** used to the stores being closed on Sundays here.

 He's been starting work at 6am for three months now, so he **gets** / **is** used to it.

 As we live in the north of Norway, we **get** / **are** used to very cold weather in winter.

 I'm still **getting** / **being** used to the fast pace of activity in my new company.

 When he first went to live in Australia, he **wasn't** / **didn't get** used to the heat and got burned.

 You've been working with us for some time, so you **got** / **are** used to the way we work now.

 I just can't **get** / **be** used to working every weekend. I don't think I'll ever like it.

 Don't worry about Rachel! She **gets** / **is** used to traveling on her own.

 When we had our first child, we had to **get** / **be** used to not having very much sleep.

 We've had our new boss for six months now, but I'm still **getting** / **being** used to her style.

 Jeremy lives in Los Angeles, so he **gets** / **is** used to living through minor earthquakes.

🔊

53.2 COMPLÉTEZ LES PHRASES EN UTILISANT LA FORME CORRECTE DE « BE » ET « GET ».

> Once Laura _____ *gets* _____ used to working from home, she'll realize how much better it is for her.

1 Three years after moving, I think we _____ finally used to life in the country and really like it.

2 After a while you'll _____ used to the rhythm of the train and fall asleep.

3 He _____ used to sleeping on a very soft bed at home, so he doesn't like hard beds.

4 I was just _____ used to our old English teacher when she left and we got a new one.

5 He _____ now so used to wearing glasses that he doesn't even notice them anymore.

6 I _____ used to taking the train every day and I knew the timetable by heart.

🔊

53.3 RÉCRIVEZ LES PHRASES EN CORRIGEANT LES ERREURS.

> I'm get used to waiting for Simon outside his house because he's always running late.
> *I'm used to waiting for Simon outside his house because he's always running late.*

1 Our customers from other countries get used to getting very high quality products from us.

_____

2 I don't think Christina will ever got used to living on her own. She doesn't like it.

_____

3 We're get used to being able to communicate with people from all over the world online.

_____

4 My friend is not get used to eating spicy food, so it makes him go red in the face.

_____

5 He is still being used to the new house he bought last year.

_____

6 Our children Joseph and Liz are used to be away from the two of us while we're at work.

_____

🔊

53.4 RELIEZ LE DÉBUT DE CHAQUE PHRASE À LA FIN QUI LUI CORRESPOND.

We're not used to getting such bad

① You will have to get used to working

② We were used to bringing lunch

③ Jack's slowly getting used to living

④ The new shoes were uncomfortable,

⑤ I'm used to sitting through long and

in a dorm instead of at home.

boring lectures. I do it every day.

long hours if you want to be on this team.

service at this restaurant. What has happened?

to work, but now we eat in the canteen.

but she soon got used to them.

53.5 ÉCOUTEZ L'ENREGISTREMENT, PUIS COCHEZ LES BONNES RÉPONSES.

Un homme parle de partir s'installer dans un nouveau pays et de s'habituer à y vivre.

How long has the speaker lived in China?
Two weeks ☐
Two months ☐
Two years ☑

① Where did the speaker live before this?
China ☐
The UK ☐
Japan ☐

② Who told the speaker that he had to move?
His wife ☐
His boss ☐
His colleague ☐

③ Which other option did the speaker have?
Germany ☐
Japan ☐
India ☐

④ How does he find the people in China?
Direct ☐
Quiet ☐
Rude ☐

⑤ Who sometimes asks personal questions?
Colleagues ☐
Neighbors ☐
Strangers ☐

⑥ Where do you not necessarily find the best food?
Nice restaurants ☐
Fast-food outlets ☐
Street markets ☐

⑦ Where is the speaker now used to going to eat?
Nice restaurants ☐
Fast-food outlets ☐
Street markets ☐

53.6 COMPLÉTEZ LES PHRASES, PUIS LISEZ-LES À VOIX HAUTE.

I'm _____ used to _____ traveling a lot, so making two trips in one week is OK with me.

1. Our neighbors are so loud, but we'll just have to _____ the noise.

2. I've lived in Tokyo for ten years now, so I'm _____ Japanese food.

3. My boss was pleased about how quickly I _____ giving presentations.

4. We may have to _____ traveling a little farther to get to the shops soon.

5. We were just _____ the new office when we had to move to another one.

6. He's been working in virtual teams for a long time now, so he's _____ it.

53.7 RÉCRIVEZ LES PASSAGES SURLIGNÉS EN CORRIGEANT LES ERREURS.

get used to

1. _____
2. _____
3. _____
4. _____
5. _____
6. _____
7. _____
8. _____
9. _____

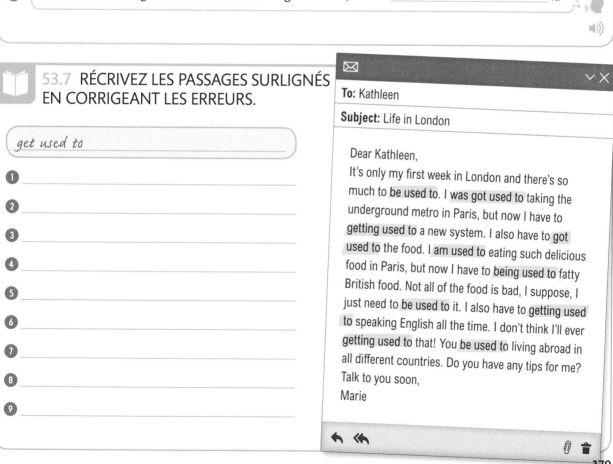

✉

To: Kathleen

Subject: Life in London

Dear Kathleen,
It's only my first week in London and there's so much to **be used to**. I **was got used to** taking the underground metro in Paris, but now I have to **getting used to** a new system. I also have to **got used to** the food. I **am used to** eating such delicious food in Paris, but now I have to **being used to** fatty British food. Not all of the food is bad, I suppose, I just need to **be used to** it. I also have to **getting used to** speaking English all the time. I don't think I'll ever **getting used to** that! You **be used to** living abroad in all different countries. Do you have any tips for me?
Talk to you soon,
Marie

54 Les articles

L'article est l'un des mots les plus courts et communs de la langue anglaise. Des règles précisent quel article, si article il y a, doit être utilisé.

 Grammaire Les articles

Aa Vocabulaire Les fautes d'orthographe les plus courantes

Compétence Prononcer les mots avec des lettres muettes

54.1 BARREZ LES MOTS INCORRECTS DANS CHAQUE PHRASE.

MOMA is a / an / ~~the~~ excellent art museum that you could visit when you go to New York.

① A / An / **The** investors who come to us have a lot of money to invest in companies.

② We paid for a / an / **the** audio guide in the palace and it gave us some interesting information.

③ A / An / **The** CEO of our company is surprisingly young. He's only 30 years old!

④ If you want to travel cheaply in Paris, you should take a / an / **the** Métro.

⑤ After dinner, I bought a / an / **the** ice cream cone and ate it while I was sitting by the fountain.

⑥ The Eiffel Tower is probably a / an / **the** most famous landmark in Paris.

⑦ We were so busy and did so much walking that I need a / an / **the** early night tonight.

⑧ The flag is up, so a / an / **the** Queen must be in the palace today.

⑨ It's amazing how quickly a / an / **the** company's share price is going up at the moment.

⑩ We're thinking about hiring a / an / **the** boat tomorrow and taking it out on the water.

⑪ My hotel has a / an / **the** beautiful view of the harbor and the sea.

54.2 RELIEZ LE DÉBUT DE CHAQUE PHRASE À LA FIN QUI LUI CORRESPOND.

People who aren't willing to help you

want to stay in an all-inclusive hotel.

1 The people who live in our town

usually aren't as good as ones you pay for.

2 The restaurant we went to last night

is the one where pizza was invented.

3 I don't know why, but spaghetti

are really irritating, in my opinion.

4 A large number of vacationers

don't want the new road to be built.

5 City tours that are free

always tastes better when you're in Italy.

 54.3 RÉCRIVEZ LES PHRASES EN CORRIGEANT LES ERREURS.

Last year I went on vacation to Kuala Lumpur in Malaysia and had the great time.
Last year I went on vacation to Kuala Lumpur in Malaysia and had a great time.

1 A Petronas Towers are the tallest buildings in Kuala Lumpur and they dominate the skyline.

_____

2 If you go up to the top of the tower, you get a excellent view of the Kuala Lumpur.

_____

3 Street food stands on the side of an road are great places to try Malaysian food.

_____

4 You can also visit Islamic Arts Museum if you go to Kuala Lumpur. It's interesting.

_____

5 Taking the day trip to the nearby Batu Caves is a good idea if you have time.

_____

6 Have you walked through a colorful China Town market in Kuala Lumpur?

_____

54.4 COMPLÉTEZ LES PHRASES EN CHOISISSANT L'ARTICLE APPROPRIÉ. LAISSEZ UN BLANC POUR L'ARTICLE ZÉRO.

They had ___*an*___ amazing dinner in the restaurant at the top of the tower.

1. This is _____ old typewriter that my mother always used to use.

2. People from Brazil are known for their love of _____ football.

3. I've never seen such _____ wide selection of foods for breakfast as they had there.

4. They love _____ Chinese food, so I'm sure they'll enjoy their trip to China.

5. Our tour guide is _____ older lady who's lived in Dublin all her life.

6. There's _____ university in Bologna which is nearly 1,000 years old.

7. Here's our guide to _____ travel destinations that will be the most popular next year.

8. _____ waitress who served us at that restaurant was very friendly and helpful.

9. Children usually enjoy visiting _____ zoo in Edinburgh. You can even see pandas there.

10. Churros are very popular in _____ Spain. People eat them with chocolate sauce.

11. I wasn't sure whether we should leave _____ tip for the waiter or not.

12. _____ music festival we went to was brilliant. There were a lot of good bands playing.

13. _____ hotel where we stayed is a five-star hotel, so it was very luxurious.

54.5 ÉCOUTEZ L'ENREGISTREMENT, PUIS COCHEZ LES BONNES RÉPONSES.

George et Carla parlent des différents pays où ils ont vécu.

Germans and Brazilians both love soccer. George thinks Germany has some top class teams.
True ✓ **False** ☐

1 George supports the Bayern Munich team and thinks it's the best team around at the moment.
True ☐ **False** ☐

2 George says German food is filling and tasty, but it is quite salty for him.
True ☐ **False** ☐

3 Carla says steak is the most popular food in Brazil. Brazilians love meat, especially barbecued beef.
True ☐ **False** ☐

4 Carla thinks the famous statue of Christ the Redeemer is the most popular landmark in Brazil.
True ☐ **False** ☐

5 Carla thinks the Brandenburg Gate is the symbol of Brazil.
True ☐ **False** ☐

54.6 ENTOUREZ LES LETTRES MUETTES, PUIS LISEZ LES PHRASES À VOIX HAUTE.

I know you want to go out later.

4 I like to listen to music while I'm traveling.

1 Let's call a plumber to fix the water heater.

5 To be honest, I don't think I like him.

2 Foreign visitors think we speak good English.

6 It's so cold. My fingers are numb.

3 I hurt my knee while we were trekking.

7 He has just trapped his thumb in the door!

55 Les idées abstraites

La plupart des noms abstraits sont indénombrables. Toutefois, certains peuvent être à la fois dénombrables et indénombrables, et les deux formes ont souvent un sens légèrement différent.

⚙ **Grammaire** Les noms concrets et abstraits
Aa Vocabulaire Les systèmes éducatifs
🧩 **Compétence** Parler d'idées abstraites

 55.1 BARREZ LE MOT INCORRECT DANS CHAQUE PHRASE.

Please accept our ~~apology~~ / apologies for the cold soup you were served in our restaurant.

1. We often find that men aren't as good at taking care of their health / healths as women are.

2. She made her anger / angers at the graffiti on the wall clear to everyone in the room.

3. Unfortunately, the funding for all of the library / libraries in our area has been cut this year.

4. He's been having some trouble / troubles getting his computer to start all week.

5. Could you please email me all of the information / informations I need for my trip to Peru?

6. Our company specializes in creating beauty / beauties products for young women.

7. He has a lot of knowledge / knowledges about the history of the Middle Ages.

8. I've made a list of all the deadline / deadlines for the project in this document.

9. We take a lot of pride / prides in our work and always do our very best.

10. It's absolutely freezing today. It must be about minus fifteen degree / degrees outside!

11. We're facing some fierce competition / competitions from companies in South America.

🔊

55.2 COMPLÉTEZ LES PHRASES AVEC LES MOTS DE LA LISTE.

There's so much more _____*space*_____ in our new flat than in our old flat in Birmingham.

1 My _____ are with the families of the victims of the disaster at this terrible time.

2 I come from Nigeria and my _____ is very important to me. I keep the traditions alive.

3 Our _____ is that our daughter will go to college and get a good job.

4 Your _____ is really important to me, and I hope you feel the same.

5 My happiest childhood _____ are of spending the summer in Sweden with my family.

6 I save some money every month and then at the end of the year I give it to local _____ .

charities   memories   ~~space~~   culture   friendship   hope   thoughts

🔊

55.3 RELIEZ LE DÉBUT DE CHAQUE PHRASE À LA FIN QUI LUI CORRESPOND.

Everyone needs some relaxation | birth to are real beauties.

1 You can now all find out what | a letter of apology for all of the noise.

2 My car has a top speed | computers for a living.

3 The kittens your cat gave | after a long week at work.

4 I'm going to write the neighbors | grades you got on the exam.

5 My cousin Matthew repairs | competitions. You can win so much!

6 We're here today because we're | of 100 miles per hour.

7 Nowadays it's more and more | semesters before you get your degree.

8 I make a living from entering | important to have good communication skills.

9 You have to study for six | interested in learning more about other cultures.

🔊

55.4 RÉCRIVEZ LES PHRASES EN CORRIGEANT LES ERREURS.

> He's had so much successes as the CEO of this company, but now he wants to move on.
> *He's had so much success as the CEO of this company, but now he wants to move on.*

1 The temperatures this summer are some of the highest in living memories.

_____

2 I work hard on my friendship because friends are an important part of my life.

_____

3 She hopes that she will complete her study and graduate next summer.

_____

4 We're collecting money for charities, but we haven't decided which one we'll give it to yet.

_____

5 There are a lot of free parking space at the front of the building if you're still looking.

_____

6 You will be in our thought while you're away and we'll call you as often as we can.

_____

7 There's always a lot of competitions in the soft drink market. It's hard to break through.

_____

8 He takes so much prides in his garden and he wants other people to enjoy it, too.

_____

9 There are so many time when I wish I had a robot who could do the housework for me.

_____

10 She decided to take all of her knowledges about marketing and put it into a book.

_____

11 The skills he has for soccer is unbelievable for someone of his age.

_____

12 The company is known for the very high qualities of their kitchen products.

_____

◀))

56 Vocabulaire

Aa 56.1 **LA TECHNOLOGIE ET L'AVENIR** ÉCRIVEZ LES MOTS DE LA LISTE SOUS LA DÉFINITION CORRESPONDANTE.

The most modern and up-to-date

state-of-the-art

❼ The most recent version of a product

❶ Say what you think might happen in the future

❽ An important discovery or achievement

❷ What will happen in the future

❾ Plan ahead so that something can happen

❸ Something that will happen but it is not possible to say when

❿ Have good or positive plans

❹ Change or affect something

⓫ An era based on digital information, when technology is dominant

❺ Design something to work in the future, even if technology changes

⓬ Hope for a successful or positive outcome

❻ A huge change in ideas or methods

⓭ Extremely modern and innovative

---

have good intentions   digital age   revolution   hope for the best   what the future holds

only a matter of time   breakthrough   make arrangements   the latest model   ~~state-of-the-art~~

cutting-edge   make predictions   future-proof   have an influence on something

57 Les espoirs

Pour parler de souhaits, souvent lorsque vous voulez que quelque chose change, utilisez les modaux « would » et « could » au passé.

⚙️ **Grammaire** « Wish » avec « would » ou « could »
Aa Vocabulaire Les espoirs
🧩 **Compétence** Parler de souhaits et d'espoirs

 57.1 RÉCRIVEZ LES PHRASES EN CORRIGEANT LES ERREURS.

> I wish I can go to the movies with you this weekend.
> *I wish I could go to the movies with you this weekend.*

1 My job at the supermarket is so boring, I wish I would find another one.

_____

2 I wish Rosemary is stopping talking about herself all the time. It's so annoying!

_____

3 I wish my teacher will give me more help. I don't understand any of this.

_____

4 They wish they would take some time off work so they could go on vacation.

_____

5 He wishes he can win the first prize in the competition he's entered.

_____

6 She would she could get a leading role in the play, but she never goes to auditions.

_____

7 I wish I would afford to get a new kitchen. This one is so old it's falling apart.

_____

8 Adam wishes his teacher will give him more homework. He doesn't have enough to do.

_____

9 I wish they will make it easier to work out how much tax you have to pay.

_____

🔊

57.2 COMPLÉTEZ LES PHRASES AVEC « COULD » OU « WOULD ».

The company wishes its employees _____*would*_____ take advantage of the training it offers.

1 I wish my boss _____ be a little more polite. He's always rude to everyone.

2 Linda wishes she _____ drive to work, but she still hasn't passed her driving test.

3 They wish their neighbors _____ be a bit quieter. They're always making noise.

4 I wish they _____ tell us what's going to happen now instead of making us wait.

5 Jacob wishes he _____ relax, but he can't because he's having a stressful time at work.

6 I wish we _____ go on a helicopter ride around Manhattan, but we can't afford it.

7 Susanne wishes her daughter _____ call her more often. She only calls once a month.

8 I wish the people on the train _____ move their bags off the seats next to them.

9 They wish they _____ get a good espresso in this town, but they can't find one anywhere.

◀))

 57.3 RELIEZ LE DÉBUT DE CHAQUE PHRASE À LA FIN QUI LUI CORRESPOND.

The printer keeps jamming. I wish   they would make them simpler.

1 My job is really boring. I wish   someone would turn it off.

2 The snails are eating my plants. I wish   I could drive instead.

3 The rules are so complicated. I wish   I could find one that works.

4 I can't type very quickly. I wish   I could go to bed.

5 They always leave a mess. I wish   I could get rid of them once and for all.

6 The bus always takes so long. I wish   my boss would let me take a course.

7 I'm so sleepy. I wish   they would think about other people.

8 That machine is very noisy. I wish   I could find something more interesting.

◀))

57.4 COMPLÉTEZ LES PHRASES AVEC « COULD » OU « WOULD », PUIS LISEZ-LES À HAUTE.

I wish the airline _____*would*_____ make it easier to change flights.

1. The students wish they _____ speak perfect English.

2. He wishes his teacher _____ give him more help.

3. She wishes she _____ go to the party.

4. We wish they _____ let us leave work early.

57.5 ÉCOUTEZ L'ENREGISTREMENT, PUIS COCHEZ LES BONNES RÉPONSES.

Cheryl parle de son travail avec son patron, Michael.

Which department does Cheryl work in?
- Human Resources ☐
- Sales ☑
- Service ☐

1. What change does Cheryl want to make to her working life?
- She wants to work from home ☐
- She wants to travel more ☐
- She wants to travel less ☐

2. Where are the customers of Cheryl's company located?
- In Cheryl's home town ☐
- Close to headquarters ☐
- Far away from headquarters ☐

3. According to Cheryl's boss, what does the CEO not want to do?
- Move the headquarters to a better place ☐
- Lose the customers the company has ☐
- Keep the head office where it is now ☐

4. What would be Cheryl's ideal job if she could pick one?
- CEO of the company ☐
- Internal sales team leader ☐
- Her boss' job ☐

5. Why will there be a vacancy within the next two years?
- Geoff wants to leave the company ☐
- Geoff is going to retire ☐
- Geoff is going to take a new position ☐

57.6 LISEZ LE COURRIEL, PUIS RÉPONDEZ AUX QUESTIONS.

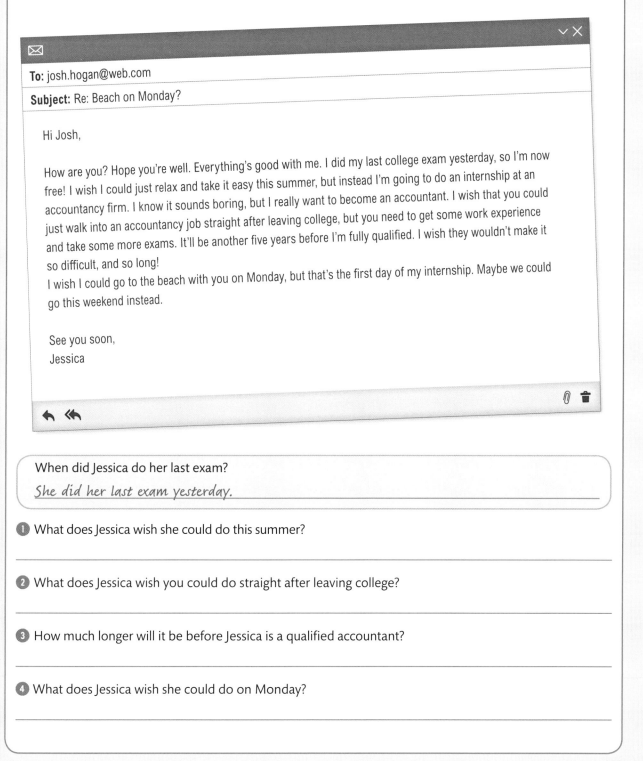

To: josh.hogan@web.com

Subject: Re: Beach on Monday?

Hi Josh,

How are you? Hope you're well. Everything's good with me. I did my last college exam yesterday, so I'm now free! I wish I could just relax and take it easy this summer, but instead I'm going to do an internship at an accountancy firm. I know it sounds boring, but I really want to become an accountant. I wish that you could just walk into an accountancy job straight after leaving college, but you need to get some work experience and take some more exams. It'll be another five years before I'm fully qualified. I wish they wouldn't make it so difficult, and so long!

I wish I could go to the beach with you on Monday, but that's the first day of my internship. Maybe we could go this weekend instead.

See you soon,
Jessica

When did Jessica do her last exam?

She did her last exam yesterday.

1 What does Jessica wish she could do this summer?

_____

2 What does Jessica wish you could do straight after leaving college?

_____

3 How much longer will it be before Jessica is a qualified accountant?

_____

4 What does Jessica wish she could do on Monday?

_____

58 Le futur continu

Vous pouvez utiliser le futur continu avec « will »
pour faire des prédictions et pour faire des hypothèses
sur ce qui peut se passer au moment où l'on parle.

🔧 **Grammaire** Le futur continu avec « will »

Aa **Vocabulaire** Les demandes polies

🧩 **Compétence** Planifier votre carrière

58.1 COMPLÉTEZ LES PHRASES EN CONJUGUANT LES VERBES AU FUTUR CONTINU AVEC « WILL ».

 This book is so long, I think I ____'ll be reading____ (read) it for the whole of next year!

① Sheila is sick, so she _____ (work) from home for the rest of the week.

② This time next week, I _____ (sit) on a beach in the Caribbean.

③ The boss thinks that in 10 years' time I _____ (run) this company myself.

④ They _____ (travel) for the next two hours and won't be able to take any calls.

⑤ It looks like we _____ (spend) a lot of time together over the next few months.

⑥ The pilots are on strike, so I think I _____ (wait) at the airport for a while.

⑦ Will you _____ (bring) your husband and children with you tomorrow?

⑧ He _____ (stand) near the entrance waiting for us when we get there.

⑨ I _____ (drive) past the stores later if you want me to get some groceries.

⑩ We _____ (not launch) our new perfume until the trade fair next year.

⑪ James has applied for some jobs, so I think he _____ (leave) the company soon.

🔊

58.2 UTILISEZ LE SCHÉMA POUR CRÉER 12 PHRASES, PUIS LISEZ-LES À VOIX HAUTE.

By this time next week, I'll be working in a big city.

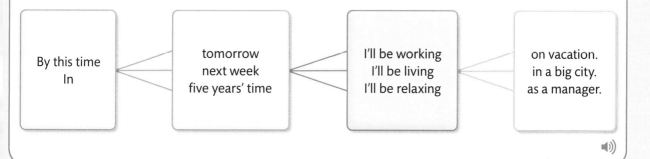

| By this time
In | tomorrow
next week
five years' time | I'll be working
I'll be living
I'll be relaxing | on vacation.
in a big city.
as a manager. |

58.3 RÉCRIVEZ LES PHRASES EN CORRIGEANT LES ERREURS.

We will be fly at 35,000 feet until we start our descent into Vancouver.
We will be flying at 35,000 feet until we start our descent into Vancouver.

1 The next time I go to the mountains, I'll be ski like an expert.
_____

2 In a few years' time, I be playing basketball professionally.
_____

3 We will being hosting some visitors from China next week.
_____

4 This evening they be serving snacks and drinks for everyone.
_____

5 In five years' time, I won't be teach at a primary school any more.
_____

6 Will you asking for input from the audience during your presentation?
_____

58.4 ÉCRIVEZ LES MOTS SUIVANTS DANS LE BON ORDRE AFIN DE RECONSTITUER LES PHRASES.

| vacation. | I'll | Spain | traveling | to | be | on | my |

I'll be traveling to Spain on my vacation.

❶ | be | in | 10 | time. | software | We'll | this | using | years' |

_____

❷ | will | 6pm | today. | until | be | Lisa | working |

_____

❸ | five | bus | will | leaving | minutes. | The | in | be |

_____

❹ | stopping | Station. | Central | at | This | be | train | will |

_____

❺ | be | I | will | Next | working | from | home. | week, |

_____

🔊

 58.5 ÉCOUTEZ L'ENREGISTREMENT, PUIS COCHEZ LES BONNES RÉPONSES.

 Charles téléphone à Rachel pour savoir où se trouve Bill.

Charles wants to find Bill.
True ☑ **False** ☐ **Not given** ☐

❶ Bill usually eats his lunch at 12:30pm.

True ☐ **False** ☐ **Not given** ☐

❷ Charles is giving a presentation in two weeks.

True ☐ **False** ☐ **Not given** ☐

❸ Charles and Bill work in market research.

True ☐ **False** ☐ **Not given** ☐

❹ Bill likes to go for a walk around the building.

True ☐ **False** ☐ **Not given** ☐

❺ Charles will leave the office at 4pm today.

True ☐ **False** ☐ **Not given** ☐

58.6 LISEZ L'ARTICLE, PUIS RÉPONDEZ AUX QUESTIONS.

Where are we heading?

The march toward global connectivity

The number of internet users is increasing rapidly and it's predicted that in a few years' time, five billion of us will be shopping online. Around half of these people will be using tablets to access the internet. By 2020, connected devices will be so integrated into our lives that we will see them as "digital assistants."

At this very moment someone, somewhere will be buying something online and it is expected that every retail company will be selling their products on the web in 10 years' time.

Whole cities will become increasingly connected, with free public wi-fi in more and more areas. The internet user of the future will be browsing on the go, wherever they are.

According to the article what is going up very quickly at the moment?

The number of internet users is going up very quickly at the moment.

---

① According to the article, how many people will be shopping online in a few years' time?

_____

② How many of these people will be using tablets to access the internet?

_____

③ What will become so integrated into our lives that we'll see them as "digital assistants?"

_____

④ According to the article, what can we assume that someone, somewhere will be doing right now?

_____

⑤ Which retail companies will be selling their products on the web in 10 years' time?

_____

⑥ Where will future internet users be able to get online?

_____

59 Le futur perfect

Vous pouvez utiliser le « futur perfect » pour parler d'événements qui vont chevaucher, ou finir avant, un autre événement du futur.

Grammaire Le futur perfect
Aa Vocabulaire Les projets de vie
Compétence Faire des projets et des prédictions

59.1 COMPLÉTEZ LES PHRASES EN CONJUGUANT LES VERBES AU FUTUR PERFECT.

By next March, I ___*will have bought*___ (buy) my own house.

1. I _____ (finish) my degree by the time I am 22.

2. You _____ (be) married for one year in a week's time.

3. We _____ (complete) all our essays by the end of June.

4. By the time I am 24, I _____ (find) a good job.

5. I think my son _____ (propose) to his girlfriend by the end of the year.

6. By the time we are 30, we _____ (have) our first child.

7. Liza _____ (move) to London by the end of the month.

8. I _____ (graduate) from college by this time next year.

9. By the time I am 25, I _____ (leave) my parents' house.

10. I _____ (make) one million dollars by the time I'm 40.

11. They _____ (start) their new business by the end of the month.

59.2 RÉCRIVEZ LES PASSAGES SURLIGNÉS EN CORRIGEANT LES ERREURS.

will have taken

1 _____

2 _____

3 _____

4 _____

5 _____

6 _____

7 _____

8 _____

9 _____

Hot Cakes

HOME | ENTRIES | ABOUT | CONTACT

POSTED AT 8:55PM
MY BUSINESS PLAN

By the end of this month, I will have take out a bank loan. I also will has found the perfect location for my new cupcake shop, and I will have perfect the recipes for my cupcakes. By the end of next month, I will have open my new shop and I hope I will has been featured in all the local newspapers. By the end of the first week, I hope that I will have sell at least 1,500 cupcakes. By the end of the first month, I hope that I will increased this number to 8,000 cupcakes. I expect that I will have make a profit of $12,000 by the end of the first six months. By the end of the first year, I have taken on two members of staff and I will have launch my online business. It's an ambitious plan, but I know I can do it!

59.3 COMPLÉTEZ LES PHRASES, PUIS LISEZ-LES À VOIX HAUTE.

Ken _____will have read_____ (read) all his textbooks before lessons start next week.

1 They _____ (choose) the best candidate by the end of the day.

2 Jenny _____ (buy) a new dress before the wedding.

3 By the end of the year, I _____ (complete) three marathons.

4 I _____ (open) all my presents by the end of the party.

5 By the time he starts his new job, Hans _____ (have) his hair cut.

6 We _____ (visit) 15 countries by the end of this year.

59.4 RÉCRIVEZ LES PHRASES AU FUTUR PERFECT CONTINU.

In a year's time, I (study) English for 10 years.
In a year's time, I will have been studying English for 10 years.

1 By the time we arrive in Spain, we (drive) for eight hours.

_____

2 Jenna (run) her own business for five years in May.

_____

3 In June, I (work) as a teacher for 10 years.

_____

4 By the time the cake is decorated, we (cook) for six hours.

_____

5 I (do) yoga for 10 years by the end of the year.

_____

6 In November, Becky and I (live) together for three years.

_____

7 By midday, Jonas (wait) to see the doctor for three hours.

_____

8 By the time I have finished, I (clean) the house for five hours.

_____

9 By the time the plane lands in Malaysia, we (travel) for 13 hours.

_____

10 By December, I (learn) to paint for six months.

_____

11 I (study) medicine for four years by the end of June.

_____

12 By the end of next month, the police (look) for the criminals for a year.

_____

59.5 COCHEZ LES PHRASES CORRECTES.

Next week, I will have finished my course at the university. ☑
Next week, I will have been finishing my course at the university. ☐

1 At the end of the week, Lise will have studied in France for three months. ☐
At the end of the week, Lise will have been studying in France for three months. ☐

2 This time tomorrow, I will have been having my operation. ☐
This time tomorrow, I will have had my operation. ☐

3 I will have finished this report by the time you get here. ☐
I will have been finishing this report by the time you get here. ☐

4 Next week, I will have been studying for two years. ☐
Next week, I will have studied for two years. ☐

5 By the end of January, I will have been finishing my Italian course. ☐
By the end of January, I will have finished my Italian course. ☐

6 In two hours, I will have written my last report for this client. ☐
In two hours, I will have been writing my last report for this client. ☐

◀))

59.6 RÉCRIVEZ LES PASSAGES SURLIGNÉS EN CORRIGEANT LES ERREURS.

owned

1 _____

2 _____

3 _____

4 _____

✉

To: Bill

Subject: Our anniversary

My dearest Bill,
On January 8, we will have been owning this house for 10 years. We will have being married for 11 years, and we will have been having children for six years. What a fantastic 10 years. Thank you! I hope the next 10 years will be just as happy. By then, we will have been knowing each other for 25 years, and being together almost as long! I can't believe how fast the time flies.
All my love,
Anabel

↩ ↩↩ 📎 🗑

60 Le futur dans le passé

En anglais, vous pouvez utiliser plusieurs constructions pour décrire les pensées concernant l'avenir qu'une personne a eues à un certain moment du passé.

⚙ **Grammaire** « Would » et « was going to »
Aa **Vocabulaire** Changer ses plans
🧩 **Compétence** Dire ce que vous pensiez

60.1 BARREZ LE MOT INCORRECT DANS CHAQUE PHRASE.

I ~~will~~ / would love to see a basketball game in the US. I'm a big basketball fan.

1 I always thought that I will / would go to college, but I then decided to get a job instead.

2 As soon as I get home, I will / would give you a call to let you know I've arrived safely.

3 I'm sure that we will / would still be friends when we're older. There's no doubt about that.

4 He said that he will / would try to get me some tickets for the soccer game if he could.

🔊

60.2 COCHEZ LES PHRASES CORRECTES.

It's strange that he failed the exam. I thought he's going to get the highest grade. ☐
It's strange that he failed the exam. I thought he was going to get the highest grade. ☑

1 I got up so late, I knew I wasn't going to get to the airport in time. ☐
I got up so late, I knew I wouldn't going to get to the airport in time. ☐

2 Sarah's an excellent swimmer, so I knew it's going to be hard to beat her. ☐
Sarah's an excellent swimmer, so I knew it was going to be hard to beat her. ☐

3 My mother promised she won't going to embarrass me by hugging me in public. ☐
My mother promised she wasn't going to embarrass me by hugging me in public. ☐

4 I found the exam easy, so I believed I was going to get a good grade. ☐
I found the exam easy, so I believed I will going to get a good grade. ☐

5 He knew he wasn't getting the job, but he wanted to apply for it anyway. ☐
He knew he wasn't going to get the job, but he wanted to apply for it anyway. ☐

🔊

60.3 RÉCRIVEZ LES PHRASES EN CORRIGEANT LES ERREURS.

> I got up at 9 o'clock, so I know I was going to miss my flight at 10 o'clock.
> *I got up at 9 o'clock, so I knew I was going to miss my flight at 10 o'clock.*

1 They couldn't come last week because they are going to a soccer game that evening.

_____

2 She had taken her English exam the next day, so she felt a little nervous.

_____

3 They would meeting with their lawyers that afternoon to decide what to do.

_____

4 Sandra is planning to fly to Tenerife with her daughter yesterday, but the pilots are on strike.

_____

5 Gareth is making a big announcement that afternoon, but then he lost his voice.

_____

6 Camy and Charlie were have a big party to celebrate their anniversary that weekend.

_____

7 Harren is getting married to Jennifer at 2 o'clock that afternoon in New York.

_____

60.4 ÉCOUTEZ L'ENREGISTREMENT, PUIS INDIQUEZ SI LES ÉVÉNEMENTS ONT RÉELLEMENT EU LIEU OU PAS.

Yes ✓ No ☐

1 Yes ☐ No ☐

2 Yes ☐ No ☐

3 Yes ☐ No ☐

60.5 RÉCRIVEZ LES PHRASES EN UTILISANT LE FUTUR DANS LE PASSÉ.

> She is nervous as she is taking her English speaking exam this morning.
> *She was nervous as she was taking her English speaking exam that morning.*

1 I know that I will be the marketing head of a leading company one day.

2 When I see him I know that I'm going to marry him and move to another country.

3 I'm taking my last exam in chemistry at college this afternoon.

4 I think I will travel around the world working as a part-time photographer.

5 She believes she will get a recording contract as soon as she finishes her course at college.

6 I know I will be late when I see how much traffic there is on the road.

7 I'm meeting some Chinese customers this morning for a presentation on distribution.

8 I think Shania and Jo will go somewhere warm for their holiday this year.

9 He is building an extension on the back of their house in Germany.

10 I decide I will retire early and spend more time with my family and close friends.

11 I know I'm going to be able to climb to the top of the mountain sooner than the others.

12 The company is interviewing some more people for the marketing job this week.

61 Vocabulaire

Aa 61.1 L'ART ET LA CULTURE ÉCRIVEZ LES SYNTAGMES DE LA LISTE SOUS LA DÉFINITION CORRESPONDANTE.

Be extremely absorbed in something

be engrossed in something

1 Complicated / simple artistic or cultural ideas

2 Long, written stories that are fictional

3 Say what you feel, even if it is controversial

4 Say that something is very good and tell others about it

5 The fictional people in a book, film, or play

6 The series of events that makes up the story in a book, film, or play

7 Say that something is extremely good / bad

8 Very positive reviews

9 A feeling or effect that lasts a long time

10 Alter or change a decision or feeling about something

11 Finally make a decision

12 The first / last moments of a book, film, or play

13 To set a particular mood or tone

---

glowing reviews   heap praise / criticism on something   ~~be engrossed in something~~   plot

highly recommend   lasting impression   characters   make up your mind   speak your mind

opening / closing scenes   create an atmosphere   highbrow / lowbrow   change your mind   novels

62 Omettre des mots

Il peut être utile d'éviter les répétitions, lorsque vous voulez communiquer clairement. Pour cela, vous pouvez supprimer tous les mots inutiles.

⚙ **Grammaire** L'ellipse
Aa Vocabulaire Les divertissements
🧩 **Compétence** Omettre les mots inutiles

⚙ **62.1 BARREZ LES MOTS QUI PEUVENT ÊTRE SUPRIMÉS DE LA PHRASE.**

 They could have gone to Spain on vacation, but they didn't want to ~~go to Spain on vacation~~.

1 The ceremony honored firemen and the ceremony honored paramedics.

2 We could go to the session on marketing or we could go to this talk on public relations.

3 It would be nice to go to the theater or to go to a film. You can decide.

4 This process was described by Gutmann and it was also described by Quirke.

5 She could have directed the TV series or she could have directed the film version.

6 They should use paper bags and they should recycle more of their garbage.

7 He might have become a great writer, but he didn't want to become a great writer.

8 The problem is that he wants to leave work early, but she doesn't want to leave work early.

9 He was chosen to play the lead role and he did an excellent job.

10 I could wear this yellow dress for the wedding or I could wear this blue skirt.

11 You could eat at the new Italian restaurant or you could eat at the Mexican restaurant.

🔊

SILVER SCREEN

What to watch

Your one-stop guide to films this week

First Kiss Fans of romantic comedies will go to see *First Kiss* and fall in love with it. You could go to see it with your friends or that special someone in your life.

★★★★☆

Starship Ipsilon This is a fun remake of an old science-fiction film and makes fun of the genre of sci-fi. Die-hard sci-fi fans may not like the new actors and storylines, but will go and see it anyway, I imagine.

★★☆☆☆

Dead of Night The plot of this horror film is slightly ridiculous and could have been written by any 10 year old. The director has directed many well-known horror films, but we won't count this one among his best work.

★★☆☆☆

Bobby IV Bobby Johnson is definitely back and shows us why he's the greatest wrestler of all time in this new sequel in the Bobby series. Bobby never gives up and does everything in his power to regain the world championship.

★★★☆☆

What type of film is *First Kiss*?
Action ☐
Horror ☐
Romantic comedy ☑

❶ Who should you not go to see *First Kiss* with?
Your friends ☐
Your partner ☐
Your parents ☐

❷ What is wrong with *Dead of Night*?
Its plot ☐
Its special effects ☐
Its music ☐

❸ How would you describe *Starship Ipsilon*?
Blockbuster ☐
Spoof ☐
Prequel ☐

❹ Who will go to see *Starship Ipsilon*?
Dedicated sci-fi fans ☐
Those who are new to sci-fi ☐
Actors from the original film ☐

❺ What kind of film is *Bobby IV*?
Remake ☐
Sequel ☐
Documentary ☐

62.3 COMPLÉTEZ LES PHRASES AVEC LES MOTS QUI ONT ÉTÉ OMIS.

> It's a shame. I liked the film, but my brother didn't [_____ *like the film* _____].

1 I'm so sorry! I broke your television, but I didn't mean to [_____].

2 We can't go to the movies tonight but we can [_____] tomorrow.

3 He told me he could speak French, but I don't think he can [_____] .

4 My daughter loves horror films and [_____] thrillers.

5 We went to Venice and [_____] rode in a gondola this summer.

6 She could sit in the kitchen or [_____] the garden.

7 Do we need a new computer? We could get a laptop or [_____] a tablet instead.

8 It's such a beautiful day. We should go to the park or [_____] the beach.

9 The critics loved the latest blockbuster and [_____] said it was worth watching.

10 I need to borrow your car. I will email shortly to explain why [_____].

🔊

62.4 ÉCOUTEZ L'ENREGISTREMENT, PUIS COCHEZ LES BONNES RÉPONSES.

Rachel et Simon discutent dans la salle de cinéma en attendant le début du film.

> Simon and Rachel are going to see *Death Kiss*.
> **True** ☑ **False** ☐

1 The film starts at 7:30pm.
True ☐ **False** ☐

2 Simon has booked the tickets.
True ☐ **False** ☐

3 Rachel wants a hotdog.
True ☐ **False** ☐

4 Simon wants buttered popcorn.
True ☐ **False** ☐

5 The last film Simon saw was very boring.
True ☐ **False** ☐

6 Rachel went to the film with Gavin.
True ☐ **False** ☐

7 Gavin is 15 years old.
True ☐ **False** ☐

62.5 BARREZ LE MOT INCORRECT DANS CHAQUE PHRASE.

> The people I met when I was on vacation were **surprisingly** / ~~**highly**~~ good at speaking English.

1. I worked really hard on my entry, so I was **ridiculously** / **bitterly** disappointed that I didn't win.

2. The line for tickets at the museum was **painfully** / **heavily** slow. I thought we would never get in.

3. I won't go to that restaurant again. The prices were **heavily** / **astronomically** high!

4. The trip was **painfully** / **ridiculously** long because we were stuck in traffic for two hours.

5. I was **deeply** / **bitterly** moved by the poem she read at her mother's funeral.

6. Everyone knows that farmers in this country are **heavily** / **deeply** subsidized.

7. I think you should avoid mentioning any **astronomically** / **highly** controversial topics in your talk.

62.6 RELIEZ LE DÉBUT DE CHAQUE PHRASE À LA FIN QUI LUI CORRESPOND.

She always works long hours	she knew who might be able to help.
1. We went for a walk in the woods	a beach or city break?
2. She emailed and called everyone	or go out for dinner tonight?
3. The cathedral is beautiful	and doesn't take very much time off.
4. Do you think we should go on	but not his face. It's been a long time.
5. He went cycling along the Rhine	and took some wonderful photos of the trees.
6. I want to move,	and ask him to confirm the details.
7. Could you call or email him	and is the seat of the Bishop of Rouen.
8. I can remember his name,	stayed at a wonderful resort on the coast.
9. They went to Mauritius and	and visited a lot of vineyards.
10. Do you want to cook	but he doesn't.

63 Substituer des mots

De même qu'avec les ellipses (omission de mots), vous pouvez éviter de vous répéter en remplaçant certaines phrases par des phrases plus courtes. On appelle ce procédé la substitution.

⚙ **Grammaire** La substitution
Aa Vocabulaire Les livres et la lecture
🧩 **Compétence** Remplacer des phrases

⚙ 63.1 BARREZ LE MOT INCORRECT DANS CHAQUE PHRASE.

 We saw a lot of dogs at the rescue center, but the **one** / ~~ones~~ we adopted was the cutest.

1 I've eaten a lot of pizza in my time, but the **one** / **ones** I ate in Rome last year was the best.

2 I love these high-heeled shoes, but I think it's time I got some new **one** / **ones**.

3 Kirsten did well on both parts of the exam, but she did especially well on the first **one** / **ones**.

4 I really like the movies he's in, especially the earlier **one** / **ones** from the start of his career.

5 Our daughter likes a lot of subjects at school, but the **one** / **ones** she enjoys the most is science.

6 Mike has written a few books, but I think the first thriller he wrote is the best **one** / **ones**.

7 Ann tried on 10 different wedding dresses before she found the **one** / **ones** she wanted.

8 There are many activities for older children and some for younger **one** / **ones**.

9 I love all of the cakes Sam makes, but the **one** / **ones** she made today was really delicious.

10 I've been to a lot of countries, but the **one** / **ones** I enjoyed visiting the most was Japan.

11 Sarah isn't happy with her office assistant, so she wants to get a new **one** / **ones**.

🔊

63.2 COMPLÉTEZ LES PHRASES AVEC « ONE », « ONES » OU « SOME ».

> We still have _____*some*_____ issues to resolve before the project is completed.

1 If you need any pens to write with, I have _____ here.

2 If you'd like a copy of my notes, I will print _____ for you.

3 They need some more batteries because the _____ I gave them last time have run out.

4 If you find anywhere selling cups of coffee, could you get me _____ ?

5 There's water here in case you need to use _____ while you're painting.

6 My new computer is slower than the _____ I got rid of when I bought it.

7 This cheeseburger tastes as good as the _____ I ate in the other restaurant.

◀))

63.3 RÉCRIVEZ LES PHRASES EN CORRIGEANT LES ERREURS.

> Our car is so old and unreliable these days. We need to get a new ones.
> *Our car is so old and unreliable these days. We need to get a new one.*

1 If you need any more paper to write on, there's one on my desk.

_____

2 If you're looking for some new running shoes, I'd recommend the some on the left.

_____

3 I have three tickets and I only need two, so I could give you some if you like.

_____

4 If you need any information about the building, ask me and I'll give you ones.

_____

5 If they like Italian restaurants, there's a great some just down the road.

_____

6 I think Jenny and Matthew's wedding was the best ones I've ever been to.

_____

◀))

63.4 RELIEZ LE DÉBUT DE CHAQUE PHRASE À LA FIN QUI LUI CORRESPOND.

If you need a pencil,

① I know you want a new computer,

② My sister bought me an album,

③ If you're looking for bookstores,

④ I think my favorite authors

⑤ We should buy new flowers

⑥ Please help yourself to tea or coffee

⑦ I wanted to bring a cake,

but it wasn't the one I wanted.

are the ones who write about vampires.

if you would like some.

I have one over here.

but I didn't have time to bake one.

and get rid of these old ones.

there are some on Upper Street.

but we can't afford one.

63.5 COCHEZ LES PHRASES CORRECTES.

I like spicy food, but my wife doesn't like. ☐
I like spicy food, but my wife doesn't. ☑

① I didn't enjoy it, but my friend enjoyed. ☐
I didn't enjoy it, but my friend did. ☐

② Did you see the new movie? We did see. ☐
Did you see the new movie? We did, too. ☐

③ You bought a blue hat! I did, too. ☐
You bought a blue hat! I do, too. ☐

④ Do I still cycle to work? Yes, I do. ☐
Do I still cycle to work? Yes, I did. ☐

⑤ He works downtown, but she doesn't. ☐
He works downtown, but she isn't. ☐

⑥ My mom went, but my dad didn't. ☐
My mom went, but my dad didn't went. ☐

⑦ Did you bring your camera? I didn't. ☐
Did you bring your camera? I didn't bring. ☐

⑧ You baked cookies! I did, too. ☐
You baked cookies! I do, too. ☐

⑨ Does she like reading? Yes, she does. ☐
Does she like reading? Yes, she do. ☐

⑩ They went skiing last year, but we didn't. ☐
They went skiing last year, but we don't. ☐

⑪ My friend found it difficult. I did, too. ☐
My friend found it difficult. I found, too. ☐

63.6 ÉCOUTEZ L'ENREGISTREMENT, PUIS COCHEZ LES BONNES RÉPONSES.

Michael parle à Kristen d'une Smartwatch onéreuse qu'il a reçue en cadeau.

Michael has a new smartwatch.	True ☑	False ☐
❶ Kristen has the same smartwatch as Michael.	True ☐	False ☐
❷ You can only use the smartwatch as a smartphone.	True ☐	False ☐
❸ Hi-tech watches are on sale at a shop in the mall.	True ☐	False ☐
❹ Michael's mother gave him the smartwatch.	True ☐	False ☐
❺ Michael and his mother couldn't afford to replace the smartwatch.	True ☐	False ☐
❻ Kristen wants Michael to bring her a voucher for the online shop.	True ☐	False ☐

63.7 RÉPONDEZ AUX QUESTIONS DE L'ENREGISTREMENT EN UTILISANT DES SUBSTITUTIONS, PUIS LISEZ-LES À VOIX HAUTE.

Would you like to go to the mall?

[suppose] _Yes, I suppose so._

❸ Didn't Tarkovsky direct your favorite movie?

[did] _____

❶ Is it going to be sunny later?

[hope] _____

❹ Will the drinks be free tonight?

[imagine] _____

❷ Did you remember to lock the door?

[think] _____

❺ Will Sarah be at the party tonight?

[assume] _____

64 Réduire les propositions infinitives

En plus de l'ellipse et de la substitution, vous pouvez réduire les propositions infinitives pour éviter des répétitions. Ce procédé vous permettra de parler anglais de façon plus naturelle.

⚙ **Grammaire** Réduire les propositions infinitives
Aa Vocabulaire La musique et le monde du spectacle
🧩 **Compétence** Éviter les répétitions

64.1 BARREZ TOUS LES MOTS QUE VOUS POUVEZ SUPPRIMER.

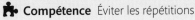 I want to get the best tickets for the show but I can't afford to ~~get them.~~

 ❶ I wanted to wake up early today, but I wasn't able to wake up early today.

 ❷ Stefan was enjoying the ballet. At least, he seemed to be enjoying it.

 ❸ I'm so nervous! I'm singing on stage tonight, but I really don't want to sing on stage tonight.

 ❹ Your dog likes chasing people a lot more than he used to like chasing people.

 ❺ I'm so thirsty! I meant to buy a drink before the movie, but I forgot to buy one.

 ❻ Don't be nervous. There's no need to be nervous.

 ❼ Darren said he'd help us unpack, but it seems that he won't be able to help us.

 ❽ I really wanted to go to that concert, but I couldn't afford to go to it.

 ❾ If you want to be promoted, you have to show me that you deserve to be promoted.

 ❿ Helena asked me to join the college choir, but I didn't want to join the choir.

 ⓫ I'm sorry I'm so late! I didn't mean to be so late.

64.2 RÉCRIVEZ LES PHRASES EN CORRIGEANT LES ERREURS.

Richard usually forgets to send me a birthday card but this year he's promised not.

Richard usually forgets to send me a birthday card but this year he's promised not to.

1 I'd really like to go away this year, but I won't able to.

_____

2 Keisha said I should go to her party tonight, but I don't really want.

_____

3 I tried to find out Will's email address, but I wasn't to.

_____

4 Frankie liked the birthday present we bought her. At least, she seemed.

_____

5 I didn't realize that it was necessary to wear a tie, but apparently we have.

_____

6 I'm very concerned about my test results, even though the doctor says there's no need be.

_____

🔊

64.3 ÉCOUTEZ L'ENREGISTREMENT, PUIS COCHEZ LES BONNES RÉPONSES.

Paul et Jess discutent d'un concert auquel ils aimeraient aller.

Jess definitely wants to see the horror movie.
True ☐ **False** ☑

1 Paul invites Jess to see a rock band.
True ☐ **False** ☐

2 The musicians' instruments are recycled.
True ☐ **False** ☐

3 The musicians are originally from South Africa.
True ☐ **False** ☐

4 Paul is not sure that he can get the tickets.
True ☐ **False** ☐

5 Paul will call Jess when he has the tickets.
True ☐ **False** ☐

64.4 RELIEZ LE DÉBUT DE CHAQUE PHRASE À LA FIN QUI LUI CORRESPOND.

I wasn't planning to go to the concert,

but I wasn't able to.

1 I'd really like to buy a new pair of shoes,

though I don't need to.

2 I'm not sure if I can visit my aunt this weekend,

but he can't afford to.

3 Jonas would really like to buy a car,

but I would love to.

4 I'll watch a movie if all my friends want to,

although I prefer to.

5 I don't insist on going to warm countries for vacations,

but I hope to.

6 I tried to get tickets for the concert,

but I wouldn't choose to.

64.5 COMPLÉTEZ LES PHRASES AVEC LES MOTS DE LA LISTE.

I said we should get coffee first, and she _____ *agreed* _____ .

1 I am always really nervous before I go to the doctor's. It's difficult not _____ .

2 It's not certain that I'll do well on my exams, but I _____ to.

3 Marie wants me to go shopping with her, but I really don't _____ to.

4 I've never been to the US. I'd love the _____ .

5 You can get a vaccination before your trip, but you don't _____ to.

| need | agreed | chance | expect | to be | want |

64.6 ÉCRIVEZ LES MOTS SUIVANTS DANS LE BON ORDRE AFIN DE RECONSTITUER LES PHRASES.

can | We | to | movie theater | go | you | want | tonight | the | if | to.

We can go to the movie theater tonight if you want to.

1 but | listening | sister | to. | music, | hates | to | I | loud | love | my

_____

2 can | work | to. | early | You | leave | afternoon | if | like | this | you | would

_____

3 be | me | to. | I'd | her | Gigi | asked | delighted | and | said | go | wedding | to | I | to

_____

4 agree | do | Don't | the | want | don't | fun run | if | you | to. | really | to

_____

🔊

64.7 RÉPONDEZ AUX QUESTIONS DE L'ENREGISTREMENT, PUIS LISEZ LES PHRASES À VOIX HAUTE

Are you going to go to the show?

[decide] No, _I decided not to_ .

1 Would you like to come to the gig with me?

[delighted] Yes, _____ .

2 Do you want to go swimming tonight?

[want] No, _____ .

3 Should I dress up for the party?

[need] No, _____ .

4 Did Miranda enjoy the play?

[seem] Yes, _____ .

5 Are you going on vacation this year?

[afford] No, _____ .

🔊

65 Décrire des réactions

Bien que les marqueurs rhétoriques n'aient pas souvent de contenu sémantique, ils peuvent rendre la conversation plus fluide et apporter un complément d'information concernant l'opinion du locuteur.

⚙ **Grammaire** Les marqueurs rhétoriques informels
Aa Vocabulaire Les préfixes niveau avancé
🧩 **Compétence** Structurer une conversation

⚙ **65.1 BARREZ LES MOTS QUI CONVIENNENT LE MOINS DANS CHAQUE PHRASE.**

 ~~Anyway~~ / Actually, the great thing was that everyone in Canada could understand me.

 ① Sorry, I had to take that call. So by the way / as I was saying, the gallery opened in 1903.

 ② I've been to that museum, too. Hey, I love your shoes, actually / by the way.

 ③ This gallery is beautiful. Oh, anyway / by the way, did you see there's a new café downstairs?

 ④ You think he's an expert? Anyway / Actually, he doesn't really know anything about art.

 ⑤ Anyway / By the way, I'm afraid I will have to say goodbye now, but thank you for today.

 ⑥ No, actually / by the way, it was George who thought we should buy this painting, not me.

 ⑦ Mike's very happy because, as I was saying / anyway, he's getting married next September.

 ⑧ Yes, I'd like some coffee. So, actually / as I was saying, we've got a lot of paintings at home.

 ⑨ Anyway / Actually, I'm sure you'll have a great time in Tokyo. See you when you get back!

 ⑩ So, as I was saying / by the way, Jenny and I have known each other for a long time.

 ⑪ Yes, by the way / actually, I've already been here a few times, so I know my way around.

🔊

65.2 RÉPONDEZ AUX QUESTIONS DE L'ENREGISTREMENT AVEC LES MOTS DE LA LISTE, PUIS LISEZ LES PHRASES À VOIX HAUTE.

Andy Warhol is your favorite artist, isn't he?

_____Actually_____ , my favorite artist is David Hockney.

actually

Actually

1 Oh, that's right! I think they have a few Warhol pieces upstairs.

Yes, but _____ before, I prefer Hockney.

as I was saying

2 Did you go to the exhibition of his work last year?

No, it was sold out. _____ , we should get moving!

~~Actually~~

3 Yes, it's getting late already. Do you want to see the new installation?

I've already seen it, _____ . I came here last month.

Anyway

4 I'm going to go to the gift shop before it closes.

_____ , I've already been. But you go.

🔊

65.3 COCHEZ LES PHRASES CORRECTES.

He's really superactive. He always solves problems before they arise. ☐
He's really proactive. He always solves problems before they arise. ☑

1 The fastest aircraft travel through the air at antisonic speeds. ☐
The fastest aircraft travel through the air at supersonic speeds. ☐

2 Powerful computers can prodict the outcomes of some experiments with amazing accuracy. ☐
Powerful computers can predict the outcomes of some experiments with amazing accuracy. ☐

3 The first farms in human history were established in the Postlithic, or New Stone Age. ☐
The first farms in human history were established in the Neolithic, or New Stone Age. ☐

4 The prewar period, after the fighting had ended, saw an economic boom. ☐
The postwar period, after the fighting had ended, saw an economic boom. ☐

🔊

65.4 LISEZ L'ARTICLE, PUIS COCHEZ LES BONNES RÉPONSES.

The writer visited a school of fashion.
True ☐ **False** ☑

❶ The writer attended a freshman show.
True ☐ **False** ☐

❷ A reception event took place before the show.
True ☐ **False** ☐

❸ Skye Tyler's work is traditional and conservative.
True ☐ **False** ☐

❹ There was no postmodern art in the show.
True ☐ **False** ☐

❺ Neo-Gothic art reinvents and revises Gothic styles.
True ☐ **False** ☐

Fresh blood

What influences young artists?

Yesterday I attended the graduation show of young artists who've been studying at the Royal College of Art in London.

During the preshow reception, I mingled with some of the artists in an anteroom next to the exhibition hall. I took the opportunity to ask some of them about what had influenced their work. Skye Tyler, 22 from London, told me she tries to be very antiestablishment.

When we went into the exhibition hall, I noticed that a lot of the artists had produced some interesting postmodern pieces. Others were influenced by a style that could only be described as neo-Gothic, as it is a reinvention and updating of Gothic art from the Middle Ages.

Aa 65.5 RELIEZ CHAQUE DÉFINITION AU MOT À LAQUELLE ELLE CORRESPOND.

a room leading into another room → anteroom

❶ see something in advance — preview

❷ something built on top of something else — antibacterial

❸ harmful to bacteria — superstructure

❹ made longer — postpone

❺ a new interpretation of classical ideas — superhuman

❻ do something later than planned — preassigned

❼ cure for poison — antidote

❽ better than human — prolonged

❾ allocated in advance — neoclassical

🔊

65.6 COMPLÉTEZ LES PHRASES AVEC LES PRÉFIXES DE LA LISTE.

I'm afraid you can't come in. All tickets for the exhibition have been __*pre*__ assigned.

1 He's interested in _____ liberalism. I'm not sure what that is, but it's a new type of liberalism.

2 I've been enjoying the _____ game buildup, but now I just can't wait for the game to start.

3 _____ classical architecture became popular when interest in ancient Greece rose again.

4 We've organized a _____ conference event so people can meet before the meetings start.

5 James must be _____ human! It's amazing how he manages to work and travel so much.

6 She specializes in _____ natal care, so she looks after newborn babies.

7 _____ modern art was a reaction by artists against the modernist art that came before it.

8 Instead of finishing her degree, she's decided to _____ pone her studies and go traveling.

9 You first go into the _____ chamber of the tomb of Tutankhamun and then the main chamber.

10 If I could have any _____ power I wanted, I think it would be the ability to fly.

11 I've had enough of our neighbors' _____ social behavior, they're always making noise!

12 We're celebrating the 50th anniversary of the introduction of _____ discrimination laws.

pre	post	post	ante	anti	neo
super	pre	neo	pre	anti	neo	super

66 Réaliser ses projets

Vous voudrez parfois parler de personnes qui font des choses pour vous. Pour cela, vous devrez utiliser une construction différente.

⚙ **Grammaire** « Have/get something done »
Aa Vocabulaire Les services et les réparations
🧩 **Compétence** Décrire ce que d'autres personnes font pour vous

66.1 RELIEZ LE DÉBUT DE CHAQUE PHRASE À LA FIN QUI LUI CORRESPOND.

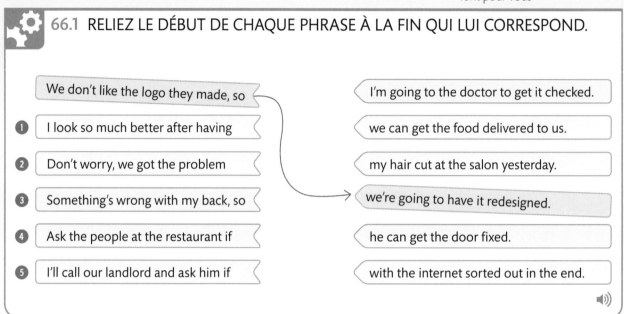

We don't like the logo they made, so ——————→ we're going to have it redesigned.

1. I look so much better after having

2. Don't worry, we got the problem

3. Something's wrong with my back, so

4. Ask the people at the restaurant if

5. I'll call our landlord and ask him if

I'm going to the doctor to get it checked.

we can get the food delivered to us.

my hair cut at the salon yesterday.

we're going to have it redesigned.

he can get the door fixed.

with the internet sorted out in the end.

66.2 ÉCRIVEZ LES MOTS SUIVANTS DANS LE BON ORDRE AFIN DE RECONSTITUER LES PHRASES.

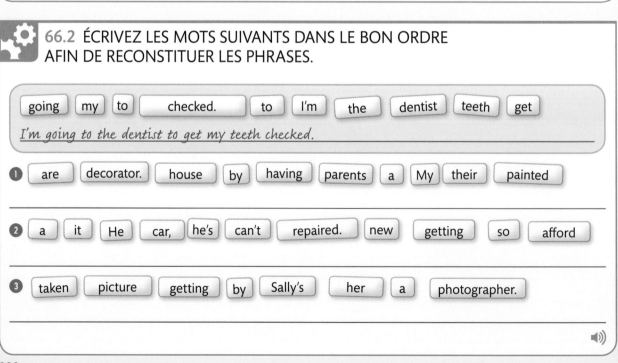

going | my | to | checked. | to | I'm | the | dentist | teeth | get

I'm going to the dentist to get my teeth checked.

1. are | decorator. | house | by | having | parents | a | My | their | painted

2. a | it | He | car, | he's | can't | repaired. | new | getting | so | afford

3. taken | picture | getting | by | Sally's | her | a | photographer.

220

66.3 ÉCOUTEZ L'ENREGISTREMENT, PUIS COCHEZ LES BONNES RÉPONSES.

> Joanne checked her car battery.
> **True** ☑ **False** ☐

1 Joanne changed the spark plugs.
True ☐ **False** ☐

2 Joanne will have to get the car repaired.
True ☐ **False** ☐

3 Lou got oil on Joanne's coat.
True ☐ **False** ☐

4 Joanne will have to get the coat dry cleaned.
True ☐ **False** ☐

5 Romesh will iron his own shirts.
True ☐ **False** ☐

6 Someone is going to cut Romesh's hair.
True ☐ **False** ☐

7 Romesh is interviewing someone for a new job.
True ☐ **False** ☐

66.4 COMPLÉTEZ LES PHRASES EN CONJUGUANT LES VERBES À LA BONNE FORME.

> She's been _____getting_____ (get) her articles translated by a young German student at the university.

1 Leah needs to go to the dentist as soon as possible _____ (have) her teeth fixed.

2 He's _____ (get) his birth certificate translated into English, so he can get married.

3 They _____ (have) a marquee built in the grounds of the castle for their party last year.

4 She always _____ (have) her essays checked by her mother before she hands them in.

5 My wedding ring _____ (get) stolen when someone broke into our house last week.

6 We've been having problems with our website, but we're _____ (get) them sorted out.

7 Jessica can't come to the phone right now because she's _____ (have) her nails done.

8 We've _____ (have) a lot of changes made to the house since we moved in five years ago.

9 He's been _____ (have) his hair cut at that barber's shop since he was five years old.

66.5 RÉCRIVEZ LES MOTS SURLIGNÉS EN CORRIGEANT LES ERREURS.

> *get*

1. _____
2. _____
3. _____
4. _____
5. _____
6. _____
7. _____
8. _____

Organize a conference

Here's a list of things to keep in mind

If you want to organize a conference, you need to have organized. The first thing you need to do is have a venue sorted out. You can do this yourself or get someone find one for you. Once you've get this organized, get someone who works at the venue give you an overview of the costs. You can then write a call for papers and get colleagues share it with people they know. Make a program and got it printed. If you're have the programs delivered, make sure the printer knows whether they should deliver them to your home or to the venue. On the day before the conference, get all of the lights and equipment check by the venue staff and then checked them again yourself! If you've have your conference staff trained in how to deal with the delegates at the conference, they'll know exactly what to do on the day.

 66.6 RÉCRIVEZ LES PHRASES AVEC « HAVE » OU « GET ».

> The hairdresser cut my hair. (**have**)
> *I had my hair cut.*

1. I ordered a pizza delivery for dinner. (**get**)

   _____

2. A mechanic fixed my car. (**get**)

   _____

3. A decorator is painting our house. (**have**)

   _____

4. My shirts are being dry-cleaned. (**get**)

   _____

5. A photographer took my picture. (**get**)

   _____

6. Someone repaired the oven. (**get**)

   _____

7. A dentist checked my teeth. (**get**)

   _____

8. Someone is landscaping their garden. (**have**)

   _____

9. A student translated my essay. (**have**)

   _____

10. My eyesight was tested at the hospital. (**get**)

    _____

11. The hotel staff did my laundry. (**get**)

    _____

Where's Gina?

She's in the bathroom. She's still _____*getting ready*_____ for the party.

1 Where did you go?

I'm having problems with my eyes, so I went to the optician to _____ .

2 Where is your purse?

You won't believe it. I _____ when we were on vacation!

3 I'm really hungry. How can I get a pizza?

You can either pick the pizza up from the restaurant or you can _____ .

4 When will I get my business cards?

The business cards are here. Would you like me to _____ to your home address?

5 Is that an old jacket you're wearing?

No, but I can't believe how filthy it is. I need to _____ as soon as possible.

6 Is your internet up again?

No, the internet at home still isn't working properly. We need to _____ this week.

7 Are you allowed to have long hair at your new job?

No, I'm going to the hairdresser's to _____ .

get it sorted out	had it stolen	~~getting ready~~	get them checked
have it dry-cleaned	have it cut	have it delivered	have them sent

223

Les accords complexes

L'un des principes fondamentaux de la langue anglaise est que les sujets et les verbes doivent s'accorder. Néanmoins, certains sujets peuvent se comporter comme des noms singuliers ou pluriels en fonction du contexte.

⚙ **Grammaire** Les accords complexes
Aa Vocabulaire Les noms collectifs
✚ **Compétence** Utiliser l'accord correct

⚙ 67.1 COMPLÉTEZ LES PHRASES AVEC LES MOTS DE LA LISTE.

 The whole ___*fleet*___ is out today and it's sailing across to the other side of the channel.

① The _____ was so appreciative of our performance that they gave us three encores.

② All the _____ at the hotel where we stayed were extremely friendly and helpful.

③ My son's _____ is doing a concert at the town hall on Saturday evening.

④ Jake's _____ is always arguing. His brother and sister are the worst.

⑤ Next week, all the _____ in the office are going to do extra training.

⑥ The _____ is holding an emergency session to discuss foreign policy issues.

⑦ Our _____ is known for being the most environmentally friendly in the company.

⑧ My _____ is the market leader in the digital industry and has been for 10 years now.

⑨ Later this afternoon our _____ is going to be discussing the issues you mentioned.

family	orchestra	government	staff	~~fleet~~
teams	department	audience	panel	company

🔊

67.2 COCHEZ LES PHRASES CORRECTES.

Singing Stars are my favorite TV program. I watch it every Saturday night. ☐
Singing Stars is my favorite TV program. I watch it every Saturday night. ☑

❶ Spain have a very long border with Portugal. It's one of the longest in Europe. ☐
Spain has a very long border with Portugal. It's one of the longest in Europe. ☐

❷ The Netherlands are of the best countries to go on vacation if you like cycling. ☐
The Netherlands is one of the best countries to go on vacation if you like cycling. ☐

❸ He's great at soccer, but athletics is the sport that he wants to focus on from now on. ☐
He's great at soccer, but athletics are the sport that he wants to focus on from now on. ☐

❹ Politics were my favorite subject at school, so I decided to study it in college. ☐
Politics was my favorite subject at school, so I decided to study it in college. ☐

❺ The news about the celebrity couple were very hard to believe. ☐
The news about the celebrity couple was very hard to believe. ☐

◀))

67.3 RELIEZ LE DÉBUT DE CHAQUE PHRASE À LA FIN QUI LUI CORRESPOND.

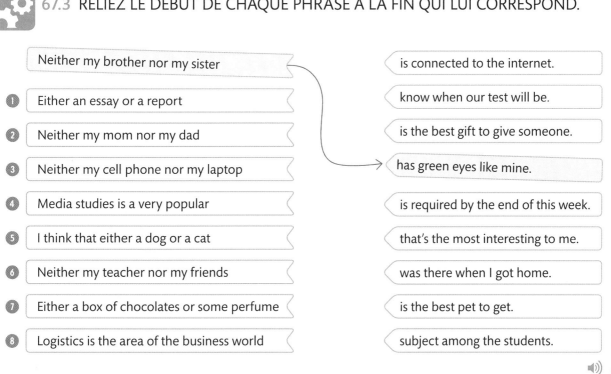

Neither my brother nor my sister — is connected to the internet.

❶ Either an essay or a report — know when our test will be.

❷ Neither my mom nor my dad — is the best gift to give someone.

❸ Neither my cell phone nor my laptop — has green eyes like mine.

❹ Media studies is a very popular — is required by the end of this week.

❺ I think that either a dog or a cat — that's the most interesting to me.

❻ Neither my teacher nor my friends — was there when I got home.

❼ Either a box of chocolates or some perfume — is the best pet to get.

❽ Logistics is the area of the business world — subject among the students.

◀))

225

67.4 BARREZ LE MOT INCORRECT DANS CHAQUE PHRASE.

The news **is** / ~~are~~ always depressing. There are so many stories about bad things that are happening.

1 All of the information about this **is** / **are** available to you on the college's website.

2 Neither my dad nor my mom **was** / **were** very happy when I got suspended from school.

3 **Is** / **Are** *The Dragon Leader* a good book or do you not like fantasy novels?

4 Either pop music or rock music **is** / **are** what I like to listen to when I'm relaxing.

5 Physics **is** / **are** what Charlie studied in college, too.

6 Politics **is** / **are** slowly moving more to the left in this country at the moment.

7 **Is** / **Are** the mathematics you're doing in your class very difficult or can you do it easily?

8 Neither my presentation nor my essay **was** / **were** good enough to get me a passing grade.

9 The Bahamas **has** / **have** very warm weather at this time of year, so I'd recommend going there.

10 Either English or Spanish **is** / **are** the language that people most commonly learn at our school.

67.5 ÉCOUTEZ L'ENREGISTREMENT, PUIS COCHEZ LES BONNES RÉPONSES.

Neil, un étudiant, parle d'une matière populaire à l'université.

Economics is very popular in college.
True ☑ **False** ☐ **Not given** ☐

1 There are 400 new economics students this year.
True ☐ **False** ☐ **Not given** ☐

2 Economics with tourism is popular.
True ☐ **False** ☐ **Not given** ☐

3 Neil is studying mathematics now.
True ☐ **False** ☐ **Not given** ☐

4 Neil thinks mathematics is too difficult for him.
True ☐ **False** ☐ **Not given** ☐

5 Both of Neil's parents went to college.
True ☐ **False** ☐ **Not given** ☐

6 Neil's parents don't put a lot of pressure on him.
True ☐ **False** ☐ **Not given** ☐

7 Neil still lives near his family.
True ☐ **False** ☐ **Not given** ☐

67.6 CHOISISSEZ LE MOT CORRECT, PUIS LISEZ LA PHRASE À VOIX HAUTE.

The Netherlands **is** / ~~are~~ the country where I grew up, but now I live in France.

1 *Jungle Adventures* **is** / are the new television show that everyone is talking about.

2 The US **is** / are the largest country in North America when it comes to population.

3 This information **need** / needs to be shared with everyone else in the team right away.

4 Neither the adults nor the children **was** / were interested in the entertainment they provided.

5 I think politics **isn't** / aren't a topic that you should discuss when you're making small talk.

6 Neither my black suit nor my dark blue one **is** / are clean enough to wear.

7 Neither my phone nor Clark's phone **is** / are getting any signal at the moment.

8 Either the lemon or the lime **was** / were too strong in the sauce he made.

9 Everyone in Jack's family **is** / are interested in birdwatching, so he's going on a trip with them.

10 Neither history nor business **is** / are interesting to me.

68 « So » et « such »

Vous pouvez utiliser « so » et « such » avec certains mots pour ajouter de l'emphase. Les deux ont une signification similaire mais sont employés différemment.

 Grammaire « So » et « such » emphatiques
Aa Vocabulaire La science médicale
Compétence Accentuer des descriptions

68.1 BARREZ LE MOT INCORRECT DANS CHAQUE PHRASE.

You're so / ~~such~~ amazing! You've had three operations this year and you're still smiling!

1. Last night my mom called me to say that my grandma was very ill. It was so / **such** a shock.

2. Hong Kong is so / **such** a fascinating city. You should go there if you get the chance.

3. You've got so / **such** a difficult job. I don't think I'm patient enough to be a teacher.

4. He carried the baby **so** / such gently, as if he was scared she might break.

5. I can't believe I've got a job in Paris! It's **so** / such exciting!

6. That movie was **so** / such gripping. It was almost three hours long, but the time flew past!

7. You've got so / **such** a beautiful smile. Has anyone ever told you that?

8. It's always so / **such** a pleasure to spend time with Tom. He's a lovely man.

9. Keira is **so** / such generous. Did you know that she gave $250 to charity last month?

10. I'm not surprised the police stopped Mick. He drives **so** / such dangerously.

11. Thanks for responding **so** / such quickly. That was really efficient of you.

12. It was so / **such** a surprise when my cat turned up after being missing for six months!

13. You behaved **so** / such rudely in front of our guests. I felt quite embarrassed.

14. You learn languages **so** / such easily! Can you share your secret with me?

15. I think Martin is **so** / such brave. I couldn't do a bungee jump.

16. Your present job is **so** / such interesting. Is it also well paid, unlike the previous one?

17. *Back to City Life* was so / **such** a great book. I want to read it again!

18. It was so / **such** a relief when the doctor told me the good news. I've been celebrating.

19. I've had so / **such** a fun evening. Can I see you again tomorrow?

68.2 RELIEZ LE DÉBUT DE CHAQUE PHRASE À LA FIN QUI LUI CORRESPOND.

The doctor was so tired — that he nearly fell asleep!

that everyone was surprised.

1. The medicine works so effectively — that she was off work for months.

2. It was such a bad injury — that he's sure to go on to college.

3. It was such an unexpected result — that he nearly fell asleep!

4. He recovered so quickly — that I didn't really feel worried.

5. Brian is so intelligent — that we have a 98 percent cure rate.

6. The doctor was so reassuring — that he was back at work within two weeks.

68.3 COMPLÉTEZ LES PHRASES AVEC « SO » OU « SUCH ».

Elizabeth had ___so___ little experience in her role as teacher that she was really nervous.

1. It's _____ a beautiful day. Why don't we go for a walk on the beach?

2. I am _____ grateful to the doctors that I'm going to send them a thank you card.

3. It was _____ a thrill to spend time with my grandchildren.

4. The movie was _____ boring that Pauline and I fell asleep.

5. It was _____ a surprise that I didn't know what to say.

6. Chantelle is _____ helpful. She's a lovely young woman.

7. Tom reacted _____ bravely when the doctor told him he had to go into the hospital.

So much surgeons have to work extremely long hours these days.
So many surgeons have to work extremely long hours these days.

1 Such few people eat enough fruit and vegetables every day.

2 Such little funding is available for research into age-related diseases.

3 There are so much medicines to choose from for your condition.

4 Such many wonderful people work in our health service.

5 Charis feels so better since she started doing more exercise.

6 Such few students are bright enough to become doctors and engineers.

7 So many effort goes into making sure the patients are comfortable.

8 Such little money is spent on healthcare services for the disabled.

9 Such many people know someone who has been in the hospital.

10 There has been so many amazing progress in the field of medicine in the last decade.

11 So many time and money has been put into designing this new hospital.

12 It's so easier to play sports since I lost a lot of weight.

68.5 COCHEZ LES PHRASES CORRECTES.

Medical treatments today are such much better than they used to be. ☐
Medical treatments today are so much better than they used to be. ☑

1 Lyndsey is so an inspiration to me. I follow everything she posts on her blog. ☐
Lyndsey is such an inspiration to me. I follow everything she posts on her blog. ☐

2 Jamie made such an effort to find the right present for my birthday. ☐
Jamie made much an effort to find the right present for my birthday. ☐

3 I have so many free time these days, I've started some new hobbies. ☐
I have so much free time these days, I've started some new hobbies. ☐

4 The exam was such easy that I wondered whether I had missed something. ☐
The exam was so easy that I wondered whether I had missed something. ☐

5 You play the piano so beautifully! Can you play it again, please? ☐
You play the piano such beautifully! Can you play it again, please? ☐

6 There are such few opportunities for people who can't read or write. ☐
There are so few opportunities for people who can't read or write. ☐

🔊

68.6 ÉCRIVEZ LES PHRASES EN AJOUTANT « SO » OU « SUCH » AU BON ENDROIT, PUIS LISEZ-LES À VOIX HAUTE.

The party was a success. [such]

The party was such a success. 🗣

1 These stray cats are a nuisance. [such]

🗣

2 I feel much calmer after a walk in the rain. [so]

🗣

3 You opened the door quietly last night. [so]

🗣

4 *Color* was amazing that I watched it again. [so]

🗣

5 There are many shirts to choose from. [so]

🗣

6 It's a lovely dress that I'm going to buy it. [such]

🗣

7 My dog is always hungry. She eats much. [so]

🗣

🔊

« The » est le mot le plus couramment usité dans la langue anglaise. Il peut être employé dans de nombreuses situations, tout comme l'article indéfini « a » et l'article zéro.

Grammaire Le « the » générique

Aa Vocabulaire Les explorations et les inventions

Compétence Utiliser les articles de niveau avancé

69.1 BARREZ LES MOTS INCORRECTS DANS CHAQUE PHRASE.

 A̶ / A̶n̶ / The internet is probably the most important invention of the last 50 years.

 ❶ My brother has a / an / the pet spider. I hate it!

 ❷ I'd like a piece of cake and a / an / the orange juice, please.

 ❸ A / An / The airplane was invented by the Wright brothers.

 ❹ Can I ask you a / an / the question?

 ❺ I can see a / an / the man over there with blond hair. But I'm not sure that it's Josh.

 ❻ A / An / The bicycle is a very common form of transportation all over the world.

 ❼ I have a / an / the arrangement with my colleague, where we share the commute to work.

 ❽ There was a / an / the awkward silence when I asked Tami how her job was going.

 ❾ A / An / The hummingbird is one of the smallest birds on the planet.

 ❿ Would you like a / an / the cup of coffee?

 ⓫ A / An / The sandwich is named after the Earl of Sandwich, who supposedly invented it.

69.2 COMPLÉTEZ LES PHRASES AVEC L'ARTICLE APPROPRIÉ EN LAISSANT UN BLANC POUR L'ARTICLE ZÉRO.

> ___The___ telescope was invented in the 16th century.

1 _____ apple a day keeps the doctor away.

2 _____ women are still rarely paid as much as men.

3 _____ human beings are the number-one predator on Earth.

4 There's _____ advertisement for a new smartwatch in today's paper.

5 _____ electric car is now a reality in many countries.

6 _____ students usually don't have very much money.

7 _____ panda is in danger of becoming extinct.

◀))

69.3 COCHEZ LES PHRASES CORRECTES.

> I'd like to introduce my colleague, Sophie Brennan. ☑
> I'd like to introduce my colleague, the Sophie Brennan. ☐

1 I'm afraid there isn't a Mark Wilson in this office. Have you got the right name? ☐
  I'm afraid there isn't the Mark Wilson in this office. Have you got the right name? ☐

2 Are you saying you're good friends with a John Smith? ☐
  Are you saying you're good friends with John Smith? ☐

3 This is my sister's best friend, a Kristin Wyatt. ☐
  This is my sister's best friend, Kristin Wyatt. ☐

4 Let me introduce you to the manager of our company, Isaac Myers. ☐
  Let me introduce you to the manager of our company, the Isaac Myers. ☐

5 I don't know of a Lucy Armitage. Is there anyone else you'd like to speak to? ☐
  I don't know of the Lucy Armitage. Is there anyone else you'd like to speak to? ☐

6 You don't mean a Cherry Baldwin, the famous actress, do you? ☐
  You don't mean the Cherry Baldwin, the famous actress, do you? ☐

◀))

69.4 RÉCRIVEZ LES PHRASES EN CORRIGEANT LES ERREURS.

> Thomas Edison is widely acknowledged as an inventor of the moving picture.
> *Thomas Edison is widely acknowledged as the inventor of the moving picture.*

1 I can't find the Mikaela Zimmerman in the company directory. Are you sure she works here?

2 Did you manage to get yourself ticket for the concert?

3 Cell phone has become a much smaller and lighter device in recent years.

4 Allow me to introduce you to my fiancé, a Brad Livingstone.

5 I had delicious meal at that new Italian restaurant last night.

6 There's no record of the Thomas Luckett ever having lived here.

7 Dog is often described as man's best friend.

8 Can you believe I was sitting next to an Elizabeth Parker? She's such a huge star!

9 Dress is often the most important thing for a bride at her wedding.

10 This is my boss, a Francesco Coppola.

11 We usually have the breakfast at about 7:15am.

12 Internet has revolutionized our lives since its invention.

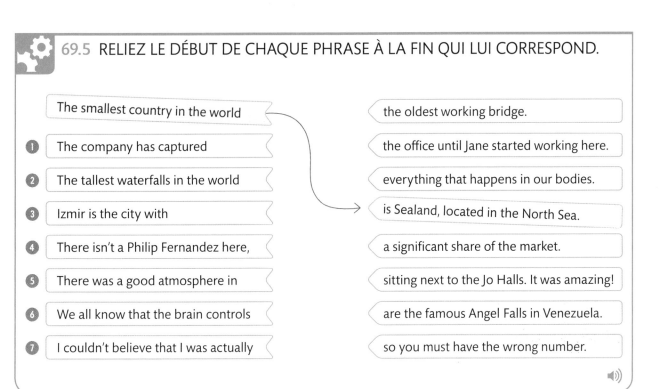

The smallest country in the world — is Sealand, located in the North Sea.

the oldest working bridge.

the office until Jane started working here.

everything that happens in our bodies.

① The company has captured

② The tallest waterfalls in the world

③ Izmir is the city with

a significant share of the market.

④ There isn't a Philip Fernandez here,

⑤ There was a good atmosphere in

sitting next to the Jo Halls. It was amazing!

are the famous Angel Falls in Venezuela.

⑥ We all know that the brain controls

⑦ I couldn't believe that I was actually

so you must have the wrong number.

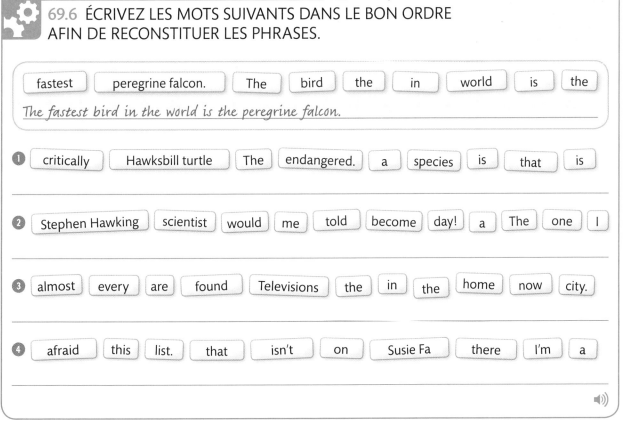

fastest | peregrine falcon. | The | bird | the | in | world | is | the

The fastest bird in the world is the peregrine falcon.

① critically | Hawksbill turtle | The | endangered. | a | species | is | that | is

② Stephen Hawking | scientist | would | me | told | become | day! | a | The | one | I

③ almost | every | are | found | Televisions | the | in | the | home | now | city.

④ afraid | this | list. | that | isn't | on | Susie Fa | there | I'm | a

Réponses

1.1 🔊

1 I'm a sales assistant in a department store that opened recently.
2 Hurry up! The bus is coming. If we miss it, we will be late for work.
3 I'm meeting my new team leader right now to discuss plans for next year.
4 I get up at 7 o'clock every day to get to the office on time.
5 I always have a coffee break at 10 o'clock so I can work faster.
6 Today I'm wearing a new white blouse I bought from the store near my office.
7 She's working in the New York office at the moment, but she's planning to move to California.
8 I think I'm in the wrong building. Cathy lives in building number seven.
9 I'm having lunch in 30 minutes. Would you like to join me?
10 I go home at 5 o'clock every day after I finish work.

1.2 🔊

1 **I'm** the new member of the team.
2 **He always** sits at that desk. You'll have to move!
3 The train **arrives** at 7:22am every morning.
4 The bus is **usually on** time, but not today.
5 **I'm talking** to my boss at the moment.
6 **I'm working** on the new project with David today.
7 We **are** a very good team!
8 **I have** a meeting at 9 o'clock every day.
9 **I'm waiting** for you in front of the office.

1.3 🔊

1 I**'ve been trying** to call him all day, but he **hasn't answered** yet.
2 He**'s been working** all day, so he **hasn't had** a break yet.
3 I'm glad I**'ve finished** that project because I**'ve been working** on it for ages.
4 Jo**'s been cooking** all night, but Jim still **hasn't arrived** for dinner.
5 I**'ve been driving** for two hours now and I still **haven't made** it to work.
6 He**'s got** his schedule now and he**'s been meeting** the team all day.

1.4 🔊

1 Rebecca is from Australia, **isn't she?**
2 Gary doesn't live far from the office, **does he?**
3 They went to college in the US, **didn't they?**
4 You're working in the Singapore office, **aren't you?**
5 The new employees have their badges, **don't they?**
6 She's been waiting for 20 minutes, **hasn't she?**
7 Angelina worked as an engineer in New York, **didn't she?**
8 Mark has traveled to many countries in Europe, **hasn't he?**
9 They are planning to move out of the city, **aren't they?**
10 Alan should go on the training course next week, **shouldn't he?**
11 You have been to Singapore on a business trip, **haven't you?**

1.5

1 False 2 False 3 False 4 True
5 False

1.6 🔊

1 Maxine always takes the 7:45 train to work like Paul, **doesn't she?**
2 Your car is parked on the road in front of the company reception, **isn't it?**
3 Jonathan doesn't work in the sales department anymore, **does he?**
4 She worked for one of our competitors before she started working here, **didn't she?**
5 Nick and Philip have visited a lot of different countries on business trips, **haven't they?**
6 You would like to join us for lunch in the cafeteria today, **wouldn't you?**
7 Jessica didn't go to the strategy meeting we had last Tuesday, **did she?**
8 The boss should be showing the new employees around the office, **shouldn't he?**
9 Katrina and John know each other from their days in college, **don't they?**
10 He's been waiting for some time to talk to the boss about his promotion, **hasn't he?**
11 James isn't going to be the next head of the Human Resources department, **is he?**
12 Daniel should present the results of his research to the rest of the team, **shouldn't he?**
13 You worked with Janet on the project we did in Singapore, **didn't you?**
14 He works from home two days a week so he can spend time with his family, **doesn't he?**
15 Simon and Gregory are working on a prototype for the new product, **aren't they?**

2.1 🔊

1 Action 2 Action 3 State 4 State
5 State 6 Action 7 State 8 State
9 Action 10 Action

2.2 🔊

1 She's concentrating hard at the moment.
2 I hate video games. They're so boring.
3 He wants to move to a bigger place.
4 She seems to be a reliable employee.
5 He's reading a science-fiction novel.
6 I'm just cooking some pasta for dinner.
7 The package weighs four pounds.
8 I can't hear you at all.
9 Laura is appearing in the show this evening.
10 What do you think of me?

2.3 🔊

1 The items that the bags **contain** are heavy.
2 **I see** the mountains in the distance.
3 He **is weighing** the boxes on the scales right now.
4 We **spent** two hours doing our work.
5 I **believe** everything you say.
6 I'm sorry, but **I feel** that you're wrong.
7 I **was listening** to the radio when you came in.
8 This milk **smells** bad.
9 Shaun **usually arrives** at work at 8am.

2.4 🔊

1 William **wants** to travel around the world when he's older.
2 I **am tasting** the soup to see if it needs more salt or pepper.
3 I **am seeing** my dentist later this afternoon for a consultation.
4 My knees **hurt** when I walk too far or sit for too long.
5 My colleagues **are having** lunch right now in the cafeteria.
6 Michael **is being** all shy and quiet now that you're here to visit.

3.1 🔊

1 Laura **went into business** straight after school, at the age of 18.
2 The difference between these two cars is **clearly visible**.
3 You've studied so much for the exam. Now all that's left is to **do your best.**
4 I **distinctly remember** asking you to pack the passports. Don't tell me you forgot!

5 I think it's **extremely unlikely** that you'll win the lottery tonight.

6 I don't think Steffi likes me. She seems to have a **low opinion** of me.

7 The smell of fresh bread always **stirs up memories** of my grandma.

8 Bill made a big mistake at work and it has **ruined his career.**

9 I'm very lucky to have a **close family.** We meet up every Sunday for lunch.

3.2

1 True **2** False **3** Not given **4** True
5 Not given **6** True **7** Not given
8 False **9** True

3.3 ◄))

1 I met my wife while I was in college.
2 When I was young, I loved climbing trees.
3 After I retired, I moved to Florida.
4 During the summer I worked in a café.
5 I worked part-time while I was studying abroad.

3.4

1 25 years ago
2 23 years ago
3 15 years ago

3.5 ◄))

1 Stephanie **graduated** from college with an honors degree **last** year.

2 Bill **had been running** for many years when **he decided** to run a marathon.

3 Matthew **started** working at the company 33 years **ago.**

4 Leah **had** a baby **last** month. Her name's Sophie and she's beautiful.

5 Peter **arrived** very early **this** morning because he has an important meeting.

6 Jenny **was working** in a bar in London when she **met** Stephen.

7 Jenny and Stephen **got married** this year **on** June 7.

8 Stuart **had been living** in the US **for** 10 years before he moved to the UK.

9 When they **were** five years old, Anna and Jasmine **were** best friends.

3.6 ◄))

1 Whether too much sleep is bad for you **is a matter of opinion.**

2 There is a popular belief that **the number 13 is unlucky.**

3 Lionel has gone into business, **selling clothes he has designed himself.**

4 There's forecast to be light rain later on, **so take an umbrella.**

5 When I smelled that perfume, it stirred **up memories of my first love.**

6 The airport is still closed, so **it's extremely unlikely we'll fly today.**

7 I'm not sure why Rebecca has **such a low opinion of me.**

8 The scandal over drug-taking ruined **her career in athletics.**

04

4.1 ◄))

1 She's **an intelligent little** girl. She always does well at school.

2 It's a **horrible, ugly old** car. I'm not going to buy it as I don't like it.

3 We're going on a **fantastic, cheap** train trip across Europe for our vacation.

4 This is such **a comfortable old** sweater. I love wearing it in winter.

5 Gio always wears **stylish Italian** clothes. He is a fashion designer in London.

6 Today we're going to present our **innovative new** tablet to you for the first time.

7 Don't forget to try these **delicious spicy** sauces, which we've created ourselves.

8 I was one of the first to ride in a **unique high-speed** train while I was there.

9 Sometimes a **reliable low-tech** product is a better option than a more hi-tech one.

4.2

4.3 ◄))

1 My grandma is a **wonderful, generous old** lady.

2 I bought this **awful, ugly expensive** dress on the internet.

3 What a **pleasant, friendly young** man Peter is!

4 Jon's got a **beautiful, stylish new** car.

4.4 ◄))

1 Lana's **dis**honest. She hides information and never tells the truth.

2 You're so **in**considerate. Think about other people for a change!

3 It was very **un**kind of you to make your sister cry. You should apologize to her.

4 Leon always has a solution for a problem. Unfortunately, he's often **in**correct.

5 Susanne is always being rude to her parents. She's so **dis**respectful.

6 Stop behaving like a five-year-old! You're so **im**mature!

4.5

1 inexperienced **2** arrogant **3** Esther
4 seven years **5** popular

4.6 Réponses modèles

1 He solved the problem by taking charge of the situation and seeking help from others.
2 He wants to be promoted into management.
3 He might appear rude because he is shy and awkward in social situations.
4 He can go on training programs to help him with his social skills.
5 Jenson needs to improve his social skills before he can be considered for promotion.
6 The review is generally positive.

05

5.1 ◄))

1 It's **a shame that** some people aren't interested in learning languages.

2 It's **interesting that** you chose that book because it's the book that I chose, too.

3 It's **not important to** win. What you should be focused on is doing your very best.

4 It is **easy to** learn English vocabulary, but it's difficult to learn the grammar.

5 It's **good that** our neighbors are so understanding because we make a lot of noise!

6 When it's so cold outside, it's **important to** wrap yourself up as warmly as possible.

7 It's **essential that** everyone has enough water to drink while we're out walking in the heat.

8 It's **bad to** look at your phone while you're driving. You could have an accident.

9 Joshua has been doing so badly at school that he's **unlikely to** do well in his exams.

10 It is **difficult to** understand people when they speak English very quickly.

11 Look at those black clouds over there. I think it's **likely to** rain sometime soon.

12 Our train is so delayed. I think it's **unlikely that** we'll get home before midnight!

13 It's really **bad that** some people don't care about the environment. They should!

14 It's **important that** our children do their best at school and get a good education.

15 It's **good to** have all of the family here together again. I've missed everyone.

5.2 ◄))

1 It is unlikely **that** I will finish this assignment on time.

2 It's difficult **to** decide what to order because it all sounds delicious.

3 **To** lose at this point would be very difficult after coming so far.

4 It's easy **to** start writing an essay, but it's not always easy to finish one!

5 It's essential **that** everyone follows the rules and does what they're told.

6 **To** read English is easy, but to write in English is more difficult.

7 It's important **to** choose an interesting topic to give a presentation about.

5.3 🔊

1 I have a certain aptitude for **navigating with a map, but I still get lost.**

2 My friend has a complete inability **to plan ahead. He's always late!**

3 It seems like some people have a **natural ability to run long distances.**

4 Dr. Finn had a remarkable capacity **to memorize huge passages of text.**

5.4

1 At a college
2 Surfing the internet
3 Natural
4 Tonal

5.5 🔊 Réponses modèles

1 Because it's important **to be able to communicate with people from all over the world.**

2 I think English is likely **to be a popular language for a long time.**

3 I think I have **a natural ability for learning languages.**

4 It's difficult **to remember all of the words and say them when you need them.**

06

6.1 🔊

1 once-in-a-lifetime
2 thirst for adventure
3 check out
4 go sightseeing
5 hopelessly lost
6 see somebody off
7 leg of a journey
8 look around
9 check in
10 feel homesick
11 culture shock
12 get away from it all
13 stop off

07

7.1 🔊

1 I usually get up at 7am.
2 I would like to check in early.
3 I need to check out by 9am.
4 He works out for two hours.
5 We always go out on Fridays.

6 Please line up here to go in.
7 Martin showed up at the party.

7.2 🔊

1 They want to check in at the hotel.
2 He keeps on complaining about his job.
3 She doesn't like getting up early.
4 She works out in the morning.
5 We're going out for Sheila's birthday.
6 He showed up late to work yesterday.
7 Jo, please come in and join us here.
8 Tim is coming down for my birthday.
9 Cooking is hard, but you should keep at it.
10 He always checks out early.

7.3 🔊

1 She really needs to **clean** her desk **up**. It's full of papers and old coffee cups.

2 The sixth grade students are **putting** a show **on** to celebrate the end of their time at this school.

3 Everyone needs to **hand** their forms **in** by Friday. Otherwise you can't go on the trip.

4 I need you to **look** a few words **up** in the dictionary for me. Can you do that?

5 I'll **check** the hotels in Monte Carlo **out** and let you know what the prices are.

7.4 🔊

1 It's not a problem. We'll come over and pick **it** up from your place.

2 He was so angry he tore **it** up and threw it around the room.

3 You should put **it** on when you go outside. It's absolutely freezing.

4 If you cut **it** out, you can use it to get two for the price of one at the supermarket.

7.5 🔊

1 He's always trying to **live up to** his reputation as a big spender.

2 We're **coming up with** some really good ideas at the moment.

3 I should just **get rid of** the things that I don't need.

4 She's so fast. I can't **keep up with** her.

5 Melissa's great. I really **look up to** her.

7.6 🔊

1 We all went to the airport with John and **saw him off**.

2 Her plane **took off** at 9:20am, so she should land at 2:50pm.

3 He always **stops off** to see his mother on his way home from work.

4 Hi Jonathan, it's me again. I'm sorry we were **cut off** just now.

5 The traffic was so bad that we **set off** at 9 o'clock and didn't arrive until 12.

6 I'm worried about my new dog. I don't think he **gets along with** Buster.

7.7

1 True **2** True **3** False **4** Not given
5 False **6** False **7** True **8** False
9 False **10** True

08

8.1 🔊

1 I **learned** a lot of Japanese while I **was living** in Japan.

2 While I **was waiting** for the train, I **met** my favorite singer.

3 As we **were walking** home last night, we **saw** a firework display.

4 We **stopped** at the café while we **were visiting** the castle.

5 I **got** off my bike a few times while I **was cycling** to work.

6 I **saw** a lot of cafés when I **was strolling** around town.

7 While I **was wandering** around, I **found** a good bookstore.

8 She **took** so many pictures when she **was traveling**.

9 I **was having** problems with my car until he **helped** me.

8.2 🔊

1 We tried a local restaurant because **the hotel receptionist had recommended it (to us).**

2 I went in the sauna after I **had been in the swimming pool (at the hotel).**

3 We rented a bike because **a friend of ours had said it was a good idea.**

4 They gave us a welcome drink just after **we had arrived at the hotel.**

5 We didn't have to wait in line to go in because **we had bought advance tickets.**

8.3 🔊

1 The Miller family **had been going** to Croatia for years before it became popular with tourists.

2 We needed to move around after we **had been sitting** on the plane for 14 hours.

3 I **had been waiting** for them at the airport for half an hour before they arrived.

4 Our team **had been losing** in the first half of the game, but they came back in the second.

5 She **had been studying** Spanish for six months before she went to Mexico.

6 It **had been raining** for five days in a row before we had some sunshine.

8.4 🔊

1 She **had been planning** to cycle across China, but then she **had** an accident on her bike.

2 When they **got** back home, they discovered that someone **had burgled** their house.
3 After I **had been traveling** around Asia for six months, I **felt** very happy to be back home.
4 Before I **went** to South America, I **hadn't tried** tango dancing.
5 He **wanted** to visit the fjords because he **had heard** they were beautiful.

8.5 🔊
1 I had written some practice answers **before the exam, so I was well prepared.**
2 When I got back to the parking lot, **I realized that someone had stolen my car.**
3 Before I started working here, I had **been working in the US for six months.**
4 I had given the matter a lot of thought **before I decided to change jobs.**
5 They were eating at a restaurant when **a famous author came in.**
6 She wanted to go to Spain because **her parents had told her it was fantastic.**
7 They had been planning to go out, **but they decided to go to bed early.**
8 I was feeling extremely tired because **I had not been sleeping very well.**

8.6 Réponses modèles
1 Jason had moved to New York a few months earlier.
2 Jason had been doing an internship in London before he moved to New York.
3 Jason saw the woman again a few days later.
4 The woman was the first person to write a message.

09

9.1 🔊
1 When you're in Berlin, you ought to visit the television tower.
2 I know! You really should take the kids down to the swimming pool.
3 You might want to take a boat trip around the lake while you're here.
4 Jonas could make a reservation. Then he'll definitely get a seat on the train.
5 Yes, it's awesome. You really must do that.

9.2 ❸

9.3 🔊
1 We had some outstanding food at Lionel's restaurant! **You ought to try the pasta.**
2 The room wasn't bad, although ours was a lot smaller than some of the others. **You could ask for a larger room if this is an issue.**
3 We can't praise our tour guide enough. She gave us such a lot of interesting information. **You must ask for Irene if you go there.**

4 I had trouble sleeping because the sheets were very rough. **You might want to bring a sheet!**
5 The staff at the bar had fantastic recommendations for drinks. **You really must try the cocktails.**

9.4
1 Like **2** Like **3** Like **4** Dislike

9.5 🔊
1 You **must** put on a lot of sun cream or you'll burn.
2 You **had better** take your walking boots if you're going to go hiking while you're there.
3 The firework display will be absolutely stunning. You **must** go and see it.
4 If I were you, I **would** take the train from Paris to London instead of flying.
5 You **should** ask if they have any vacancies at the Hotel Bennetton.

9.6
1 car **2** photographs **3** car doors
4 dish **5** photographs

9.7 Réponses modèles
Hi Jake!
How are you? It's been a long time since I sent you a letter, so I thought I would tell you about our family trip to Paris. **We went to** France in August and it was wonderful. **The highlight for me was** all the incredible French food! **I really enjoyed the** museums and galleries too. **You ought to** go when you get the chance. **If I were you, I'd** make it the next family adventure! **You must** come and visit us soon, too.
Look forward to hearing from you. **You'd better** not take a month to reply this time!
Best wishes,
Jaya

10

10.1 🔊
1 The plane is two hours late now, **so we will miss our connecting flight.**
2 Sadly, the project won't be finished **by the end of June after all.**
3 We might have time to visit the spa **if we leave now and we hurry up.**
4 Ask the rep from the travel agency, as **she will probably know the answer.**
5 He definitely won't be trying beef **because he's a vegetarian.**
6 It's unlikely that he will call, as **I don't think he has my phone number.**
7 When we arrive at the airport, **we will wait for you in the arrivals hall.**

8 It's very unlikely that it will rain, since **there isn't a cloud in the sky today.**

10.2
1 Likely **2** Unlikely **3** Unlikely
4 Unlikely

10.3 🔊
1 The internet has **fundamentally** changed how we book our vacations.
2 **Luckily**, we had nice weather every day when we were on vacation.
3 **Unfortunately**, Emma was sick when we were on vacation.
4 The trip home was **predictably** slow. There are always problems on that route.
5 They make their pancakes in **essentially** the same way that we do.
6 **Interestingly**, Winston Churchill had stayed at our hotel when he was in the region.
7 **Fortunately**, we were fit enough to be able to hike back down the coast.

10.4 🔊
1 **Luckily**, we made it to the hotel before the reception closed for the night.
2 Windsurfing is **essentially** sailing with a surfboard.
3 **Unfortunately**, the hotel is completely booked up.
4 **Interestingly**, the café was also an art gallery.
5 **Surprisingly**, Richard actually went in the pool. You know how he normally hates water.
6 **Predictably**, Donald got sunburned again. He never puts any sun tan lotion on.

10.5
1 Not given **2** True **3** True **4** False
5 False **6** True **7** True **8** Not given
9 True

11

11.1 🔊
1 grow up
2 run in the family
3 stick up for somebody
4 see eye to eye with somebody
5 make friends with somebody
6 click with somebody
7 give birth
8 drift apart
9 bump into somebody
10 put your foot down
11 look up to somebody
12 close friend
13 break up with somebody

12.1 🔊

1 I have bright blue eyes **like my mother.**
2 We live in different countries, **but we all get together at Christmas.**
3 My siblings are all very intelligent, **especially my brother, who's a scientist.**
4 My dad loves to play board games, **particularly chess.**
5 They like different TV channels **so they watch them in different rooms.**
6 We can video chat with each other **since we all have smartphones or laptops.**
7 She is interested in my life at college **because she wasn't able to go.**
8 I enjoy going fishing **just as my father does. He's great at it.**
9 My father is a great cook, **so he always makes dinner for us.**
10 We only see each other once a month **because we're all so busy now.**
11 It's hard to buy a present for dad and, **as a result, he always gets socks!**
12 We cook something different for her **as she's a vegetarian.**
13 My relatives all talk a lot, **especially when they all get together.**
14 Ann and I still stay up late chatting **just as we used to do when we were kids.**
15 I love cooking Chinese food, **though my family doesn't eat it often.**

12.2 🔊

1 My brother loves sports, **especially** ice hockey.
2 Our family usually goes to Greece on vacation, **though** last year we went to Turkey.
3 My brother got great grades at school, **so** he studied at a good university.
4 My dad works in the garden every day **as** he has a lot of free time after retiring.
5 My mother loves cats **just as** my grandmother did.
6 My sister loves music, **particularly** rock and pop bands.
7 My mother's always wanted to go to Paris, **so** we organized a trip for her 50th birthday.
8 We do sometimes argue with each other, **but** we never stay angry at each other for long.
9 My two younger brothers are very close **as** they shared a room when they were growing up.
10 My family isn't very big **like** my husband's.
11 We will have a big family gathering this year **as** all my cousins will be here.
12 Sonya is a talented painter **just as** her grandmother was.
13 All my relatives are good singers, **particularly** my aunt.

12.3 🔊

1 She searched for her mother's last name **online, yet she didn't find anything helpful.**
2 As a result of a friend's recommendation, **she decided to look at family records online.**
3 Her mother had many fascinating ancestors, **notably one who was an army general.**
4 Whereas her mother's side was interesting, **her father's ancestors were all dull.**
5 Therefore, she decided to concentrate on **finding out more about her mother's side.**
6 As well as the army general, **other ancestors of hers were very interesting.**
7 As a result of her research, **she felt more connected to her family.**

12.4 🔊

1 **Due to** the delay to our flight from Atlanta, we missed our connecting flight.
2 It was raining heavily, **so** we decided to cancel the barbecue.
3 My mother is always late, **but** my father is always on time.
4 Ronald Tuft received a number of awards, **notably** the Victoria Cross.
5 Her early work is very radical and her later work is **equally** innovative.
6 Hotels have to be careful **since** it's easy for guests to write bad reviews nowadays.

12.5

1 False 2 True 3 Not given 4 True
5 True 6 False 7 False 8 Not given

13.1 🔊

1 When I was young, we would **visit** our grandparents every weekend.
2 I didn't **use** to like olives. Now I love them!
3 Did they **use** to have a car?
4 In the summer break, we **would spend** all day at the beach if it was sunny.
5 We **used** to live in an apartment in Milwaukee before we moved to Chicago.
6 When I was a student, I **would look** for special offers to save money.
7 In my old job, I **would listen** to customers' complaints all day long.
8 Did **you** use to play soccer?
9 When I was very young, I **would not eat** any vegetables.
10 At school, my best friend was Leo. We **used to do** everything together.
11 My brother didn't **use to like** swimming. Now he loves it.

13.2 🔊

1 Did you use to have a computer at home when you were a child?
2 I worked in Paris from 2005 to 2009.
3 Liam has been to Los Angeles twice.
4 We didn't use to have to wear a school uniform at my school.
5 I used to ride a bicycle to school every day, even in the rain.

13.3

1 would get up 2 would cycle
3 used to spend 4 would get
5 used to moan 6 used to complain
7 never used to

13.4

1 Not given 2 False 3 True
4 Not given 5 False

13.5

3

13.6 🔊

1 Janine has similar **values** to us. She loves animals and she's a vegetarian.
2 Your dog is so **greedy**! He's eaten a bowl of food and still wants more.
3 I take **honesty** very seriously. I can't employ people who lie to me.
4 These days there is greater **acceptance** of people with differing points of view.
5 The best thing about Philip's **character** is that he is so kind.

13.7 🔊

1 Did you **use** to go to dance classes when you were young?
2 I **did** a lot of housework yesterday afternoon.
3 I didn't **use** to enjoy jogging, but now I do.
4 When I was young, my parents **would** take us to the beach every summer.

13.8 🔊

1 When I was young, I wouldn't clean up my bedroom. It made my mom really angry!
2 My brother and I would play video games for hours when we were young.
3 I didn't use to drink tea when I was little. Now I drink it all day long!
4 In college, I would often meet my friends for coffee after classes had finished for the day.

14.1 🔊

1 This train ticket is **half as** expensive as that one because of the 50 percent discount.
2 He is **just as** intelligent as his brother. They both got high grades.

③ Peter is **nearly as** good at soccer as the others. He'll catch up quickly.

④ My new place is **nowhere near as** big as my old one. It only has one bedroom instead of four.

⑤ The new album is **not quite as** catchy as their old stuff. I liked their first album a little more.

⑥ My new computer is **not quite as** fast as my old one. It's actually a little slower.

⑦ This new soft drink tastes **nearly as** good as SodaUp, but it's not quite the same.

⑧ The car was **nowhere near as** expensive as we'd thought. It was a real bargain.

⑨ They both worked hard. She deserved to win **just as** much as he did.

14.2

① Frank's ② Neither ③ Morello's
④ Morello's ⑤ Frank's ⑥ Morello's
⑦ Neither

14.3 ◄))

① This train isn't quite as fast as we'd thought.
② He can't type as quickly as she can.
③ It was nowhere near as good as I'd hoped.
④ It tasted just as good as it did last time.
⑤ She doesn't shop as much as she used to.
⑥ They ran as quickly as they could.
⑦ The car wasn't nearly as fast as we thought.
⑧ He told us to do it as efficiently as possible.
⑨ Cooking took half as long as usual today.
⑩ I wasn't as confident as I was before.
⑪ These pastries are just as good as Ann's.

14.4 ◄))

① Most people think that if a product has a **high price**, it must be good quality.
② My friend Robbie is a very **heavy sleeper**. Nothing wakes him up!
③ I was very pleased to hear that my teacher has a **high opinion** of me.
④ After traveling for thirty hours with very little sleep, I needed some **strong coffee**.
⑤ Discount retailers like this one sell everything at a **low price**.
⑥ Everyone leaves work at about 5pm, so there's always **heavy traffic** at that time.
⑦ I like **weak coffee** with lots of milk in it.

14.5 ◄))

① I love cakes and candy. You could say **that have a sweet tooth**.
② Sometimes it's fun to spend money **on a three-course meal**.
③ My brother is a businessman **so he has to wine-and-dine clients**.
④ The dinner party was amazing. My friends **went out of their way to cook for us**.
⑤ He cooked an interesting **savory dish using tofu and fish**.

14.6 Réponses modèles

① Catherine was not quite as enthusiastic about banking as her sister was.
② Catherine's friends were working about half as many hours as she was.
③ Catherine's mom was just as worried as her dad about how much she was working.
④ Catherine thought her second experience of studying was not quite as scary as her first.
⑤ The photography major was just as interesting as Catherine had thought it would be.

15

15.1 ◄))

① The more I think about the exam, **the more nervous I feel.**
② The older you are, **the wiser you become.**
③ The more the boat shook, **the more frightened we felt.**
④ The more advanced the course becomes, **the more difficult it gets.**
⑤ The higher up the mountain you go, **the colder it gets.**

15.2 ◄))

① The more I earn, the more I save.
② The more time we spend outdoors, the happier we feel.
③ The harder Joel works, the unhappier he becomes.

15.3 ◄))

① The **more** difficult a challenge is, the **more** I enjoy it.
② The **earlier** you start working on the project, **the** sooner you'll finish.
③ **The longer** an action film is, **the** less I want to watch it.
④ The **hotter** it is, **the thirstier** I become in the summer months.
⑤ The **angrier** Peter gets, **the less** sure I become of how to react.
⑥ **The** more successful my sister becomes, **the** more stressed she gets.
⑦ The **friendlier** a person is, the more popular they are at work.
⑧ The more I study, the less **certain** I become of what I know.
⑨ The **more** dangerous an adventure sport is, the more I like it.
⑩ **The** further you swim in the mornings and evenings, **the** fitter you'll become.
⑪ The **less** junk food you eat in the day, the **slimmer** you'll get.
⑫ **The** more interviews with successful people I read, **the** more I realize success is down to hard work.

15.4

① busier and busier ② and more tired
③ the earlier the better ④ and more stressful
⑤ the sooner the better

15.5 ◄))

① Because of climate change, temperatures on Earth are getting **hotter and hotter**.
② In developed countries, people are getting **richer and richer**. Is this fair?
③ Ben practices the piano every day so he's getting **better and better**.
④ Every time I look at my baby daughter she seems **more and more beautiful** to me.
⑤ I waved as the boat got **farther and farther** away, and a tear slid down my cheek.

16

16.1 ◄))

① enrol in
② attend classes
③ strikingly different
④ take a test / take an exam
⑤ contrast differences
⑥ undergraduate
⑦ meet a deadline
⑧ a world of difference
⑨ miss a deadline
⑩ continuous assessment
⑪ postgraduate
⑫ give someone feedback on something
⑬ clear distinction

17

17.1 ◄))

① such as = **for example**
② additionally = **in addition**
③ furthermore = **moreover**
④ therefore = **as a result**
⑤ to conclude = **in conclusion**

17.2 ◄))

① It is, therefore, easier to study **in a place where you know the language.**
② There are a lot of possibilities. For **example, studying at a university.**
③ First, you have to think about **what the benefits would be.**
④ In conclusion, I think studying **abroad is something everyone should try.**
⑤ Moreover, you also have the chance **to meet people from other countries.**
⑥ If you know Spanish, for instance, **go to a Spanish-speaking country.**

17.3

1 False 2 False 3 True 4 False
5 True 6 False

17.4

17.5 🔊

1 If **they want** to go on the trip, they'll need to sign up today.
2 Unless **we get** three more registrations, we won't be able to run the class.
3 If he wants to join the Spanish class, he **will need** to email me this evening.
4 If **you join** the committee, you will have to give up a lot of your free time.
5 If you want to meet up for coffee later, I **will be** in the library.
6 I **will have** to cancel Tuesday's class unless we find another room.
7 If **they want** to find out more about our club, we **will be** at the fair tomorrow.
8 Unless **we hear** from them in the next five minutes, we will start without them.
9 If **you are** a biology student, you will need to buy a lab coat by Friday.
10 If **you need** a study partner next semester, I might be available.
11 If **they are able** to come to the film night, it will be a great evening.

17.6 🔊

1 If you sign up for this study group, **you have to come to weekly meetings.**
2 When you are a student ambassador, **you are a representative of the university.**
3 You will fail the exam **unless you work a lot harder.**
4 When I give you homework, **I expect you to do it.**
5 Send me an email **if you have any further questions.**
6 If you want to find a part-time job, **you can go to our career center.**
7 If you're interested in hiking, **you can join the Expeditions Society.**
8 Unless you can pay a big fine, **don't take your library books back late.**
9 When you go into the second year, **you can apply to study abroad.**
10 I am always ready to listen **if you need someone to talk to.**
11 If you want to study French, **you should visit the language center.**
12 Unless you attend classes regularly, **you will not understand this subject.**

17.7

3

18

18.1 🔊

1 approximately half 2 a small minority
3 the vast majority 4 just under a third

18.2 🔊

1 In **a few** cases students are asked to retake the year.
2 In **a number** of cases students drop out and leave college.
3 In **some** cases students can ask to defer and start college a year later.
4 In **a majority** of cases students make friends for life while in college.
5 In **most** cases students live on campus in their first year.
6 **Just under** a quarter of students have part-time jobs.

18.3

1 False 2 True 3 True 4 Not given
5 True 6 False 7 Not given 8 True
9 True 10 Not given 11 False

18.4 🔊

1 In a **few** cases, the company will hire candidates who do not have a degree
2 Approximately **two-thirds** of students regularly buy fast food.
3 I'm not prepared to pay as **much** as $180 to go to a music festival.
4 In **some** cases, patients are asked to stay at home so they don't infect others.
5 The plane tickets are really cheap. They cost as **little** as $30.
6 Can you believe it? Out of 120 professors, as **many** as 90 can speak three languages.
7 **Well over** 90 percent of students complete their studies.
8 In a **minority** of cases, students will have to find their own accommodation.
9 In **most** cases, you'll feel much better within a week.
10 The yoga class isn't very popular. There are as **few** as three people at most classes.
11 Just **under** a quarter of students take more than a year to find a job.
12 **Just over** half of students meet their future partner in college.

18.5

1 False 2 Not given 3 True 4 False
5 False 6 Not given

18.6 🔊

1 Really? I heard that the class sizes are **really small**.
2 Is that so? My experience is very **different** from that.

---

3 Is that right? I heard that it is **clean and comfortable**.

19

19.1

2

19.2 🔊

1 Money for setting up a new business **can be raised** through these websites.
2 Rachel **had been selling** at local events before she decided to get serious.
3 Rachel found out that social media **was being used** by other entrepreneurs.
4 Rachel **set up** her own website by using a simple web platform.
5 Within a week, Rachel **had been offered** funding by eight investors online.
6 Rachel **took on** someone to work for her as her business grew.
7 Later Rachel **found** another crowdfunding website.
8 Rachel's new tea shop **will be located** in London.

19.3 🔊

1 Their products **were being sold at the baseball club last weekend.**
2 Social media **can easily be used by entrepreneurs to promote their businesses.**
3 Our detailed business plan **for the next 12 months will be written this weekend.**
4 His old catering business **had already been sold when he bought the hairdressing business.**
5 All of the cooking equipment **was delivered to our new shop yesterday.**

19.4 🔊

1 **Check-in** time at this hotel is 2pm. Your room won't be free until then.
2 Just put the **leftovers** in the fridge. We'll have them for lunch tomorrow.
3 Don't forget to make a **backup** of your files.
4 The police are looking for an **onlooker** who may have seen the bank robbers.
5 Let me make it clear from the **outset** what I expect from you.
6 In the first part of the lesson I'll give you a lot of **input** and then you'll be able to use it.
7 Getting angry with the boss in the boardroom was his **downfall**. He'll never work here again.
8 The police have announced a **crackdown** on bicycle thieves.

19.5
❶ True ❷ False ❸ True ❹ False

19.6 🔊
❶ When my dad cooks, **there are never any leftovers.**
❷ After losing my data, I know **it's essential to have a backup.**
❸ Never share your login **with anyone for security reasons.**
❹ There has been a crackdown **on social media use during class.**
❺ I always prefer an early check-in **to make the journey easier.**
❻ The police put up a line **to hold back onlookers.**

20

20.1 🔊
❶ I'm taking my dictionary **in case I need to look some words up.**
❷ What if I run out of time? **Then I won't finish the exam.**
❸ Suppose I don't understand a question. **I will ask the examiner to repeat it.**
❹ What if catch a cold? **That would make it difficult to concentrate.**
❺ Suppose I forget to turn my phone off. **I would fail the exam if someone calls me.**
❻ I'm going to set two alarms **in case I don't hear the first one.**

20.2
❶ Likely ❷ Unlikely ❸ Likely ❹ Unlikely
❺ Unlikely ❻ Likely

20.3 🔊
❶ I know it's not likely, but suppose I **had** an accident on the way to school.
❷ What if I **help** you review and you help me with my essay?
❸ Suppose we **found** a rat in our classroom and the test was delayed.
❹ You should ask if you can have more time just in case they **say** yes.
❺ Suppose another fire alarm **goes** off during the exam. Will they give us more time?
❻ What if we **didn't** know the answers to any of the questions? What would we do?

20.4 🔊
❶ If you **got** 100 percent in the biology exam on Monday, I would be amazed.
❷ We **will learn** much more quickly if we use an app to help us learn the words.
❸ What if it **snowed** and we couldn't get to school on the day of the exam?
❹ If my brother **won** the prize for the best student, I would be shocked.

❺ My parents will be happy if I **pass** the chemistry exam.
❻ If we bought a new car, we **would not be** late so often!
❼ She **will not finish** in time if she doesn't start her project soon.
❽ It would be so much less stressful if the teachers **gave** us some help.

20.5 🔊 Réponses modèles
❶ If I could decide how long the weekend was, I would make it four days long.
❷ If I have time, I will watch a crime show.
❸ If I could go anywhere for six months, I'd go to Peru.
❹ If I could have dinner with anyone, I'd choose Orson Welles.
❺ If I had the chance to study abroad, I would go to the Sorbonne in Paris.
❻ If I won the lottery, the first thing I'd buy would be a house for my parents.
❼ If I won tickets to a concert, I'd go with my brother.

21

21.1 🔊
❶ dead-end job
❷ set your sights on something
❸ hands-on experience
❹ get ahead
❺ be fired
❻ be snowed under
❼ tackle something head-on
❽ take off
❾ bottom of the career ladder
❿ nine-to-five
⓫ laid off
⓬ give and take
⓭ working environment

22

22.1 🔊
❶ After **completing** my studies I decided to take a year off and go traveling.
❷ **Developing** original and innovative products is something I'm particularly interested in.
❸ **Instead of** spending the summer having fun, I want to get a job and earn some money.
❹ **Since** attending a workshop on project management, I have a deeper understanding of this area.
❺ I've applied **for** so many jobs, but I haven't had a single interview.
❻ **Before** starting my studies, I had earned very high grades at school.

❼ While **volunteering** at a school in Peru, I realized how much I enjoy helping other people.
❽ **As well as** giving me a strong theoretical grounding, my degree also gave me practical skills.
❾ **Starting** work at your company immediately would be perfect for me.
❿ They're **not only** doing interviews for the job, they're also asking people to take a test.
⓫ **After** completing my studies, I have gained some work experience in marketing.
⓬ After **seeing** the job ad, I knew this job was the one for me and I applied for it.
⓭ **Without** working in human resources for 10 years, I wouldn't be able to take on this role.
⓮ Since **qualifying** as a doctor, I've started working at a local hospital.
⓯ **Going** out into the community to work with people has been very valuable.

22.2 Réponses modèles
❶ Experience of the logistics industry would be particularly desirable.
❷ The candidate will be responsible for growing the number of visitors to the company's website.
❸ The ideal candidate would stay in the company for a long time.
❹ You need to have a Bachelor's degree or higher to apply for this job.
❺ You need to be able to speak and write English perfectly.
❻ You have to send your résumé and a cover letter to the company if you want to apply for this job.

22.3 🔊
❶ I have recently **completed** a degree in mechanical engineering.
❷ This has prepared me very **well** for working in the area of product management.
❸ One course I **did** on brand design is particularly relevant to this position.
❹ I have a keen interest in **following** developments in the food industry.
❺ Thank you for taking the time to consider my application and I look forward to **hearing** from you.

22.4 🔊
❶ The contents of my degree course have prepared me very well for **this position**.
❷ I have a **strong interest** in the energy sector and have work experience in this area.
❸ You will find that I'm a fast and accurate writer with a keen **eye for detail**.
❹ I would be able to **take on** the responsibility that this position involves.
❺ The experience I have gained in my previous jobs is **particularly relevant** to this position.

22.5 🔊
1 I think I would make an excellent office supervisor at some point in the future.
2 In my old job I experienced some conflict with colleagues.
3 I've organized a lot of events such as trade fairs and product launches.
4 Since graduating from college, I've gained a lot of experience in public relations.
5 I may look to move into a managerial job in a few years' time.
6 I would like to be involved with the organization of marketing campaigns.
7 As you can see, I have extensive work experience in the area of retail.
8 My skills are significantly superior to those of the average candidate.
9 Thank you for taking the time to consider my application.
10 My work experience is particularly relevant to this position.
11 I have an in-depth knowledge of product development processes.
12 I've wanted to be an electrician for a very long time.
13 I very much look forward to hearing from you.

23

23.1 🔊
1 Could you tell me if **you have any relevant experience in this area**?
2 I was wondering whether **your studies are relevant to this area**.
3 We'd like to know whether **you've applied for any other jobs**.
4 I was wondering if **you like working on a team**.
5 We'd like to know if **you're a good team player**.
6 Do you have any idea what **you would like to be doing in 10 years' time**?
7 Could you tell me what **your weaknesses are**?
8 I was wondering where **you worked after completing your studies**.
9 I'm curious to know where **in China you studied**.
10 Could you tell us which **area of our activities you're particularly interested in**?
11 I'd like to know if **you've ever worked abroad**.

23.2 🔊
1 Could you tell us which projects you've worked on?
2 I'd like to know how long you plan to work for us.

3 I was wondering where you studied abroad.
4 We'd like to know if you'd like to do further training.

23.3 🔊
1 Could you tell us **how you got along with your last boss**?
2 Do you have any idea **where you want to be in five years' time**?
3 I'm curious to know if **you've ever worked with children before**.
4 I was wondering whether **you've ever managed a website before**.
5 Could you tell us **why we should employ you**?

23.4 🔊
1 Would you be prepared to travel a lot? **Let's see. It would depend where you wanted me to go.**
2 Would you like to lead a team one day? **Well, I don't know. Managing a team is something I might be interested in.**
3 Could you come in for an interview? **Let me see. I'll check my schedule and let you know.**
4 Could you send us references from your previous employers? **Well, yes, that should be possible. I'll check with them.**
5 Can we count on you to stay with us long-term? **Maybe we should wait and see how I settle in here first.**

23.5
1 How many people are on her team
2 She likes to control everything
3 Her energy inspires the people on her team
4 She wouldn't want to earn less than before
5 Rose will think about what she would expect

23.6 🔊 Réponses modèles
1 **Yes, where to start?** I'm a dedicated worker and a great communicator.
2 **Oh, let me see.** I'd like to have a position in management.
3 **Well,** it's something that I enjoy and would like to continue doing.
4 **Good question, let me see.** I have a keen eye for detail and I always give 100 percent.
5 **Let me see.** I did once take over from my boss while he was on vacation.
6 **I'm not sure.** It would depend how much you needed me to do.
7 **Let's see. I suppose** I could start next month.

24

24.1 🔊
1 She finally managed **to cut** down the number of hours she works from 40 to 35.
2 I think our manager should allow us **to leave** work a bit earlier on Friday afternoon.
3 This new piece of software enables me **to make** updates very quickly.
4 Sam threatened **to leave** if the boss doesn't find a new employee to help him.
5 I'm the person in my office who always **volunteers** to stay late.
6 This is the first time that a colleague has invited me **to have** dinner at their home.
7 The merger deal we completed last month has caused our profits **to** increase.
8 He doesn't like people **telling** him what to do while he's at work.
9 The boss has offered **to send** me on a training course to improve my computer skills.
10 He enjoys **playing** the role of the hot-shot manager when visitors come.

24.2 🔊
1 My colleague enjoys **hearing** from satisfied customers.
2 My new smartphone **enables** me to stay connected with my office wherever I am.
3 She hates her colleagues **telling** her what she should do in her department.
4 We like our customers **to give** us feedback on the services we provide them.
5 My boss has **offered to** give me an office of my own next year.

24.3
1 False 2 True 3 Not given
4 True 5 False

24.4 🔊
1 She always stops **to look** at what's on at the movie theater when we walk past it.
2 I remember **watching** that movie with Brian Owen, but it was a very long time ago.
3 She reminded him **to go** to the supermarket after work, but he still forgot!
4 I wish they would stop **looking** at us like that. They're making me nervous.
5 He finally remembered **to buy** me some flowers for my birthday. He usually forgets.
6 When I was a child, my mother always encouraged me **to eat** fruit and vegetables.
7 The turbulence caused the airplane **to move** from side to side for about 10 minutes.
8 He knew that we weren't interested in what he had to say, but he still went on **talking**.
9 I would advise you **to take** an aspirin for your headache.

⑩ Did you see Donald volunteering **to organize** the office party this year?
⑪ He tried **to push** the table through the door of our new living room, but it was too big.
⑫ The boss threatened **to make** us work all weekend if we didn't finish the project by Friday.

24.5 🔊
① Jade remembered giving me that doll as a birthday present when I was a child.
② The inspector advised us to change our safety procedures in the factory.
③ She likes people talking about how great she is. She has a very big ego!
④ The loan we got from the bank enabled us to build an extension on our house.
⑤ I'll write a note to remind myself to bring that book with me next week.

24.6 Réponses modèles
① Jackie advises Lynn to talk to her boss.
② Jackie suggests Lynn's boss could allow her to do a training course.
③ Jackie says that Lynn should leave her job and look for something else.
④ Jackie believes that Lynn is very talented.
⑤ Jackie thinks Lynn shouldn't accept people telling her she's not good enough to become a manager.

25

25.1 🔊
① Jake lent me a pencil.
② The teacher offered me some help.
③ She borrowed a book from Liz.
④ Susanne sent me a postcard from her vacation.
⑤ We donated some old clothes to the families.
⑥ They paid 20 dollars for the book.
⑦ John sent me an email yesterday.
⑧ I'm sure she told you the truth.
⑨ We gave the dog some biscuits.
⑩ He brought his computer to her house.
⑪ Joanne gave him her notes.
⑫ She lent her car to her son.
⑬ They bought the teacher some chocolates.
⑭ Brian passed the message on to Fiona for me.
⑮ Richard lent me his pen.
⑯ She always gives me a ride to work.
⑰ The teacher gave bad grades to those students.
⑱ Jason passed a note to me in class.
⑲ Kathryn lent her son some money.
⑳ They brought a lot of energy to the discussion.
㉑ He sold his old car to the neighbor.
㉒ They gave her some candy.

㉓ She gave some books she didn't need to them.

25.2 🔊
① Robert gave me a lot of help.
② Emma gave that book to me.
③ He lent his bike to a friend.
④ They passed the message on to me.
⑤ He gave his wife a great birthday present.

25.3 🔊
① He sold his books to another student.
② She bought a car for her daughter.
③ He passed the message on to her.
④ They donated money to the charity.
⑤ He lent some money to his son.
⑥ I sent him an email.

25.4
① True ② Not given ③ True ④ True
⑤ True ⑥ Not given

25.5 🔊
① However, I thought **nothing ventured, nothing gained** and I decided to just go for it anyway.
② Things really took off when I met an angel investor who basically wrote me a **blank check**.
③ Her faith in my abilities was the **ace up my sleeve** that gave me an edge over the competition.
④ As a result, I was able to **hit the ground running** and everyone was coming to me.
⑤ I had really **cornered the market** there.

26

26.1 🔊
① take minutes
② give a presentation
③ take questions
④ get down to business
⑤ sum up
⑥ show of hands
⑦ set a date
⑧ run out of time
⑨ on the agenda
⑩ board of directors
⑪ attend a meeting
⑫ conference call
⑬ absent

27

27.1 🔊
① Anna, you're welcome to help **yourself** to tea or coffee and cookies.
② I taught **myself** to use this computer program.
③ He is very proud of **himself** for getting the highest grade in his class.
④ You can all sit **yourselves** down anywhere you like.
⑤ We helped **ourselves** to the free food at the staff party.
⑥ I'm annoyed with **myself** for not thinking about that.
⑦ She accidentally cut **herself** while she was cooking.
⑧ The members of the team argued among **themselves** for about half an hour.
⑨ They're very pleased with **themselves** because their boss praised their work.
⑩ I often ask **myself** why I decided to leave the country and move to the city.
⑪ He felt that he had let **himself** down.

27.2 🔊
① My grandparents are 90 years old, but they can still do everything for **themselves.**
② He prides **himself** on his honesty and integrity.
③ Ramona is really busy today. Could you take this package to the post office for **her**?
④ You don't need to translate that for me. I can do it for **myself**.
⑤ They got the contract because they worked much harder than **us**.
⑥ You are all very welcome. Please make **yourselves** at home here.
⑦ Our neighbors were shouting at **each other** until 10 o'clock last night.

27.3 🔊
① We want you to prepare the presentations yourselves.
② The CEO himself mentioned me during his annual speech.
③ I am very proud! I repaired the bike myself.
④ We should be proud that we've achieved all of this by ourselves.
⑤ Food itself is changing and so are our eating habits.
⑥ They congratulated themselves on a job well done.
⑦ The shop manager herself came down to apologize to me for her mistake.

27.4 🔊
① I'm glad that we were able to do it **ourselves** without asking the boss for help.
② The presentation **itself** went well, but the meeting afterwards went badly.

3 All of the children behaved **themselves** really well during the flight.

4 The president's wife **herself** came to shake my hand and give me the award.

5 I felt very pleased with **myself** when I found out that my painting had won the prize.

6 This is the first time that he's been able to walk by **himself** since the accident.

7 I'm looking forward to having the house to **myself** while my parents are away.

8 You should all help **yourselves** to any books on my bookcase that you're interested in.

9 Your mother isn't going to wash your clothes anymore. You'll have to do it **yourself.**

27.5 ◀))

1 I can't come to the English lesson as **I'm completely snowed under at work.**

2 The boss has asked her to **stay behind this evening.**

3 Customer service is something we **need to work on this year.**

4 My computer is not working. Can **you sort it out?**

5 On Fridays we usually **knock off at 12 o'clock.**

27.6 ◀))

1 Sometimes, I'm so snowed **under** at work that I don't have time to eat my lunch.

2 I need to sort **out** these customer queries.

3 She allowed **herself** enough time to drive to the bank and park her car before the meeting.

4 Our project manager has given **us** more responsibility.

5 I'm still trying to catch **up** with the work I should have done last week.

6 We can't tear him **away** from the video game he's playing for more than ten minutes.

7 I think I have taken **on** too much work. I'm absolutely exhausted!

8 I always ask for challenging projects, but my boss never lets **me** do them.

9 Here's the safety information for working in this building. Could you all familiarize **yourselves** with it?

10 I'm sorry, but I'll have to ask Jason to deal with this. I'm completely snowed **under** at the moment.

11 When students fail their exams, they usually don't blame **themselves.**

12 When I take my children on the train, I bring some toys that they can occupy **themselves** with.

28.1 ◀))

1 He can't stand **waiting** for people. He doesn't understand why people can't be on time.

2 I have to say that I prefer **cooking** for myself to eating out. I can eat whatever I want then.

3 I hate **moving**, but fresh flowers make a new house feel more like home.

4 How would you propose **solving** the big problems that we have?

5 Your flight had such a long delay that I began **to wonder** if you would ever make it back home.

6 He likes **to go** to a concert or the opera once a month or even more frequently if he can.

7 You continued **to ignore** my concerns even after you had seen the negative effects yourself.

8 I love **swimming** outdoors in a lake or in the ocean, even if the water's quite cold.

9 We started **to plan** our wedding last year as we knew it would take a long time.

28.2 ◀))

1 In our family we usually prefer **beach vacations to city breaks.**

2 The design department proposed **making some changes to the sizes.**

3 Despite being tired, he continued **to run for the last six miles.**

4 We've always really loved **walking in the countryside.**

5 When I was younger I hated **getting up early, but now I like it.**

6 I have to say I can't stand **hearing music from people's phones.**

7 The music was so good that I started **dancing along to it.**

8 Ten years ago he began **saving money so he could buy a house.**

9 Marjorie proposed **putting more time between our meetings.**

28.3 ◀))

1 Now I regret **asking** him about his family. I had no idea what had happened to them.

2 He graduated at the top of his class and we think that he will go on **to be** a successful lawyer.

3 We regret **to inform** you that on this occasion your application was not successful.

4 I remember **putting** my car keys on the table, but then someone must have moved them.

5 Don't worry, he won't forget **to call** you when he arrives in Australia.

6 After our success this season, we're sure the hotel will go on **being** popular next season.

7 Please remember **to write** to catering and ask if they can cater for 80 instead of 60.

8 Can we stop **to buy** some snacks and get coffee at the next service station we get to?

28.4 ◀))

1 We stopped to get coffee.

2 I remembered to buy her a present.

3 I regret telling him that.

4 Did you forget going to Paris with me?

5 They went on celebrating until 2am.

6 I stopped going to the gym in February.

7 Sometimes I forget to charge my phone.

8 I regret to inform you about the changes.

9 I remember visiting you when I was a child.

28.5 ◀))

1 I forgot to ask Valerie if she wanted to join us for dinner this evening.

2 I always remember to close all of the windows when I leave the house.

3 Who would have thought he would go on to be such a successful ballet dancer in the future?

4 The views along the coast road were so beautiful we decided to stop to take photos.

5 I regret saying that he doesn't work as hard as everyone else. He hasn't spoken to me since.

28.6 ◀))

1 She had to go on working into her sixties.

2 We regret to inform you about the flight cancelations.

3 They stopped accepting paper applications two years ago.

4 Please remember to turn your computer off.

28.7 ◀))

1 Why do you always forget **to buy** milk when you go to the supermarket on your own?

2 When are you going to stop **working** there and do something you really want to do?

3 Do you regret **getting** that tattoo of a dolphin on your neck now?

4 Do you think you would like **to run** the whole company one day?

5 Can we stop **to have** dinner at that nice restaurant in town on our way home?

29.1 ◀))

1 She's a **brilliant** scientist. I'm sure she'll win the Nobel Prize for physics one day.

2 The fact that smoking can damage your health was **unknown** to most people until the 1970s.

3 It's amazing that such a **tiny** chip can contain so much data.

4 This scarf was handmade in Malaysia and the design is completely **unique.**

5 Could you please send me this document in a **digital** format? I can then upload it to our site.
6 The weather was **awful** last weekend. It wouldn't stop raining and it was really cold, too.
7 I think it's **disgusting** that there's so much bacteria on our phones.
8 She tries to avoid using cosmetic products that have too many **chemical** ingredients in them.
9 We're very proud of our **industrial** heritage, such as these 19th-century factory buildings.

29.2 ◀))
1 They had an absolutely fantastic trip to South Africa. They're already planning their next trip.
2 He's absolutely fascinated by trains so we decided to buy him a train set for his birthday.
3 The delegates at the conference were largely European with a few North Americans.
4 We wanted to create a completely digital product for today's young people.
5 It's completely impossible to put this table together. I'll never be able to do it.

29.3 ◀))
1 It's **hugely** important that as many people as possible see these billboards.
2 This product is **extremely** useful if you don't have very much time to spend on housework.
3 We think that our customer base will be **rather** interested in this new feature.
4 Our competitors' products are **wholly** inadequate to deal with these challenges.
5 The first design was **absolutely** awful, so we had to get rid of it and create a new one.
6 The coffee machine has a **totally** unique feature that enables you to make hot or cold milk.
7 I'm **utterly** exhausted after putting so much effort into the product launch last week.
8 The CEO can speak **quite** good English, but he's much better at Spanish or Portuguese.
9 Have you noticed that our new packaging designer is **really** talented?

29.4 ◀))
1 I loved it! I thought it was **thoroughly enjoyable** and very funny.
2 I'm shy, so I'd feel **absolutely terrified** if I had to do that.
3 It would be so inconvenient! I'd be **utterly miserable**.

29.5 ◀))
1 I thought the test was fairly **difficult, but my friend found it easy.**
2 Our product will be really **popular with consumers everywhere.**
3 The presentation was pretty **interesting and I learned a lot from it.**

4 My boss sometimes gets quite **annoyed if we fall behind schedule.**

29.6
1 False **2** True **3** Not given **4** True
5 True **6** True **7** Not given
8 Not given **9** False **10** Not given

30

30.1 ◀))
1 He wrote a bad review of the movie **to let everyone know it's terrible.**
2 She took the toaster back **not to get a new one, but to get a refund.**
3 I looked everywhere in the store **in order to find the items I needed.**
4 The store gave them a voucher **so as to keep their business.**
5 He called the restaurant manager **to complain about a rude waiter.**
6 She raised her voice **so that everyone would hear her.**
7 We called the airline **to ask them to cancel our flights.**
8 You need to fill in this form **in order to get your money back.**
9 I called our internet provider **to find out when they will connect us.**
10 I talked to our neighbors **to let them know they're being too noisy.**
11 Now we check all of the pallets **to ensure the goods in them aren't broken.**
12 He looked for the company online **to find out what others think about it.**
13 I called the HR department **to find out about vacancies.**
14 He asked to speak to the chef **to compliment his cooking.**
15 She talked to the salon manager **in order to complain about her haircut.**
16 I covered the goods in shrink wrap **in order to protect them.**

30.2 ◀))
1 She took her car to the garage so that the mechanics could fix it.
2 We use RFID technology so that we can track the goods.
3 He wrote a positive review of the hotel so that other people would know how good it was.
4 I usually get up 5am so that I can go running before I go to work.
5 She spent a lot of time planning her presentation so that she would be well-prepared.

30.3 ◀))
1 Our products are made **to** withstand all temperatures.

2 Our career website is **for** busy professional people.
3 You can use this little USB stick **to** connect to the internet in any location.
4 This headset is **for** video-chatting and web-conferencing.
5 This hi-fi system is only **for** serious music fans, as it's very expensive.

30.4 ◀))
1 Can we offer you a voucher **to show** we are sorry for the inconvenience caused.
2 I will be making a **complaint** about your airline as soon as I get home.
3 I'm not very satisfied **with** the product I received from the company two days ago.
4 Could you **let** me know when the basket of fruit that I ordered last week will arrive?
5 These workers are employed **to** pick and pack the goods in the factory outside the city.
6 Thank you for your prompt **assistance** with the ongoing matter of delayed product delivery.
7 You can use this device **for** cleaning the windows in your house quickly and effectively.
8 I recently **ordered** a pair of running shoes from you as a gift for my sister.
9 I need a **replacement** for this kettle as soon as possible, or else I will require a refund.
10 I look forward **to hearing** from you about the meeting next week.

31

31.1 ◀))
1 extinct
2 harmful to the environment
3 wind farm
4 consume
5 fossil fuels
6 renewable energy
7 endangered
8 solar panel
9 destruction
10 climate change
11 reduce your carbon footprint
12 global warming
13 alternative energy

32

32.1 ◀))
1 If I **had known** it was raining, I **would have brought** my umbrella.
2 I **would not have known** the party was canceled if he **had not told** me.

3 If I **had arrived** at the train station earlier, I **would not have missed** the train.
4 If they **had studied** more, they **might have passed** the exam.
5 If I **had known** you didn't like onions, I **would not have used** them.
6 If I **had not gone** to college, I **might have taken** a gap year.
7 We **would not have put** the box there if we **had known** that it would fall.
8 If I **had realized** he was unhappy, I **could have talked** to him about it.
9 I **would have worn** a suit if I **had known** the CEO was coming to visit us.
10 If we **had given** out more samples, we **would have sold** more products.
11 If she **had known** there was a test, she **would have prepared**.

32.2 🔊
1 If we'd known there was a train strike on, we would've driven there. 2 If I hadn't gone to that party, I wouldn't have met my husband. 3 If I'd worked harder, I might've been promoted last year.

32.3 🔊
1 I would have called you if I had **known** you were in town.
2 If we had taken a taxi, we **wouldn't** have missed our flight.
3 If I **had** left the house at nine, I would not have been late for the interview.
4 I would **have** made it home by 7 o'clock if my train had left on time
5 If we had known the movie was that good, we **would** have gone to see it.

32.4
1 False 2 Not given 3 False
4 False 5 True 6 False 7 True

32.5 🔊
1 If only we **had asked** for a room on the second or third floor. It wouldn't have been so noisy.
2 I wish we had been able to spend more time at that museum. It **was** really interesting.
3 If only we had been there in summer. We **could have taken** a boat trip on the river.
4 I wish we **had gone** to the Eiffel Tower earlier. We might not have had to wait so long.
5 I wish we **had read** the reviews of that restaurant before we decided to eat there.
6 I love that band. If only we **had known** they were doing a concert down the road from the hotel.
7 If only we had taken the train to the airport. We **would have arrived** there faster.

32.6 🔊
1 My brother always makes fun of me. If only **I had a sister instead**!

2 Why didn't I take your advice? I wish **I'd listened to you**.
3 I left my wallet on the train. I wish **I hadn't forgotten it**.
4 My presentation was awful. If only **I'd practiced more**.
5 I got soaked outside. If only **I'd brought my umbrella**.
6 I'm so bored at work. I wish **I'd taken time off**.
7 I hate walking. If only **I hadn't crashed my car**.

33

33.1 🔊
1 You **should** have separated your waste for recycling.
2 We **ought** to have bought fair trade chocolate.
3 She **should not** have wasted so much paper.
4 The company **should not** have dumped their waste in the river.
5 They **should** have used wood from sustainable forests.
6 We **should** have found out about the risks beforehand.
7 You **should** have changed to energy-saving light bulbs.
8 He **should** have turned the lights off when he left.
9 They **ought** to have reduced the amount of traveling their employees do.
10 We **should not** have cut down so much of the rainforest.
11 You **ought** to have drunk tap water instead of bottled water.
12 She **should not** have showered for so long. She's wasting water!
13 They **should not** have flown the goods halfway across the world.
14 We **ought** to have talked to the local community about this.
15 Governments **should** have made a law to stop this happening.
16 We **should not** have buried the waste in that land-fill.
17 He **ought** to have turned his computer off at night.
18 You **should** have stopped using new plastic bags every time you go shopping.

33.2 🔊
1 We should not have dumped the waste in the river.
2 We should not have used so many pesticides in these fields.
3 We should not have overfished the oceans.
4 We ought to have switched to greener cars sooner.

5 We should have thought about the effects of the mine on the river.
6 We should have protected the wildlife from the oil spill.

33.3 🔊
1 We should not have built the dam there.
2 We ought to have started using renewable energy earlier.
3 They should have recycled all their waste materials.
4 We ought to have left the island as it was.
5 We should not have destroyed the orangutans' habitat.
6 They should have thought about the impact on fish supplies.
7 We should not have ignored what the protesters said.
8 We ought to have stored those chemicals more carefully.
9 We should have had more controls at the power plant.

33.4 🔊
1 overconfident 2 overloaded
3 overcrowded 4 overworked
5 overcautious

33.5
1 However, **following** the original explosion, a large oil leak was discovered.
2 It is estimated that oil was flowing into the sea at a rate of 62,000 gallons a day **by that time.**
3 Oil continued to flow into the ocean at this rate **throughout** the next six weeks.
4 Efforts were made to stop the flow of oil **during** that time, but none of them proved successful.
5 **Since then**, the oil spill has become known as one of the worst manmade disasters in recent history.

34

34.1 🔊
1 I'm **afraid of** getting trapped in an elevator, so I always take the stairs.
2 In recent years, there's been a huge **increase in** smartphone ownership.
3 My children sometimes **argue about** who gets to watch TV.
4 I always **ask for** a window seat when I fly so I can look out the window.
5 We'll never **agree about** how to raise children.
6 I think he'll win. All of the signs **point in** his direction.
7 There's been a **decline in** the number of letters people have written in the last decade.

8 The economic situation had the **effect of** pushing house prices down.

9 There's a **lack of** interest in the project among the people in my team.

10 I'm afraid I'm going to be **late for** our appointment this morning.

11 They're really **grateful for** all of the opportunities they've been given.

12 We **talked about** my previous work experience and career goals.

13 There's been a **decline in** the number of people watching live television in recent years.

14 When I call my sister, we **talk about** absolutely everything that's been going on in my life.

34.2 🔊

1 My husband and I sometimes argue **about** whose turn it is to do the dishes.

2 Frank is never late **for** any meetings in the office.

3 The course was canceled due to a lack **of** interest by students.

4 I know a lot of people who are afraid **of** spiders and snakes.

5 She's very grateful **for** the chance to study medicine in the US.

6 Marlon will talk **about** his travels in the Amazon rainforest this evening.

7 I'm so grateful **for** the opportunity you have given me.

34.3

1 True **2** False **3** Not given
4 Not given **5** True **6** Not given

34.4 🔊

1 We are currently searching **for** a suitable location for a new offshore wind farm.

2 The Prime Minister apologized **to** the public for not giving them all of the facts.

3 I'm so bored **with** news stories about how the Earth is getting hotter. It's freezing today!

4 If we reduce the amount of packaging we use, that will result **in** us having less waste.

34.5 🔊

1 **Environmentally-friendly** farming practices help farmers grow more food.

2 **This** government isn't going to stand by and do nothing about climate change.

3 What changes can **you** make in **your** everyday life to make it a healthier one?

4 There **isn't** a future for the nuclear power industry in this country.

34.6

1 talk about **2** suitable for **3** grateful for
4 leads to **5** effect of **6** agree about
7 points in **8** increase in **9** lack of
10 ask for **11** afraid of **12** decline in
13 argued about

35.1 🔊

1 I'm not rich, but I try to donate **a little** money to charity every month.

2 Sadly, there are **few** Sumatran tigers left in the world today.

3 I have **little** patience for people who are always late. I'm always on time!

4 There are very **few** people I would lend money to. But my brother is one of them.

5 **Little** can be done to completely stop climate change in our time.

6 Do you need some help to finish that report? I have **a little** time I can spare.

7 There are **a few** paintings in the museum I haven't seen. Can we stay a bit longer?

8 There's **little** point in explaining it to Jen. She never listens to what I say.

9 I know you're on a diet, but would you like **a little** bit of chocolate?

10 There are very **few** old buildings left in this city. It's sad that we've lost so much history.

11 I don't have lots of friends, but I've got **a few** that I'm really close to.

35.2 🔊

1 There are fewer job opportunities **than there used to be.**

2 People have less time for **hobbies and sports these days.**

3 Fewer people are interested **in local history these days.**

4 Our university offers fewer **courses than it did 10 years ago.**

5 I wish I'd brought less **luggage with me on vacation.**

6 Kelly changed jobs, but she's now **earning less money than before.**

35.3 🔊

1 Less money is spent on care for the elderly.

2 We all need to use less electricity.

3 Fewer people are worried about pollution.

4 I wish I had less work to do.

5 People are having fewer children.

6 Fewer people enjoy gardening nowadays.

35.4

1 False **2** False **3** True
4 True **5** True

35.5 🔊

1 She has been working for quite a **few** years.

2 I've earned quite a **bit** of money.

3 Amal has quite a **bit** of work experience.

4 There are quite a **few** students in this class.

5 I've spent quite a **bit** of time on this report.

6 Jo has made quite a **few** friends at university.

7 There's quite a **bit** of rice left over.

8 There are quite a **few** things I have to do.

9 It took quite a **bit** of effort to finish the race.

10 I've got quite a **few** pairs of sneakers.

11 We've got quite a **few** vacations planned.

12 She gave me quite a **bit** of useful advice.

13 There's quite a **bit** of garbage on the floor.

35.6 🔊

1 The park is empty. There must be **fewer than** 10 people here.

2 My daughter's school is tiny. It has **fewer than** five teachers.

3 Seattle is **less than** 20 miles from here. It won't take long to drive there.

4 Applicants should supply no **fewer than** two references.

5 The plane leaves in **less than** half an hour. We'd better hurry!

6 I've got **less than** $2 in cash. Could you lend me some money, please?

7 The company had to cut some jobs, so we now have **fewer than** 15 employees.

8 It's **less than** 10 minutes until the game starts. I'm so excited!

9 I'm afraid the course is canceled because **fewer than** 10 people signed up.

10 Jeremy is being paid **less than** all his friends. He wants a new job.

11 I always pack light. My suitcase weighs **less than** 12 pounds.

12 It's very disappointing that **fewer than** eight countries signed the agreement.

36.1 🔊

1 make a wish
2 set of beliefs
3 have serious misgivings / doubts
4 good / bad omen
5 gossip
6 word of mouth
7 drop a hint
8 pure luck
9 folklore
10 urban myth
11 beginner's luck
12 start / spread a rumor
13 believe in something

37.1 🔊

1 Chris hasn't turned up for training. He **might not** have realized it was today.

2 Your phone **might not** have been stolen. Have you checked in your desk?

❸ I found a wallet. It **might** have been dropped by someone walking to the station.
❹ Liz isn't answering her emails. She **may** have gone away.
❺ I **may** have forgotten to send Lola a birthday card. I'm not sure.
❻ That strange noise **could** have been a fox outside. There are a lot of them in this area.
❼ I'm sure Les **could not** have sent such a rude message. He's usually such a gentleman.
❽ Jen and Will are late. They **might** have missed the train.
❾ Helena **could not** have grown 20 inches last year. That's too much in 12 months!
❿ That bag is a fake. You **could not** have bought a real one. It was far too cheap.
⓫ You **might not** have caught the flu. It might just be a bad cold.
⓬ I **may** have left my glasses at work. I can't find them.
⓭ You **might not** need an operation. You might just need to take some medicine.
⓮ You **could not** have seen Sally in town yesterday. She's in China.
⓯ It **might not** have been Sally I saw in town. But it was someone who looks like her.
⓰ Your purse **could** have been stolen when you were waiting in line at the market.
⓱ We **may not** have bought the right ingredients for the cake. I'm not sure. Let's check.

37.2 🔊
❶ She couldn't have gone out. All her clothes are dirty!
❷ Anyone could have left the freezer door open.
❸ They may not have remembered to close the window.
❹ They may have had a party.
❺ They may have forgotten to down the hob.
❻ They might have made a big dinner for lots of people.

37.3 🔊
❶ My car has a scratch on it. Someone could have reversed into it in the parking lot.
❷ Your email could have gone into my junk folder. I'll check again.
❸ You could not have visited my old school. It was turned into an office in 2012.
❹ You could not have spoken to Jill on the phone. She's flying to Brazil right now.
❺ I might not have said the right thing to Annabel. She looked a bit upset.

37.4 🔊
❶ They **said they couldn't believe what they were seeing.**
❷ She **said she wasn't lying.**
❸ She **told me she didn't believe in things like ghosts.**
❹ He **said he had heard a terrible scream the night before.**

❺ She **said that she would never stay in a castle ever again.**
❻ She **said she took a photo and there was a ghost in it.**
❼ He **told me that they had had a lot of fun on Halloween.**
❽ They **told me they were so scared that they couldn't move.**

37.5 🔊
❶ I asked him how much his new jacket was.
❷ I asked him if / whether he felt tired.
❸ I asked her if / whether they were going to get married.
❹ I asked him what he had done last weekend.
❺ I asked her if / whether Carina was good enough to play for the team.
❻ I asked him if / whether he was busy right then.
❼ I asked him where he had gone on vacation.
❽ I asked her if / whether she would call me back when she was free.
❾ I asked her if / whether Robert was the new office manager.

37.6 🔊
❶ I asked her what her favorite food was.
❷ I asked him if / whether he was nervous about the exam.
❸ I asked him where he played tennis.
❹ I asked him if / whether she was easy to talk to.
❺ I asked her if / whether they were a difficult team to play.
❻ I asked them when they were going away.
❼ I asked him why he was sad.

38

38.1 🔊
❶ Someone could have **taken** my coat because they thought it was theirs.
❷ They **must** have already left. That's the only explanation.
❸ He couldn't have **written** such a good essay without any help from his teachers.
❹ There **may / might** have been an accident, but I'm not really sure.
❺ I know it's unlikely, but someone **may/might** have found the money and handed it in.
❻ He might have **given** me the wrong directions. He doesn't know this town very well.
❼ He couldn't **have** known that they would ask him a question about that. That's unfair.
❽ It can't have **been** a ghost. They don't really exist!
❾ She must have **been** imagining it. There's nobody upstairs.

38.2 🔊
❶ Have you checked your phone? **She could have tried to call you.**
❷ He's not answering the door. **He might have left already.**
❸ I still can't get through to her. **She might have left her phone at home.**
❹ They must have changed their address. **That's why our letters keep being returned.**
❺ Have you looked in the top drawer? **He might have left the keys there.**
❻ Their plane might have been delayed. **Is there anything on the arrivals board?**
❼ You must have dialled the wrong number. **Nobody called Sheila lives here.**
❽ We may have lost James and Katie. **They're no longer following behind us.**
❾ He can't have thrown the tickets away! **They must be here somewhere.**

38.3 🔊
❶ I **might** have won the competition if my entry had arrived in time.
❷ They **can't** have lost their way. They know this area very well.
❸ I **must** have done something to upset her. She's not speaking to me.
❹ She **couldn't** have opened that door. She doesn't have a key for it.
❺ They **may** have destroyed those documents. We haven't found them.

38.4 🔊
❶ You must **have dealt with** a lot of customers over the last 20 years.
❷ Mom and Dad might **have hidden** our presents in this cupboard.
❸ He can't **have left** without saying goodbye. He must still be here.
❹ The children might **have outgrown** these toys. They prefer video games now.
❺ They must **have run** very fast to finish the race in such good time.
❻ They can't **have told** you everything. There's a lot more that you need to know.
❼ The students might **have gone** to the classroom we were in last semester instead.

38.5
❶ True ❷ False ❸ True ❹ False ❺ False

39

39.1 🔊
❶ If he **were** more organized, he wouldn't have been late for work again today.
❷ If I had lost my job, **I would be** living with my parents again now.
❸ If he had kept on learning English, he **would be** fluent by now.

④ If they **had known** how stormy it would be, they wouldn't be outside today.
⑤ If your aunt hadn't lent you money, you **wouldn't be able to** buy a house now.
⑥ If he **were** more confident, he wouldn't have failed his driving test.
⑦ If you had gone to college, you might **have** a good job by now.
⑧ If they had finished painting the bedroom, we **wouldn't have to** sleep in the loft tonight.

39.2 🔊
① I would wear my coat **if I hadn't forgotten it**.
② If we had saved more money, **we wouldn't have to be so thrifty now**.
③ If you had believed what they said, **you would not be where you are today**.
④ He wouldn't be so bad at cooking **if his Dad had shown him how to do it**.
⑤ He might be more patient **if he hadn't already been waiting so long**.
⑥ If he had reserved a seat on the train, **he wouldn't have to stand for two hours**.
⑦ She wouldn't always be late **if she had bought herself a new watch**.
⑧ If you had read all of the questions, **you wouldn't think that the test was easy**.

39.3 🔊
① He would feel better if he had **slept** a little more last night.
② If you had **prepared** for the interview properly, you wouldn't be so nervous now.
③ You wouldn't be stuck here if you had **told** the hotel staff about the problem.
④ If you had **set** off earlier, you wouldn't have to rush so much now.
⑤ He would be less stressed if he had **taken** more time out to relax.
⑥ If they hadn't **sent** our luggage to the wrong terminal, we would be home by now.
⑦ She might not be such a good typist if she hadn't **spent** so much time at the computer.

39.4 🔊
① If he **had told** me how upset he was, I would still be there comforting him.
② If I were a good cook, I **would have invited** you to lunch at our place by now.
③ He **would have stroked** Fido if he wasn't so scared of dogs.
④ If they weren't going to France tomorrow, they **would have gone** to your party.
⑤ We **could have gone** to the theater if we weren't busy tonight.
⑥ I would be surprised if Katherine **had wanted** me to go to the ball with her.
⑦ If the teacher were here, she **would have told** you all to be quiet.
⑧ If I **had moved** to America, I might be rich and happy now.
⑨ I would be happy to help you if I **hadn't already agreed** to help Jack.

⑩ If they **had learned** to ski, they could go on a skiing vacation next year.
⑪ If we **had looked** at the map earlier, we wouldn't be so lost!
⑫ If I had taken that job, I **would be** earning a lot more money now.

40

40.1 🔊
① I can't remember what we decided about the color, but I'm sure it'll be bright, **whatever** it is.
② **Whenever** I go on vacation abroad, I always try the dishes that are typical for that country.
③ I'm sure the new boss will do a good job and treat everyone fairly, **whoever** he or she is.
④ They always believe that they will win the lottery one day, **however** small the chances are.
⑤ She always ignores any criticism she gets, **whatever** anyone says about her.
⑥ **Whenever** I fly, I always make sure that I get to the airport two hours before my flight time.
⑦ I don't think I'll be able to find the answer to this math problem, **however** hard I try.
⑧ We could talk about this on the phone or I could arrange a meeting, **whichever** you prefer.
⑨ He always finds the time to call and say goodnight to me **wherever** he is in the world.

40.2 🔊
① **Whoever** completes the questionnaire first will win an exciting prize.
② We always stay in touch by text message or email **whenever** we're apart.
③ I won't give up until I reach the top of the mountain, **however** hard it gets.
④ I can pick you up at the airport or you can take the train, **whichever** you prefer.
⑤ I'm not going to put up with this kind of behavior from him, **whoever** he is.
⑥ We can have Chinese or Italian food or something else, **whatever** you want to do.
⑦ I always take a little first aid kit with me **whenever** I go on vacation.
⑧ I'm sure she'll look beautiful in her dress, **whichever** one she chooses.
⑨ She's determined to change his mind about the Nigeria project, **however** long it takes.

40.3 🔊
① I always fear I'm going to have a bad day **whenever I walk under a ladder.**
② Whatever happens in my life, **my superstitions bring me comfort.**
③ Whoever told you that **must be very superstitious.**

④ My mother believes in superstitions, **however often they prove to be false.**
⑤ Whenever a family member gets married, **I give them something blue for luck.**
⑥ This horse shoe will bring me luck, **however difficult life gets.**
⑦ She always wears that ring, **however strange it looks.**
⑧ Whenever she sees a black cat, **she thinks that it'll bring her bad luck.**

40.4 🔊
① come rain or shine ② throw caution to the wind ③ on cloud nine ④ a bolt from the blue ⑤ steal someone's thunder
⑥ right as rain

40.5 🔊
① That's a bolt **from** the blue. I had no idea she was planning to leave the country.
② I'm going to **throw** caution to the wind and just buy that expensive car!
③ My daughter was ill with the flu last week, but she's right **as** rain now.
④ I'm afraid I'll have to **take** a rain check on that. I'm really busy this week.
⑤ Whenever I give a sales presentation, Maureen always tries to **steal** my thunder.

41

41.1 🔊
① be a household name
② attention-grabbing
③ opening night
④ red carpet
⑤ paparazzi
⑥ talent show
⑦ become a celebrity
⑧ reality show
⑨ meteoric rise
⑩ sensationalize
⑪ celebrity culture
⑫ headline news
⑬ newspaper headline

42

42.1 🔊
① These items have been **produced** in our new factory.
② It has been **reported** that a hurricane will hit the coast this evening.
③ Those tests have been **carried** out in our new laboratory next door.
④ Following the meeting, it has been **decided** that we will increase our prices.

⑤ He has been **named** by the pharmaceutical company as their new CEO.
⑥ Our products have been **exported** all over the world since 1995.
⑦ The proposal has been **rejected** by all the members of the board.
⑧ There are **alleged** to have been a series of crimes committed by this gang.
⑨ It has long been **believed** that money isn't his main motivation.

42.2 ◀))
① It is understood that there **have been many flight cancelations.**
② Our organization is thought to **be a trailblazer in the area we work in.**
③ It has been reported that **there will be massive jobs cuts.**
④ It was announced that the company **would recall its latest products.**
⑤ He is thought to have been **the most successful CEO we ever had.**
⑥ There are said to be **some nice walking trails around here.**
⑦ It is hoped that the next generation **will continue the work we've been doing.**
⑧ Norway is believed to be **among the most beautiful countries.**

42.3 ◀))
① This essay **should have been** handed in two weeks ago!
② Unfortunately, the project couldn't **be completed** on time.
③ It must **have taken** us four hours to get here because of all the traffic jams.
④ She must **have thought** that the meeting started at 11am instead of 10am.
⑤ Any feedback you may have should **be sent** to our administrator.
⑥ The machine may **have broken down** because there was some dust in it.
⑦ Traffic could **be redirected** here during the festival.
⑧ Free samples can **be obtained** from our store on the first floor.
⑨ The booking should **have been made** earlier. Then we would have better seats.

42.4 ◀))
① The bell must have rung 10 times, but he still didn't come to the door.
② There is understood to have been a car accident on Station Road this evening.
③ All of the books we sent should have been delivered to the venue by now.
④ It was announced yesterday that students can now apply for scholarships for next year.
⑤ The driver is thought to have lost his way while driving from the airport back to the city.

42.5
① Yesterday **②** Young people

③ This isn't clear yet **④** They welcome it
⑤ Positively

42.6 ◀))
① A million gallons of water **were bottled at this plant last year.**
② Our cars **are rented by business travelers at the airport.**
③ Another conference **could be organized for next September.**
④ All of our dishes **are made by hand by our chefs.**
⑤ It is hoped **that the supplier will accept the new terms and conditions.**
⑥ It is reported **that the traffic laws will be changed by the government this year.**
⑦ All of the company cars **are serviced in this garage.**
⑧ The solar panels on our roof **were installed by a Spanish company last month.**
⑨ It is agreed **that he would make an excellent team leader.**
⑩ The trucks **could have been unloaded in half the time that they actually took.**
⑪ It was announced **that she would be stepping down from the committee.**
⑫ It was claimed **that some students didn't get enough help from their teachers.**

43

43.1 ◀))
① **Approximately** 40,000 spectators watched the game at the national stadium.
② The figures **indicate** that our population is aging rapidly.
③ Harris Mode is **arguably** the most handsome man alive today.
④ To **some extent**, we can all do more to improve the state of our health.
⑤ **It has been said** that unless we stop climate change, the ice caps will melt.
⑥ It has been **suggested** that the witness lied during the trial.
⑦ People who purchase violent video games **tend** to be young men.
⑧ **It looks** like we've missed the bus. We're going to be late again.
⑨ It **appeared** that the jewelry had been stolen in the early hours of the morning.

43.2 ◀))
① The teacher suggested that **Lilian should expect good exam results.**
② If I don't have coffee in the morning, **I tend to get a headache.**
③ There are approximately 15,000 **people in the town where I live.**
④ It appears that the company **is going to make a loss this year.**

⑤ The soccer players allegedly **accepted money to lose games.**
⑥ It has been said that **there's no fool like and old fool.**
⑦ People often say **they don't have the time to exercise.**

43.3 ◀))
① The test results **suggest** that this is a new kind of bacteria.
② **To some extent**, I'm glad Gina canceled her party. I don't feel very well.
③ Jess **seems** to have gone home early.
④ Carren Lake is **arguably** the most successful British tennis player ever.
⑤ It **appears** that we have no food left in the fridge.
⑥ It would **seem** that Clarissa is not answering my text messages.

43.4 Réponses modèles
① The incident took place in Banff General Hospital.
② The medical staff was surprised to see a deer walking into the Emergency Room.
③ The deer seemed to have been injured in an accident on the roads.
④ The deer must have walked approximately 10 kilometers to get to the hospital.
⑤ The medical staff took the deer to a nearby vet.
⑥ The vet said that it looked like the animal would make a full recovery.

43.5
① True **②** False **③** Not given
④ False **⑤** True **⑥** True

43.6 ◀))
① To some **extent**, the project we worked on last month was a waste of time.
② It would seem **that** someone has hacked into our database.
③ He has **allegedly** stolen $2 million from his employer.
④ It has been **said** that absence makes the heart grow fonder.
⑤ It **appears** that you have forgotten to pay your bill.

44

44.1 ◀))
① Only after trying to reach the summit three times **did he** give up.
② Little **does she** know that we're planning a surprise party for her.
③ Only **when** it starts to snow do I stop gardening.

④ Not since the 1980s **has the team** won a major trophy.

44.2 🔊
① Only after living there for five years **did he master the Spanish language.**
② Not only is she a great mother, **but she's also a top business executive.**
③ Little did they realize **that they were in for a big surprise.**
④ Only when she read their stories **did she realize how well they can write.**
⑤ Not since his childhood **had he ridden a skateboard.**
⑥ Only after studying the instructions **did he understand how it worked.**

44.3 🔊
① Little did I know that I would meet my future husband that evening.
② Not only is he a talented pianist, he is also a writer.
③ Only when he came on stage did the fans start to scream.
④ Only after living there for six months did they talk to the neighbors.
⑤ Not only was the movie informative, but it was also entertaining.

44.4 🔊
① No sooner had I arrived home than my son asked me to help him with his homework.
② Little did she know that she would stay for 40 years when she started working there.
③ Never before have people from both communities worked together.
④ Not since I went to see *Sally's Song* have I cried this much at a film.
⑤ Rarely do you see a dog and cat that get along with each other so well.

44.5 🔊
① **Rarely** have I seen so many people running together.
② Little **did we** know that we would end up living in Italy.
③ **No sooner** had I reached the station than the train arrived.
④ Not since 1988 **have we** had such a hot summer.
⑤ **Little** did she know that she would win an award that evening.
⑥ Never before **have I seen** a child who loves reading as much as she does.
⑦ Only when I'd had time to recover **did I** realize what a lucky escape I'd had.
⑧ Only after experiencing it ourselves **could we** understand how difficult it is.
⑨ **Only after** preparing for six months did they feel ready to take the exam.
⑩ **Not since** my teenage years have I been so excited about a concert.

⑪ **Hardly** had he started to speak when someone interrupted him.
⑫ **Not only** do we produce these dolls here, but we make them all by hand.

44.6
① True ② False ③ Not given ④ True
⑤ True

44.7 🔊
① Hardly had we pitched our tent when it began to rain.
② Rarely do I feel as happy as when I'm alone.
③ Not since I was a young girl have I danced.
④ Only after calling him five times did he pick up.

45

45.1 🔊
① What I would prefer is to take the train to the international airport.
② What I really want is to hike the Inca Trail in Peru with my friends this year.
③ What I would really appreciate is some help with using the software to sort data.
④ What she was most surprised by was the party they threw for her birthday yesterday.
⑤ What we really need is some more time to get the booth ready for the annual fair.
⑥ What I hate is when people play music on their phones without using headphones.
⑦ What I really enjoyed was the day we spent at the local spa last weekend.
⑧ What he realized was that he didn't want to do that boring job for the rest of his life.
⑨ What I understood was that they aren't very happy about the sudden changes we're making.

45.2 🔊
① The **time** I'd most like to go back to is Ancient Rome so I could visit the Colosseum.
② The **meal** that I enjoy making the most is spaghetti carbonara. It's quick and easy.
③ The **subject** I liked the most at school was science, so I became a science teacher.
④ The **birthday** that I'll always remember is my twenty-first, when I had a huge party.
⑤ The **season** that I like the most is winter. I love walking in the snow.
⑥ The **famous person** I'd most like to have met is Alasdair Rove. I love his music and his style.
⑦ The **teacher** who influenced me the most is probably Mr. Lucas, my English teacher.
⑧ The **movie** that reminds me the most of my childhood is *Little Tim*. I loved it!
⑨ The **song** that always gets me up and dancing at a party is *Dancing Bells* by Claude Robert.

45.3 🔊
① **Why** do you always take on more than you can actually do in a day?
② **The place** that I would most like to be right now is a Caribbean beach.
③ **The person** I most admire and look up to is probably Shakespeare.
④ **The thing** he absolutely hates is people who talk while they're eating.
⑤ **Where** is Jonathan doing his Master's degree?
⑥ **The time of day** I like the most is first thing in the morning when I'm alone.

45.4 🔊
① You went to France last year, didn't you?
No, it was Slovakia where we went.
② Didn't we meet for the first time in 2005?
No, it was 2006 when we first met.
③ You met Sam at the party, didn't you?
No, it was Rosemary that I met.
④ Wasn't it in Paris that he proposed?
No, actually it was in New York.
⑤ Weren't we 10 when we went to Peru? **No, it was when we were 11.**
⑥ Wasn't it Mrs. Kins who taught us French?
No, it was Mrs. Bond who took that class.
⑦ Didn't John go running with Philip?
No, it was David he did that with.
⑧ Did you make this cake here?
No, it was Joanne who made that one.
⑨ He majored in history in college, didn't he?
No, it was physics that he majored in.

45.5 🔊
① It was the young man at the visitor center that helped us a lot in New York.
② It was an old lady that helped us find the way when we were lost in that Greek village.
③ It was your colleague Charles that I met at the Christmas party last year.
④ It was a restaurant in Florence where we ate the delicious steak by the river.
⑤ I think it was our second year in college when the two of us first met.

46

46.1 🔊
① (beyond) reasonable doubt ② convict a criminal ③ crime wave ④ deny all knowledge ⑤ arrest ⑥ jury
⑦ street crime ⑧ commit a crime
⑨ pass sentence ⑩ criminal record
⑪ reach a verdict ⑫ make a claim
⑬ be insured

47.1 🔊
1 Subject 2 Object 3 Subject
4 Object 5 Subject

47.2 🔊
1 The dog **which** is standing outside the police station is a drug-detection dog.
2 The woman **that** was crying had been robbed by two men on a motorcycle.
3 The man **who** was sent to prison had stolen hundreds of credit cards.
4 The man **who** is talking to the police officer had his car stolen.
5 The job **which** I'd like to do after my graduation is in crime prevention.

47.3 🔊
1 The old man **who / that** got lost in the city is 98 years old.
2 The lion **which / that** was born in captivity was released into the wild.
3 The crime **which / that** we reported is being broadcast on TV!
4 The woman **who / that** found Samantha's purse is a cleaner.
5 The cat **which / that** I recently adopted is black and white.
6 The woman **who / that** I introduced you to last Wednesday is a model.

47.4 🔊
1 The rooster **that crows loudly all day** belongs to my neighbor.
2 A movie **which won a lot of awards** is *Crazy Cuckoo*.
3 The woman **I dated last year** is now married.
4 The runner **who won the marathon** was running his first race.
5 The jacket **which I bought five years ago** is now falling apart.
6 The restaurant **that serves the best food** is in the main square.
7 The school **I went to as a little girl** is now a hotel.
8 The teacher **who I liked best at school** was Mr. Jenkins.

47.5 🔊
1 The stolen goods, which were extremely valuable, were found by the police.
2 My little brother, who is only six, is always getting into trouble at school.
3 The robbers, who were all from Southampton, were caught as they tried to leave the crime scene.
4 My house, which I moved into two months ago, has been burgled.

47.6 🔊
1 The robber, **who** left his fingerprints behind, was easily caught by the police.
2 My wallet, **which** was in my bag, was stolen while we were in the market.
3 Mr. Townsend, **who** is a suspect in a murder inquiry, has fled the country.
4 My credit card details, **which** I'd used for an online purchase, were stolen.

47.7
1 Not given 2 True 3 True
4 False 5 Not given 6 True
7 Not given 8 False 9 True

48.1 🔊
1 That's the restaurant **where** we ate that excellent chicken curry.
2 There was an agreement **whereby** both sides decided to support each other.
3 This is the church **where** my parents got married 30 years ago.
4 He's thinking about the time **when** we went to Barcelona for the weekend.
5 We use an application procedure **whereby** everything is done electronically.
6 The director talked about the area **where** the film was shot.
7 That's the office **where** my colleagues Jessica and Peter work.
8 We're now in the packing area **where** all of the items are packed.
9 Heat treatment is a process **whereby** heat is applied to metals.
10 This photo is from the semester **when** we lived in the dorm.
11 We provide a system **whereby** companies can find talented people.

48.2 🔊
1 The kitchen is **the room where** I most enjoy spending my time. I just love cooking.
2 Early morning is **the time of day when** I'm by myself and can have some peace and quiet.
3 Spring is **the season when** we most enjoy going out for walks in the country.
4 Photosynthesis is **the process whereby** plants convert sunlight into energy.
5 This is **the exhibition hall where** the last annual trade fair for construction systems was held.

48.3 🔊
1 The TV program gave us a lot of information about the process **whereby** cheese is produced.

2 That was the big museum in New York **where** they have those wonderful Picasso masterpieces.
3 That was the time **when** the car broke down and we had to wait hours before someone came to help.
4 I'm just waiting for the moment **when** everyone goes quiet so I can start speaking.
5 We're looking at the process **whereby** fuel is burned to create the steam that drives the turbine.

48.4
2

48.5 🔊
1 Fiona, whose dog is large and energetic, always walks in the park in the morning.
2 ZFF, whose CEO gave an interview on TV last night, is a company that is starting to work in China.
3 Jack, whose school has received more money for music classes, is learning to play the trumpet.
4 Francesca, whose computer has just crashed, is really stressed out right now.
5 Mandy, whose mother has suddenly become ill, took some time off work last week.
6 The company, whose employees now have unlimited time off, has innovative HR policies.
7 The tennis club, whose tennis courts are located on the outskirts of the town, is expanding every year.

48.6 Réponses modèles
1 The writer didn't notice anything unusual when he got home from work that day.
2 The writer found out that the smoke was actually coming from across the hall where Mr. Jerome lives.
3 The writer called the fire department. It arrived at the apartment building when the smoke was really starting to build up.
4 The firefighters organized a procedure whereby some of them tried to enter from the balcony and others tried to break down the door.
5 There wasn't too much damage to the apartment where the fire started.
6 Nobody was hurt in the fire.

49.1 🔊
1 Unfortunately, I will have to cancel our meeting because I won't be able to make it.
2 Will you be able to pay the fine if you park your car in this restricted zone?
3 I won't be able to get to sleep if my neighbors are making a lot of noise.

4 Will you have to stay in and study for your final exams?

5 We will have to get a good night's sleep tonight because we have an early start.

6 Will you have to take all six exams this semester?

7 We will not be able to meet our deadlines because the company hasn't delivered on time.

8 Will you be able to help me translate this text from Portuguese to English?

9 I won't be able to help you with the translation because I'm really busy at the moment.

49.2 🔊

1 We will have to work hard next month.

2 Will you have to look after the visitors all day?

3 They won't have to do everything on their own.

4 We will have to recycle more of our paper.

49.3 🔊

1 Next year we **will have to** save more money, so that we'll be able to buy a house soon.

2 I'm sorry, but I **will not be able to** come to your concert this evening. I have to work late.

3 **Will you be able to** join us for our annual school reunion next week? It would be great to see you.

4 We **will not be able to** visit the clients in person this Friday, so we will have to call them instead.

5 **Will he have to** travel a lot in his new job or will he be able to stay at home a little bit more?

49.4 🔊

1 According to the weather forecast, it will snow tomorrow, so we **will be able to** go skiing.

2 He **won't be able to** take the course he wanted to do because it's been canceled.

3 I hope that one day every person **will be able to** realize their full potential.

4 When we turn the next corner, you **will be able to** see the beach and the ocean.

5 She's so happy that she **won't have to** wear braces on her teeth any more.

6 If you want to come to the party, you **will have to** let me know by Friday at the latest.

7 If anyone would like a signed copy of the book, you **will be able to** buy one later.

8 You **won't have to** do so much paperwork now that you've got a secretary.

49.5 Réponses modèles

1 He won't be able to get very good grades and he may even fail.

2 Peter is able to make everyone think that everything's OK, even when it isn't.

3 If Peter doesn't pass his exams, he'll have to repeat the year.

4 Peter will be able to get some extra support over the next few months if Mr. Foster is able to give it to him.

49.6

1 True **2** True **3** True **4** Not given
5 False **6** Not given **7** True
8 False **9** True

50

50.1 🔊

1 He's a great runner. He **can** run twelve miles in two hours.

2 **May** I have another piece of cake? It's delicious.

3 That **can't** be Dominic at the door because he's in Spain at the moment.

4 When I was younger, I **could** party all night, but now I'm older I can't.

5 **Shall** we have lunch together on Thursday? It would be great to catch up.

6 Don't worry, I **will** make sure that everything's ready on time.

7 **Would** you go down to reception and meet the visitors for me?

8 Joanna said she **might** join us, but she probably wouldn't be able to make it.

9 You've had that cough for two weeks now. You **should** go to the doctor.

50.2 🔊

1 You **must** take your laptop out of your bag before you go through security control.

2 You **may** stay here as long as you want. Just remember to lock the door when you leave.

3 **Shall** I give you a ride home afterward? I'll be in the area at that time anyway.

4 **May** I help you carry your suitcase up the stairs?

5 When I was a child I **couldn't** do a handstand, but now I can!

6 **Will** you help me prepare the training course for our Spanish colleagues?

7 If that doesn't work, you **could** call Edward and ask him if he knows what to do.

8 Since he had his operation, he **can't** walk more than 10 steps.

50.3 🔊

1 Don't put your fingers so close to the pan. **You could burn yourself.**

2 Should I help you move those boxes, **so you don't have so much to do?**

3 Will you check that the door is **locked when you leave?**

4 You must go to reception to register **before you can go to the meeting room.**

5 May I have another cookie? **They taste delicious!**

6 I can't speak French very well, **but I can understand a lot.**

7 He ought to go to the hairdresser and **get a decent haircut for a change.**

8 Would you call and ask **if it's OK for us to arrive a little later?**

50.4 🔊

1 You should have asked your boss to pay you for the overtime you did.

2 He lost his voice, so he couldn't teach his classes last week.

3 I can't find my keys anywhere. I must have left them at home.

4 She should have asked me for advice. I would have been able to help.

5 Could you visit the museum when you were on vacation, or was it closed?

50.5 🔊

1 You should have **brought** your laptop to the meeting. Sarah reminded you yesterday.

2 They ought to **have** more respect for the neighbors when they have a party.

3 Why didn't you ask? I would **have** shared a taxi from the airport to the hotel with you.

4 I know what happened. We must **have taken** a wrong turn just after we left the hotel.

51

51.1 🔊

1 values
2 bad habit
3 lifestyle
4 stereotype
5 local custom
6 blend in
7 diversity
8 acclimate
9 manners
10 cause offense
11 nationality
12 globalization
13 dialect

52

52.1 🔊

1 The Dutch **2** Kenyans **3** The Swiss
4 The Vietnamese **5** Australians
6 Egyptians **7** Argentinians
8 Koreans **9** The Spanish **10** Greeks
11 The Japanese **12** Brazilians **13** The British

52.2 🔊

❶ We're looking for ways of helping **the homeless find accommodation.**
❷ The young often have a reputation **for being wild and irresponsible.**
❸ The British are known for their love of **fish and chips.**
❹ Some people believe that the rich **should pay a much higher level of tax.**
❺ Pets are seen as excellent companions f**or the elderly.**
❻ We have started distributing food **to the poor.**
❼ The injured were airlifted to the hospital **immediately after the accident.**

52.3 🔊

❶ We've built these ramps and put in these rails to help **the disabled** access the building.
❷ I think that **the rich** should give away more of their money to people who are in need.
❸ The emergency services have given **the injured** all of the medical attention they need.
❹ **The young** are the group who are likely to spend the most time using social media.
❺ In Nairobi, **the poor** live on the edges of the city in homes they've built themselves.
❻ Ancient **Egyptians** worshipped cats.
❼ We offer accomodation for **the elderly** who can no longer live alone.
❽ **The Swiss** are known throughout the world for making clocks and chocolate.
❾ We don't want **the healthy** to come into contact with infectious diseases.
❿ If you'd like to help **the homeless** who live on our streets, come along to our soup kitchen.
⓫ **The unemployed** sometimes aren't offered very much help with finding a new job.
⓬ He decided to become a doctor because he wanted to help **the sick.**

52.4 🔊

❶ Unemployed people are welcome to come and volunteer at the library if they want to.
❷ Our charity was set up to help the elderly by organizing a weekly social meet-up for them.
❸ The majority of Germans were in support of the decision.
❹ Our first priority is to help the injured. Then we can talk to journalists about what's happened.
❺ This fort was built by the Dutch in the late 1600s.
❻ The government wants to introduce a new law, which will make the rich pay more in taxes.
❼ These parking spaces are only for the disabled. Can you please park somewhere else?
❽ Most Brazilians are taught English at school.

❾ The homeless are sometimes seen as dangerous, but this is far from the truth.
❿ The British are coming over here to learn more about our processes and how we do things.
⓫ I decided to become a nurse because I really wanted to be able to help the sick.
⓬ The French are known for being very relaxed and this is also something I've noticed.

52.5 🔊 Réponses modèles

❶ The poor **are supported by the government and by charities.**
❷ The sick **are often reluctant to see a doctor as healthcare can be expensive.**
❸ The disabled **are considered every time a new building is constructed.**
❹ The unemployed **are encouraged to volunteer in a field that interests them.**
❺ The young **are always portrayed as loud and lazy.**
❻ The homeless **have to rely on donations from strangers.**
❼ The rich **are seen as a very lucky group of people.**

53

53.1 🔊

❶ It took me a while to **get** used to the stores being closed on Sundays here.
❷ He's been starting work at 6am for three months now, so he **is** used to it.
❸ As we live in the north of Norway, we **are** used to very cold weather in winter.
❹ I'm still **getting** used to the fast pace of activity in my new company.
❺ When he first went to live in Australia, he **wasn't** used to the heat and got burned.
❻ You've been working with us for some time, so you **are** used to the way we work now.
❼ I just can't **get** used to working every weekend. I don't think I'll ever like it.
❽ Don't worry about Rachel! She **is** used to traveling on her own.
❾ When we had our first child, we had to **get** used to not having very much sleep.
❿ We've had our new boss for six months now, but I'm still **getting** used to her style.
⓫ Jeremy lives in Los Angeles, so he **is** used to living through minor earthquakes.

53.2 🔊

❶ Three years after moving, I think we **are** finally used to life in the country and really like it.
❷ After a while you'll **get** used to the rhythm of the train and fall asleep.
❸ He **is** used to sleeping on a very soft bed at home, so he doesn't like hard beds.

❹ I was just **getting** used to our old English teacher when she left and we got a new one.
❺ He **is** now so used to wearing glasses that he doesn't even notice them anymore.
❻ I **was** used to taking the train every day and I knew the timetable by heart.

53.3 🔊

❶ Our customers from other countries **are** used to getting very high quality products from us.
❷ I don't think Christina will ever **get** used to living on her own. She doesn't like it.
❸ **We're** used to being able to communicate with people from all over the world online.
❹ My friend is **not used** to eating spicy food, so it makes him go red in the face.
❺ He is still **getting** used to the new house he bought last year.
❻ Our children Joseph and Liz are used to **being** away from the two of us while we're at work.

53.4 🔊

❶ You will have to get used to working **long hours if you want to be on this team.**
❷ We were used to bringing lunch **to work, but now we eat in the canteen.**
❸ Jack's slowly getting used to living **in a dorm instead of at home.**
❹ The new shoes were uncomfortable, **but she soon got used to them.**
❺ I'm used to sitting through long and **boring lectures. I do it every day.**

53.5

❶ The UK ❷ His boss ❸ Japan ❹ Direct
❺ Strangers ❻ Nice restaurants
❼ Street markets

53.6 🔊

❶ Our neighbors are so loud, but we'll just have to **get used to** the noise.
❷ I've lived in Tokyo for 10 years now, so I'm **used to** Japanese food.
❸ My boss was pleased about how quickly I **got used to** giving presentations.
❹ We may have to **get used to** traveling a little farther to get to the shops soon.
❺ We were just **getting used to** the new office when we had to move to another one.
❻ He's been working in virtual teams for a long time now, so he's **used to** it.

53.7

❶ was used to ❷ get used to
❸ get used to ❹ was used to
❺ get used to ❻ get used to
❼ get used to ❽ get used to
❾ are used to

54

54.1 🔊
1. **The** investors who come to us have a lot of money to invest in companies.
2. We paid for **an** audio guide in the palace and it gave us some interesting information.
3. **The** CEO of our company is surprisingly young. He's only 30 years old!
4. If you want to travel cheaply in Paris, you should take **the** Métro.
5. After dinner, I bought **an** ice cream cone and ate it while I was sitting by the fountain.
6. The Eiffel Tower is probably **the** most famous landmark in Paris.
7. We were so busy and did so much walking that I need **an** early night tonight.
8. The flag is up, so **the** Queen must be in the palace today.
9. It's amazing how quickly **the** company's share price is going up at the moment.
10. We're thinking about hiring **a** boat tomorrow and taking it out on the water.
11. My hotel has **a** beautiful view of the harbor and the sea.

54.2 🔊
1. The people who live in our town **don't want the new road to be built.**
2. The restaurant we went to last night **is the one where pizza was invented.**
3. I don't know why, but spaghetti **always tastes better when you're in Italy.**
4. A large number of vacationers **want to stay in an all-inclusive hotel.**
5. City tours that are free **usually aren't as good as ones you pay for.**

54.3 🔊
1. **The** Petronas Towers are the tallest buildings in Kuala Lumpur and they dominate the skyline.
2. If you go up to the top of the tower, you get **an** excellent view of Kuala Lumpur.
3. Street food stands on the side of **the** road are great places to try Malaysian food.
4. You can also visit **the** Islamic Arts Museum if you go to Kuala Lumpur. It's interesting.
5. Taking **a** day trip to the nearby Batu Caves is a good idea if you have time.
6. Have you walked through **the** colorful China Town market in Kuala Lumpur?

54.4 🔊
1. This is **the** old typewriter that my mother always used to use.
2. People from Brazil are known for their love of **[-]** football.
3. I've never seen such **a** wide selection of foods for breakfast as they had there.
4. They love **[-]** Chinese food, so I'm sure they'll enjoy their trip to China.
5. Our tour guide is **an** older lady who's lived in Dublin all her life.
6. There's **a** university in Bologna which is nearly 1,000 years old.
7. Here's our guide to **the** travel destinations that will be the most popular next year.
8. **The** waitress who served us at that restaurant was very friendly and helpful.
9. Children usually enjoy visiting **the** zoo in Edinburgh. You can even see pandas there.
10. Churros are very popular in **[-]** Spain. People eat them with chocolate sauce.
11. I wasn't sure whether we should leave **a** tip for the waiter or not.
12. **The** music festival we went to was brilliant. There were a lot of good bands playing.
13. **The** hotel where we stayed is a five-star hotel, so it was very luxurious.

54.5
1. False 2. True 3. True 4. True 5. False

54.6 🔊
1. Let's call a plum**b**er to fix the water heater.
2. Forei**g**n visitors think we speak good English.
3. I hurt my **k**nee while we were trekking.
4. I like to lis**t**en to music while I'm traveling.
5. To be **h**onest, I don't think I like him.
6. It's so cold. My fingers are num**b**.
7. He has just trapped his thum**b** in the door!

55

55.1 🔊
1. We often find that men aren't as good at taking care of their **health** as women are.
2. She made her **anger** at the graffiti on the wall clear to everyone in the room.
3. Unfortunately, the funding for all of the **libraries** in our area has been cut this year.
4. He's been having some **trouble** getting his computer to start all week.
5. Could you please email me all of the **information** I need for my trip to Peru?
6. Our company specializes in creating **beauty** products for young women.
7. He has a lot of **knowledge** about the history of the Middle Ages.
8. I've made a list of all the **deadlines** for the project in this document.
9. We take a lot of **pride** in our work and always do our very best.
10. It's absolutely freezing today. It must be about minus fifteen **degrees** outside!
11. We're facing some fierce **competition** from companies in South America.

55.2 🔊
1. My **thoughts** are with the families of the victims of the disaster at this terrible time.
2. I come from Nigeria and my **culture** is very important to me. I keep the traditions alive.
3. Our **hope** is that our daughter will go to college and get a good job.
4. Your **friendship** is really important to me, and I hope you feel the same.
5. My happiest childhood **memories** are of spending the summer in Sweden with my family.
6. I save some money every month and then at the end of the year I give it to local **charities**.

55.3 🔊
1. You can now all find out what **grades you got on the exam.**
2. My car has a top speed **of 100 miles per hour.**
3. The kittens your cat gave **birth to are real beauties.**
4. I'm going to write the neighbors **a letter of apology for all of the noise.**
5. My cousin Matthew repairs **computers for a living.**
6. We're here today because we're **interested in learning more about other cultures.**
7. Nowadays it's more and more **important to have good communication skills.**
8. I make a living from entering **competitions. You can win so much!**
9. You have to study for six **semesters before you get your degree.**

55.4 🔊
1. The temperatures this summer are some of the highest in living **memory**.
2. I work hard on my **friendships** because friends are an important part of my life.
3. She hopes that she will complete her **studies** and graduate next summer.
4. We're collecting money for **charity**, but we haven't decided which one we'll give it to yet.
5. There are a lot of free parking **spaces** at the front of the building if you're still looking.
6. You will be in our **thoughts** while you're away and we'll call you as often as we can.
7. There's always a lot of **competition** in the soft drink market. It's hard to break through.
8. He takes so much **pride** in his garden and he wants other people to enjoy it too.
9. There are so many **times** when I wish I had a robot who could do the housework for me.
10. She decided to take all of her **knowledge** about marketing and put it into a book.
11. The **skill** he has for soccer is unbelievable for someone of his age.
12. The company is known for the very high **quality** of their kitchen products.

56

56.1 🔊
1. make predictions
2. what the future holds
3. only a matter of time
4. have an influence on something
5. future-proof
6. revolution
7. the latest model
8. breakthrough
9. make arrangements
10. have good intentions
11. digital age
12. hope for the best
13. cutting-edge

57

57.1 🔊
1. My job at the supermarket is so boring, I wish I **could** find another one.
2. I wish Rosemary **would stop** talking about herself all the time. It's so annoying!
3. I wish my teacher **would** give me more help. I don't understand any of this.
4. They wish they **could** take some time off work so they could go on vacation.
5. He wishes he **could** win the first prize in the competition he's entered.
6. She **wishes** she could get a leading role in the play, but she never goes to auditions.
7. I wish I **could** afford to get a new kitchen. This one is so old it's falling apart.
8. Adam wishes his teacher **would** give him more homework. He doesn't have enough to do.
9. I wish they **would** make it easier to work out how much tax you have to pay.

57.2 🔊
1. I wish my boss **would** be a little more polite. He's always rude to everyone.
2. Linda wishes she **could** drive to work, but she still hasn't passed her driving test.
3. They wish their neighbors **would** be a bit quieter. They're always making noise.
4. I wish they **would** tell us what's going to happen now instead of making us wait.
5. Jacob wishes he **could** relax, but he can't because he's having a stressful time at work.
6. I wish we **could** go on a helicopter ride around Manhattan, but we can't afford it.
7. Susanne wishes her daughter **would** call her more often. She only calls once a month.
8. I wish the people on the train **would** move their bags off the seats next to them.

9. They wish they **could** get a good espresso in this town, but they can't find one anywhere.

57.3 🔊
1. My job is really boring. I wish **I could find something more interesting.**
2. The snails are eating my plants. I wish **I could get rid of them once and for all.**
3. The rules are so complicated. I wish **they would make them simpler.**
4. I can't type very quickly. I wish **my boss would let me take a course.**
5. They always leave a mess. I wish **they would think about other people.**
6. The bus always takes so long. I wish **I could drive instead.**
7. I'm so sleepy. I wish **I could go to bed.**
8. That machine is very noisy. I wish **someone would turn it off.**

57.4 🔊
1. The students wish they **could** speak perfect English.
2. He wishes his teacher **would** give him more help.
3. She wishes she **could** go to the party.
4. We wish they **would** let us leave work early.

57.5
1. She wants to travel less
2. Far away from headquarters
3. Move the headquarters to a better place
4. Internal sales team leader
5. Geoff is going to retire

57.6 Réponses modèles
1. Jessica wishes she could relax and take it easy this summer.
2. Jessica wishes you could get an accountancy job straight after leaving college.
3. It will be another five years before Jessica is a qualified accountant.
4. Jessica wishes she could go to the beach with Josh on Monday.

58

58.1 🔊
1. Sheila is sick, so she**'ll be working** from home for the rest of the week.
2. This time next week, I**'ll be sitting** on a beach in the Caribbean.
3. The boss thinks that in 10 years' time I**'ll be running** this company myself.
4. They**'ll be traveling** for the next two hours and won't be able to take any calls.
5. It looks like we**'ll be spending** a lot of time together over the next few months.
6. The pilots are on strike, so I think I**'ll be** waiting at the airport for a while.
7. Will you **be bringing** your husband and children with you tomorrow?
8. He**'ll be standing** near the entrance waiting for us when we get there.
9. I**'ll be driving** past the stores later if you want me to get some groceries.
10. We **won't be launching** our new perfume until the trade fair next year.
11. James has applied for some jobs, so I think he**'ll be leaving** the company soon.

58.2 🔊
1. By this time next week, I'll be working in a big city.
2. By this time tomorrow, I'll be working in a big city.
3. By this time tomorrow, I'll be working as a manager.
4. By this time tomorrow, I'll be living in a big city.
5. By this time tomorrow, I'll be relaxing on vacation.
6. By this time next week, I'll be working as a manager.
7. By this time next week, I'll be living in a big city.
8. By this time next week, I'll be relaxing on vacation.
9. In five years' time, I'll be working in a big city.
10. In five years' time, I'll be working as a manager.
11. In five years' time, I'll be living in a big city.
12. In five years' time, I'll be relaxing on vacation.

58.3 🔊
1. The next time I go to the mountains, I'll be **skiing** like an expert.
2. In a few years' time, **I'll be** playing basketball professionally.
3. We will **be** hosting some visitors from China next week.
4. This evening **they'll** be serving snacks and drinks for everyone.
5. In five years' time, I won't be **teaching** at a primary school any more.
6. Will you **be** asking for input from the audience during your presentation?

58.4 🔊
1. We'll be using this software in 10 years' time.
2. Lisa will be working until 6pm today.
3. The bus will be leaving in five minutes.
4. This train will be stopping at Central Station.
5. Next week, I will be working from home.

58.5
1. True
2. False
3. Not given
4. True
5. False

Réponses modèles

1 In a few years' time, five billion people will be shopping online.

2 Around half of these people will be using tablets to access the internet.

3 Connected devices will become so integrated into our lives that we'll see them as "digital assistants."

4 We can assume that someone, somewhere will be buying something online right now.

5 Every retail company will be selling their products on the web in 10 years' time.

6 Future internet users will be able to get online wherever they are.

59

59.1 🔊

1 I **will have finished** my degree by the time I am 22.

2 You **will have been** married for one year in a week's time.

3 We **will have completed** all our essays by the end of June.

4 By the time I am 24, I **will have found** a good job.

5 I think my son **will have proposed** to his girlfriend by the end of the year.

6 By the time we are 30, we **will have had** our first child.

7 Liza **will have moved** to London by the end of the month.

8 I **will have graduated f**rom college by this time next year.

9 By the time I am 25, I **will have left** my parents' house.

10 I **will have made** one million dollars by the time I'm 40.

11 They **will have started** their new business by the end of the month.

59.2

1 will have found **2** will have perfected
3 will have opened **4** will have been
5 will have sold **6** will have increased
7 will have made **8** will have taken
9 will have launched

59.3 🔊

1 They **will have chosen** the best candidate by the end of the day.

2 Jenny **will have bought** a new dress before the wedding.

3 By the end of the year, I **will have completed** three marathons.

4 I **will have opened** all my presents by the end of the party.

5 By the time he starts his new job, Hans **will have had** his hair cut.

6 We **will have visited** 15 countries by the end of this year.

59.4 🔊

1 By the time we arrive in Spain, we **will have been driving** for eight hours.

2 Jenna **will have been running** her own business for five years in May.

3 In June, I **will have been working** as a teacher for 10 years.

4 By the time the cake is decorated, we **will have been cooking** for six hours.

5 I **will have been doing** yoga for 10 years by the end of the year.

6 In November, Becky and I **will have been living** together for three years.

7 By midday, Jonas **will have been waiting** to see the doctor for three hours.

8 By the time I have finished, I **will have been cleaning** the house for five hours.

9 By the time the plane lands in Malaysia, we **will have been traveling** for 13 hours.

10 By December, I **will have been learning** to paint for six months.

11 I **will have been studying** medicine for four years by the end of June.

12 By the end of next month, the police **will have been looking** for the criminals for a year.

59.5 🔊

1 At the end of the week, Lise will have been studying in France for three months.

2 This time tomorrow, I will have had my operation.

3 I will have finished this report by the time you get here.

4 Next week, I will have been studying for two years.

5 By the end of January, I will have finished my Italian course.

6 In two hours, I will have written my last report for this client.

59.6

1 been **2** had **3** known **4** been

60

60.1 🔊

1 I always thought that I **would** go to college, but I then decided to get a job instead.

2 As soon as I get home, I **will** give you a call to let you know I've arrived safely.

3 I'm sure that we **will** still be friends when we're older. There's no doubt about that.

4 He said that he **would** try to get me some tickets for the soccer game if he could.

60.2 🔊

1 I got up so late, I knew I wasn't going to get to the airport in time.

2 Sarah's an excellent swimmer, so I knew it was going to be hard to beat her.

3 My mother promised she wasn't going to embarrass me by hugging me in public.

4 I found the exam easy, so I believed I was going to get a good grade.

5 He knew he wasn't going to get the job, but he wanted to apply for it anyway.

60.3 🔊

1 They couldn't come last week because they **were** going to a soccer game that evening.

2 She **was taking** her English exam the next day, so she felt a little nervous.

3 They **were** meeting with their lawyers that afternoon to decide what to do.

4 Sandra **was** planning to fly to Tenerife with her daughter yesterday, but the pilots are on strike.

5 Gareth **was** making a big announcement that afternoon, but then he lost his voice.

6 Camy and Charlie **were** having a big party to celebrate their anniversary that weekend.

7 Harren **was** getting married to Jennifer at 2 o'clock that afternoon in New York.

60.4

1 No **2** Yes **3** No

60.5 🔊

1 I knew that I would be the marketing head of a leading company one day.

2 When I saw him I knew that I was going to marry him and move to another country.

3 I was taking my last exam in chemistry at college that afternoon.

4 I thought I would travel around the world working as a part-time photographer.

5 She believed she would get a recording contract as soon as she finished her course at college.

6 I knew I would be late when I saw how much traffic there was on the road.

7 I was meeting some Chinese customers that morning for a presentation on distribution.

8 I thought Shania and Jo would go somewhere warm for their holiday that year.

9 He was building an extension on the back of their house in Germany.

10 I decided I would retire early and spend more time with my family and close friends.

11 I knew I was going to be able to climb to the top of the mountain sooner than the others.

12 The company was interviewing some more people for the marketing job that week.

61

61.1 🔊
1. highbrow / lowbrow
2. novels
3. speak your mind
4. highly recommend
5. characters
6. plot
7. heap praise / criticism on something
8. glowing reviews
9. lasting impression
10. change your mind
11. make up your mind
12. opening / closing scenes
13. create an atmosphere

62

62.1 🔊
1. The ceremony honored firemen and paramedics.
2. We could go to the session on marketing or this talk on public relations.
3. It would be nice to go the theater or a film. You can decide.
4. This process was described by Gutmann and Quirke.
5. She could have directed the TV series or the film version.
6. They should use paper bags and recycle more of their garbage.
7. He might have become a great writer, but he didn't want to.
8. The problem is that he wants to leave work early, but she doesn't.
9. He was chosen to play the lead role and did an excellent job.
10. I could wear this yellow dress for the wedding or this blue skirt.
11. You could eat at the new Italian restaurant or the Mexican restaurant.

62.2
1. Your parents 2. Its plot 3. Spoof
4. Dedicated sci-fi fans 5. Sequel

62.3 🔊
1. I'm so sorry! I broke your television, but I didn't mean to [**break your television**].
2. We can't go to the movies tonight but we can [**go to the movies**] tomorrow.
3. He told me he could speak French, but I don't think he can [**speak French**].
4. My daughter loves horror films and [**my daughter loves**] thrillers.

5. We went to Venice and [**we**] rode in a gondola this summer.
6. She could sit in the kitchen or [**she could sit in**] the garden.
7. Do we need a new computer? We could get a laptop or [**we could get**] a tablet instead.
8. It's such a beautiful day. We should go to the park or [**we should go to**] the beach.
9. The critics loved the latest blockbuster and [**the critics**] said it was worth watching.
10. I need to borrow your car. I will email shortly to explain why [**I need to borrow your car**].

62.4
1. True 2. False 3. True 4. False
5. True 6. False 7. False

62.5 🔊
1. I worked really hard on my entry, so I was **bitterly** disappointed that I didn't win.
2. The line for tickets at the museum was **painfully** slow. I thought we would never get in.
3. I won't go to that restaurant again. The prices were **astronomically** high!
4. The trip was **ridiculously** long because we were stuck in traffic for two hours.
5. I was **deeply** moved by the poem she read at her mother's funeral.
6. Everyone knows that farmers in this country are **heavily** subsidized.
7. I think you should avoid mentioning any **highly** controversial topics in your talk.

62.6 🔊
1. We went for a walk in the woods **and took some wonderful photos of the trees.**
2. She emailed and called everyone **she knew who might be able to help.**
3. The cathedral is beautiful **and is the seat of the Bishop of Rouen.**
4. Do you think we should go on **a beach or city break?**
5. He went cycling along the Rhine **and visited a lot of vineyards.**
6. I want to move, **but he doesn't.**
7. Could you call or email him **and ask him to confirm the details.**
8. I can remember his name, **but not his face. It's been a long time.**
9. They went to Mauritius and **stayed at a wonderful resort on the coast.**
10. Do you want to cook **or go out for dinner tonight?**

63

63.1 🔊
1. I've eaten a lot of pizza in my time, but the **one** I ate in Rome last year was the best.
2. I love these high-heeled shoes, but I think it's time I got some new **ones**.
3. Kirsten did well on both parts of the exam, but she did especially well on the first **one**.
4. I really like the movies he's in, especially the earlier **ones** from the start of his career.
5. Our daughter likes a lot of subjects at school, but the **one** she enjoys the most is science.
6. Mike has written a few books, but I think the first thriller he wrote is the best **one**.
7. Ann tried on 10 different wedding dresses before she found the **one** she wanted.
8. There are many activities for older children and some for younger **ones.**
9. I love all of the cakes Sam makes, but the **one** she made today was really delicious.
10. I've been to a lot of countries, but the **one** I enjoyed visiting the most was Japan.
11. Sarah isn't happy with her office assistant, so she wants to get a new **one.**

63.2 🔊
1. If you need any pens to write with, I have **some** here.
2. If you'd like a copy of my notes, I will print **one** for you.
3. They need some more batteries because the **ones** I gave them last time have run out.
4. If you find anywhere selling cups of coffee, could you get me **one**?
5. There's water here in case you need to use **some** while you're painting.
6. My new computer is slower than the **one** I got rid of when I bought it.
7. This cheeseburger tastes as good as the **one** I ate in the other restaurant.

63.3 🔊
1. If you need any more paper to write on, there's **some** on my desk.
2. If you're looking for some new running shoes, I'd recommend the **ones** on the left.
3. I have three tickets and I only need two, so I could give you **one** if you like.
4. If you need any information about the building, ask me and I'll give you **some**.
5. If they like Italian restaurants, there's a great **one** just down the road.
6. I think Jenny and Matthew's wedding was the best **one** I've ever been to.

63.4 🔊
1. I know you want a new computer, **but we can't afford one.**

② My sister bought me an album, **but it wasn't the one I wanted.**

③ If you're looking for bookstores, **there are some on Upper Street.**

④ I think my favorite authors **are the ones who write about vampires.**

⑤ We should buy new flowers **and get rid of these old ones.**

⑥ Please help yourself to tea or coffee **if you would like some.**

⑦ I wanted to bring a cake, **but I didn't have time to bake one.**

63.5 🔊

① I didn't enjoy it, but my friend did.
② Did you see the new movie? We did, too.
③ You bought a blue hat! I did, too.
④ Do I still cycle to work? Yes, I do.
⑤ He works downtown, but she doesn't.
⑥ My mom went, but my dad didn't.
⑦ Did you bring your camera? I didn't.
⑧ You baked cookies! I did, too.
⑨ Does she like reading? Yes, she does.
⑩ They went skiing last year, but we didn't.
⑪ My friend found it difficult. I did, too.

63.6

① False ② False ③ True ④ True
⑤ True ⑥ True

63.7 🔊 Réponses modèles

① I hope so!
② I think so.
③ No, Steven Spielberg did.
④ I don't imagine so.
⑤ I assume so.

64

64.1 🔊

① I wanted to wake up early today, but I wasn't able to.
② Stefan was enjoying the ballet. At least, he seemed to be.
③ I'm so nervous! I'm singing on stage tonight, but I really don't want to.
④ Your dog likes chasing people a lot more than he used to.
⑤ I'm so thirsty! I meant to buy a drink before the movie, but I forgot.
⑥ Don't be nervous. There's no need to be.
⑦ Darren said he'd help us unpack, but it seems that he won't be able to.
⑧ I really wanted to go to that concert, but I couldn't afford to.
⑨ If you want to be promoted, you have to show me that you deserve to be.
⑩ Helena asked me to join the college choir, but I didn't want to.
⑪ I'm sorry I'm so late! I didn't mean to be.

64.2 🔊

① I'd really like to go away this year, but I won't **be** able to.
② Keisha said I should go to her party tonight, but I don't really want **to**.
③ I tried to find out Will's email address, but I wasn't **able** to.
④ Frankie liked the birthday present we bought her. At least, she seemed **to**.
⑤ I didn't realize that it was necessary to wear a tie, but apparently we have **to**.
⑥ I'm very concerned about my test results, even though the doctor says there's no need **to** be.

64.3

① False ② True ③ False ④ True ⑤ False

64.4 🔊

① I'd really like to buy a new pair of shoes, **though I don't need to.**
② I'm not sure if I can visit my aunt this weekend, **but I hope to.**
③ Jonas would really like to buy a car, **but he can't afford to.**
④ I'll watch a movie if all my friends want to, **but I wouldn't choose to.**
⑤ I don't insist on going to warm countries for vacations, **although I prefer to.**
⑥ I tried to get tickets for the concert, **but I wasn't able to.**

64.5 🔊

① I am always really nervous before I go to the doctor's. It's difficult not **to be**.
② It's not certain that I'll do well on my exams, but I **expect** to.
③ Marie wants me to go shopping with her, but I really don't **want** to.
④ I've never been to the US. I'd love the **chance**.
⑤ You can get a vaccination before your trip, but you don't **need** to.

64.6 🔊

① I love listening to loud music, but my sister hates to.
② You can leave work early this afternoon if you would like to.
③ Gigi asked me to go to her wedding and I said I'd be delighted to.
④ Don't agree to do the fun run if you really don't want to.

64.7 🔊

① Yes, **I'd be delighted to.**
② No, **I don't want to.**
③ No, **you don't need to.**
④ Yes, **she seemed to.**
⑤ No, **I can't afford to.**

65

65.1 🔊

① Sorry, I had to take that call. So **as I was saying**, the gallery opened in 1903.
② I've been to that museum, too. Hey, I love your shoes, **by the way**.
③ This gallery is beautiful. Oh, **by the way**, did you see there's a new café downstairs?
④ You think he's an expert? **Actually**, he doesn't really know anything about art.
⑤ **Anyway**, I'm afraid I will have to say goodbye now, but thank you for today.
⑥ No, **actually**, it was George who thought we should buy this painting, not me.
⑦ Mike's very happy because, **as I was saying**, he's getting married next September.
⑧ Yes, I'd like some coffee. So, **as I was saying**, we've got a lot of paintings at home.
⑨ **Anyway**, I'm sure you'll have a great time in Tokyo. See you when you get back!
⑩ So, **as I was saying**, Jenny and I have known each other for a long time.
⑪ Yes, **actually**, I've already been here a few times, so I know my way around.

65.2 🔊

① Yes, but **as I was saying** before, I prefer Hockney.
② No, it was sold out. **Anyway**, we should get moving!
③ I've already seen it, **actually**. I came here last month.
④ **Actually**, I've already been. But you go.

65.3 🔊

① The fastest aircraft travel through the air at supersonic speeds.
② Powerful computers can predict the outcomes of some experiments with amazing accuracy.
③ The first farms in human history were established in the Neolithic, or New Stone Age.
④ The postwar period, after the fighting had ended, saw an economic boom.

65.4

① False ② True ③ False ④ False ⑤ True

65.5 🔊

① preview ② superstructure
③ antibacterial ④ prolonged
⑤ neoclassical ⑥ postpone ⑦ antidote
⑧ superhuman ⑨ preassigned

65.6 🔊

① He's interested in **neo**liberalism. I'm not sure what that is, but it's a new type of liberalism.

② I've been enjoying the **pre**game buildup, but now I just can't wait for the game to start.

③ **Neo**classical architecture became popular when interest in ancient Greece rose again.

④ We've organized a **pre**-conference event so people can meet before the meetings start.

⑤ James must be **super**human! It's amazing how he manages to work and travel so much.

⑥ She specializes in **neo**natal care, so she looks after newborn babies.

⑦ **Post**modern art was a reaction by artists against the modernist art that came before it.

⑧ Instead of finishing her degree, she's decided to **post**pone her studies and go traveling.

⑨ You first go into the **ante**chamber of the tomb of Tutankhamun and then the main chamber.

⑩ If I could have any **super**power I wanted, I think it would be the ability to fly.

⑪ I've had enough of our neighbors' **anti**social behavior, they're always making noise!

⑫ We're celebrating the 50th anniversary of the introduction of **anti**discrimination laws.

66

66.1 🔊

① I look so much better after having **my hair cut at the salon yesterday.**

② Don't worry, we got the problem **with the internet sorted out in the end.**

③ Something's wrong with my back, **so I'm going to the doctor to get it checked.**

④ Ask the people at the restaurant if **we can get the food delivered to us.**

⑤ I'll call our landlord and ask him if **he can get the door fixed.**

66.2 🔊

① My parents are having their house painted by a decorator.

② He can't afford a new car, so he's getting it repaired.

③ Sally's getting her picture taken by a photographer.

66.3

① False ② True ③ False ④ False ⑤ False ⑥ True ⑦ False

66.4 🔊

① Leah needs to go to the dentist as soon as possible **to have** her teeth fixed.

② He's **getting** his birth certificate translated into English, so he can get married.

③ They **had** a marquee built in the grounds of the castle for their party last year.

④ She always **has** her essays checked by her mother before she hands them in.

⑤ My wedding ring **got** stolen when someone broke into our house last week.

⑥ We've been having problems with our website, but we're **getting** them sorted out.

⑦ Jessica can't come to the phone right now because she's **having** her nails done.

⑧ We've **had** a lot of changes made to the house since we moved in five years ago.

⑨ He's been **having** his hair cut at that barber's shop since he was five years old.

66.5

① get ② have ③ got ④ have ⑤ have ⑥ get ⑦ having ⑧ checked ⑨ check ⑩ had

66.6 🔊

① I got a pizza delivered.
② I got my car fixed.
③ We're having our house painted.
④ I'm getting my shirts dry-cleaned.
⑤ I got my picture taken.
⑥ I got the oven repaired.
⑦ I got my teeth checked.
⑧ They're having their garden landscaped.
⑨ I had my essay translated.
⑩ I got my eyesight tested.
⑪ I got my laundry done.

66.7 🔊

① I'm having problems with my eyes, so I went to the optician to **get them checked**.

② You won't believe it. I **had it stolen** when we were on vacation!

③ You can either pick the pizza up from the restaurant or you can **have it delivered**.

④ The business cards are here. Would you like me to **have them sent** to your home address?

⑤ No, but I can't believe how filthy it is. I need to **have it dry-cleaned** as soon as possible.

⑥ No, the internet at home still isn't working properly. We need to **get it sorted out** this week.

⑦ No, I'm going to the hairdresser's to **have it cut.**

67

67.1 🔊

① The **audience** was so appreciative of our performance that they gave us three encores.

② All the **staff** at the hotel where we stayed were extremely friendly and helpful.

③ My son's **orchestra** is doing a concert at the town hall on Saturday evening.

④ Jake's **family** is always arguing. His brother and sister are the worst.

⑤ Next week, all the **teams** in the office are going to do extra training.

⑥ The **government** is holding an emergency session to discuss foreign policy issues.

⑦ Our **department** is known for being the most environmentally friendly in the company.

⑧ My **company** is the market leader in the digital industry and has been for 10 years now.

⑨ Later this afternoon our **panel** is going to be discussing the issues you mentioned.

67.2 🔊

① Spain has a very long border with Portugal. It's one of the longest in Europe.

② The Netherlands is one of the best countries to go on vacation if you like cycling.

③ He's great at soccer, but athletics is the sport that he wants to focus on from now on.

④ Politics was my favorite subject at school, so I decided to study it in college.

⑤ The news about the celebrity couple was very hard to believe.

67.3 🔊

① Either an essay or a report **is required by the end of this week.**

② Neither my mom nor my dad **was there when I got home.**

③ Neither my cell phone nor my laptop **is connected to the internet.**

④ Media studies is a very popular **subject among the students.**

⑤ I think that either a dog or a cat **is the best pet to get.**

⑥ Neither my teacher nor my friends **know when our test will be.**

⑦ Either a box of chocolates or some perfume **is the best gift to give someone.**

⑧ Logistics is the area of the business world **that's the most interesting to me.**

67.4 🔊

① All of the information about this **is** available to you on the college's website.

② Neither my dad nor my mom **were** very happy when I got suspended from school.

③ **Is** The Dragon Leader a good book, or do you not like fantasy novels?

④ Either pop music or rock music **is** what I like to listen to when I'm relaxing.

⑤ Physics **is** what Charlie studied in college, too.

⑥ Politics **is** slowly moving more to the left in this country at the moment.

⑦ **Is** the mathematics you're doing in your class very difficult or can you do it easily?

⑧ Neither my presentation nor my essay **was** good enough to get me a passing grade.

9 The Bahamas **has** very warm weather at this time of year, so I'd recommend going there.
10 Either English or Spanish **is** the language that people most commonly learn at our school.

67.5
1 Not given
2 True
3 False
4 True
5 False
6 True
7 Not given

67.6 🔊
1 *Jungle Adventures* **is** the new television show that everyone is talking about.
2 The US **is** the largest country in North America when it comes to population.
3 This information **needs** to be shared with everyone else in the team right away.
4 Neither the adults nor the children **were** interested in the entertainment they provided.
5 I think politics **isn't** a topic that you should discuss when you're making small talk.
6 Neither my black suit nor my dark blue one **is** clean enough to wear.
7 Neither my phone nor Clark's phone **is** getting any signal at the moment.
8 Either the lemon or the lime **was** too strong in the sauce he made.
9 Everyone in Jack's family **is** interested in birdwatching, so he's going on a trip with them.
10 Neither history nor business **is** interesting to me.

68

68.1 🔊
1 Last night my mom called me to say that my grandma was very ill. It was **such** a shock.
2 Hong Kong is **such** a fascinating city. You should go there if you get the chance.
3 You've got **such** a difficult job. I don't think I'm patient enough to be a teacher.
4 He carried the baby **so** gently, as if he was scared she might break.
5 I can't believe I've got a job in Paris! It's **so** exciting!
6 That movie was **so** gripping. It was almost three hours long, but the time flew past!
7 You've got **such** a beautiful smile. Has anyone ever told you that?
8 It's always **such** a pleasure to spend time with Tom. He's a lovely man.
9 Keira is **so** generous. Did you know that she gave $250 to charity last month?

10 I'm not surprised the police stopped Mick. He drives **so** dangerously.
11 Thanks for responding **so** quickly. That was really efficient of you.
12 It was **such** a surprise when my cat turned up after being missing for six months!
13 You behaved **so** rudely in front of our guests. I felt quite embarrassed.
14 You learn languages **so** easily! Can you share your secret with me?
15 I think Martin is **so** brave. I couldn't do a bungee jump.
16 Your present job is **so** interesting. Is it also well paid, unlike the previous one?
17 *Back to City Life* was **such** a great book. I want to read it again!
18 It was **such** a relief when the doctor told me the good news. I've been celebrating.
19 I've had **such** a fun evening. Can I see you again tomorrow?

68.2 🔊
1 The medicine works so effectively **that we have a 98 percent cure rate.**
2 It was such a bad injury **that she was off work for months.**
3 It was such an unexpected result **that everyone was surprised.**
4 He recovered so quickly **that he was back at work within two weeks.**
5 Brian is so intelligent **that he's sure to go on to college.**
6 The doctor was so reassuring **that I didn't really feel worried.**

68.3 🔊
1 It's **such** a beautiful day. Why don't we go for a walk on the beach?
2 I am **so** grateful to the doctors that I'm going to send them a thank you card.
3 It was **such** a thrill to spend time with my grandchildren.
4 The movie was **so** boring that Pauline and I fell asleep.
5 It was **such** a surprise that I didn't know what to say.
6 Chantelle is **so** helpful. She's a lovely young woman.
7 Tom reacted **so** bravely when the doctor told him he had to go into the hospital.

68.4 🔊
1 **So** few people eat enough fruit and vegetables every day.
2 **So** little funding is available for research into age-related diseases.
3 There are so **many** medicines to choose from for your condition.
4 **So** many wonderful people work in our health service.
5 Charis feels so **much** better since she started doing more exercise.

6 **So** few students are bright enough to become doctors and engineers.
7 So **much** effort goes into making sure the patients are comfortable.
8 **So** little money is spent on healthcare services for the disabled.
9 **So** many people know someone who has been in the hospital.
10 There has been so **much** amazing progress in the field of medicine in the last decade.
11 So **much** time and money has been put into designing this new hospital.
12 It's so **much** easier to play sports since I lost a lot of weight.

68.5 🔊
1 Lyndsey is such an inspiration to me. I follow everything she posts on her blog.
2 Jamie made such an effort to find the right present for my birthday.
3 I have so much free time these days, I've started some new hobbies.
4 The exam was so easy that I wondered whether I had missed something.
5 You play the piano so beautifully! Can you play it again, please?
6 There are so few opportunities for people who can't read or write.

68.6 🔊
1 These stray cats are **such** a nuisance.
2 I feel **so** much calmer after a walk in the rain.
3 You opened the door **so** quietly last night.
4 *Color* was **so** amazing that I watched it again.
5 There are **so** many shirts to choose from.
6 It's **such** a lovely dress that I'm going to buy it.
7 My dog is always hungry. She eats **so** much.

69

69.1 🔊
1 My brother has **a** pet spider. I hate it!
2 I'd like a piece of cake and **an** orange juice, please.
3 **The** airplane was invented by the Wright brothers.
4 Can I ask you **a** question?
5 I can see **a** man over there with blond hair. But I'm not sure that it's Josh.
6 **The** bicycle is a very common form of transportation all over the world.
7 I have **an** arrangement with my colleague, where we share the commute to work.
8 There was **an** awkward silence when I asked Tami how her job was going.
9 **The** hummingbird is one of the smallest birds on the planet.

⑩ Would you like **a** cup of coffee?
⑪ **The** sandwich is named after the Earl of Sandwich, who supposedly invented it.

69.2 🔊
① **An** apple a day keeps the doctor away.
② [-] Women are still rarely paid as much as men.
③ [-] Human beings are the number-one predator on Earth.
④ There's **an** advertisement for a new smartwatch in today's paper.
⑤ **The** electric car is now a reality in many countries.
⑥ [-] Students usually don't have very much money.
⑦ **The** panda is in danger of becoming extinct.

69.3 🔊
① I'm afraid there isn't a Mark Wilson in this office. Have you got the right name?
② Are you saying you're good friends with John Smith?
③ This is my sister's best friend, Kristin Wyatt.
④ Let me introduce you to the manager of our company, Isaac Myers.
⑤ I don't know of a Lucy Armitage. Is there anyone else you'd like to speak to?
⑥ You don't mean the Cherry Baldwin, the famous actress, do you?

69.4 🔊
① I can't find **a** Mikaela Zimmerman in the company directory. Are you sure she works here?
② Did you manage to get yourself **a** ticket for the concert?

③ **The** cell phone has become a much smaller and lighter device in recent years.
④ Allow me to introduce you to my fiancé, **Brad** Livingstone.
⑤ I had **a** delicious meal at that new Italian restaurant last night.
⑥ There's no record of **a** Thomas Luckett ever having lived here.
⑦ **The** dog is often described as man's best friend. / **Dogs are** often described as man's best friend.
⑧ Can you believe I was sitting next to **the** Elizabeth Parker? She's such a huge star!
⑨ **The** dress is often the most important thing for a bride at her wedding.
⑩ This is my boss, **Francesco** Coppola.
⑪ We usually have **breakfast** at about 7:15am.
⑫ **The** internet has revolutionized our lives since its invention.

69.5 🔊
① The company has captured **a significant share of the market.**
② The tallest waterfalls in the world **are the famous Angel Falls in Venezuela.**
③ Izmir is the city with **the oldest working bridge.**
④ There isn't a Philip Fernandez here, **so you must have the wrong number.**
⑤ There was a good atmosphere in **the office until Jane started working here.**
⑥ We all know that the brain controls **everything that happens in our bodies.**
⑦ I couldn't believe that I was actually **sitting next to the Jo Halls. It was amazing!**

69.6 🔊
① The Hawksbill turtle is a species that is critically endangered.
② The Stephen Hawking told me I would become a scientist one day!
③ Televisions are now found in almost every home in the city.
④ I'm afraid that there isn't a Susie Fa on this list.

Remerciements

L'éditeur aimerait remercier :
Jo Kent, Trish Burrow et Emma Watkins pour le texte supplémentaire ; Thomas Booth, Helen Fanthorpe, Helen Leech, Carrie Lewis et Vicky Richards pour leur assistance rédactionnelle ; Stephen Bere, Sarah Hilder, Amy Child, Fiona Macdonald et Simon Murrell pour le travail de conception supplémentaire ; Simon Mumford pour les cartes et les drapeaux nationaux ; Peter Chrisp pour la vérification des faits ; Penny Hands, Amanda Learmonth et Carrie Lewis pour la relecture ; Elizabeth Wise pour la création de l'index ; Tatiana Boyko, Rory Farrell, Clare Joyce et Viola Wang pour les illustrations complémentaires ; Liz Hammond pour le montage des scripts et la gestion des enregistrements audio ; Hannah Bowen et Scarlett O'Hara pour la compilation des scripts audio ; Richard Hughes et Jordan Killiard pour le mixage et le mastering des enregistrements audio ; Heather Hughes, Tommy Callan, Tom Morse, Gillian Reid et Sonia Charbonnier pour leur soutien créatif et technique ; Priyanka Kharbanda, Suefa Lee, Shramana Purkayastha, Isha Sharma, Sheryl Sadana pour leur assistance rédactionnelle ; Yashashvi Choudhary, Jaileen Kaur, Bhavika Mathur, Richa Verma, Ankita Yadav, Apurva Agarwal pour leur support de conception ; Deepak Negi et Nishwan Rasool pour la recherche d'images ; Rohan Sinha pour le soutien managérial et moral.

DK souhaite également remercier pour leur aimable autorisation de reproduction de photographies :

19 Peter Cook (c) **Dorling Kindersley** avec l'aimable autorisation du musée de l'Air et de l'Espace Pima, Tucson, Arizona (centre). 146 **Dreamstime.com:** Smellme (en haut à droite).

Toutes les autres images sont la propriété de DK. Pour plus d'informations, rendez-vous sur **www.dkimages.com**